IMAGES
of America

MEBANE

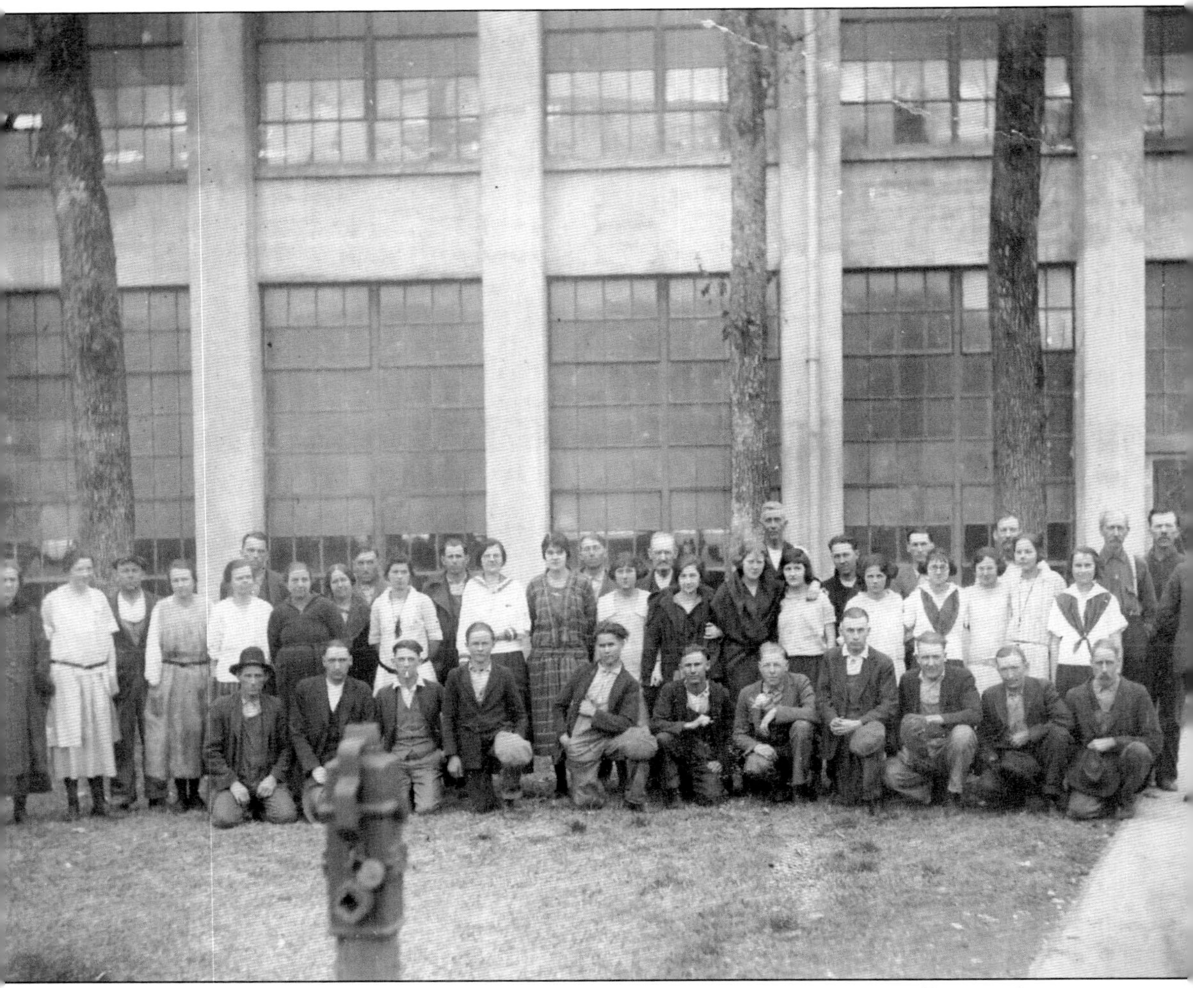

On the Cover: Male and female employees from Durham Hosiery Mills pose for a group photograph in front of the mill on South First Street some time in the 1920s. Built in 1922, this was Durham Hosiery Mill No. 2, constructed three years after Mill No. 1 was built on the corner of Washington and Second Streets. The two mills were among several textile mills located in Mebane in the early years of the 20th century. Durham Hosiery built its plants on the south side of town, while Baker-Cammack Hosiery, Kales Hosiery, and Southerland Dyeing and Finishing Mill built on the north side of town. For many years, these factories ran two and sometimes three shifts and provided low-paying but steady work for hundreds of people. Neighborhoods grew up around the mills as workers took advantage of the inexpensive rental houses the company built for them. The Durham Hosiery plants went through several ownership and name changes before closing down in 1999–2000. Both mills are still standing today. Many people refer to them as the Dixie Yarn Mills because of their long history under that name. The City of Mebane purchased the old Durham Hosiery Mill No. 1 in 2002 and transformed it into the Mebane Public Library. Durham Hosiery Mill No. 2 is being extensively renovated into loft apartments by a private developer. (Courtesy of the author.)

IMAGES
of America

MEBANE

J. Ronald Oakley

ARCADIA
PUBLISHING

ISBN 978-0-7385-9222-0

Published by Arcadia Publishing
Charleston, South Carolina

Printed in the United States of America

Library of Congress Control Number: 2011939559

For all general information, please contact Arcadia Publishing:
Telephone 843-853-2070
Fax 843-853-0044
E-mail sales@arcadiapublishing.com
For customer service and orders:
Toll-Free 1-888-313-2665

Visit us on the Internet at www.arcadiapublishing.com

This book is dedicated to my wife, Kathy, a transplanted Georgia peach who adopted my hometown as her own and helped me every step of the way in the completion of this work.

Contents

Acknowledgments

Space does not permit an acknowledgement of all the people who helped make this book possible. Many individuals responded to my requests for old photographs by rummaging through their personal collections of photographs in albums, desk drawers, and boxes stored in closets or attics and helped in the identification of the time, place, and names of the people in the photographs. Their names appear in the courtesy lines under the photographs. Traci Davenport, the director of the Mebane Historical Museum (MHM), made its archives of photographs, artifacts, and other research materials available to me, and many of the museum's images are included in this work. Museum volunteer Kelly Gauldin spent many hours scanning hundreds of photographs and travelling around town taking snapshots of historical sites I wanted to include in the book. Finally, my editors at Arcadia, James Wright, Lindsay Carter, and Mike Litchfield, patiently guided and occasionally prodded me through the rewarding process of producing a photographic history of my hometown.

INTRODUCTION

Located in eastern Alamance County near the Orange County line, Mebane is one of several factory towns that sprang up in Alamance County in the late 19th century. The original settlers of Alamance County were the Indians, but in the 19th century, many people came down to the area from Pennsylvania and other Northern areas, including Quakers, Scotch-Irish Presbyterians, Lutherans, Baptists, and Methodists.

The genesis of the town dates back to at least 1809, when a post office was established in Orange County at a stagecoach stop and inn located close to what is today's intersection of Stagecoach Road and Lebanon Road near Lake Michael. The postmaster was James Mason, and the little junction became known as Mason Hall.

Gradually, a few other settlers moved into the area, but the real growth began in the mid-1850s with the completion of the North Carolina Railroad linking Goldsboro in the east to Charlotte in the west. Stephen A. White, Frank Mebane, and other residents from Hawfields and other outlying communities moved into Mason Hall to be near the new railroad, and the trading center of what would become Mebane began to grow. In 1881, the community was incorporated as Mebanesville, named in honor of the family that had played such a big role in the history of the town, Alamance and Orange Counties, and the state. In 1883, the name was officially shortened to Mebane.

In 1881, Dave and Will White, sons of the town's first mayor, Stephen A. White, built White Furniture Company alongside the railroad. As the company prospered, it built a huge plant in downtown Mebane. In the last part of the 19th century and early years of the 20th, other industries sprang up along the railroad, including textile mills, flour and feed mills, a mattress and bedding company (Kingsdown), and a lumber company.

In the early 1920s, state Highway 70 was built, running from Morehead City on the coast through the Piedmont and mountains, into Tennessee, and eventually all the way to Barstow, California. It paralleled the railroad tracks in Mebane, giving the growing town still another major transportation artery. Buses came through Mebane several times every day, providing a comfortable and convenient ride to larger cities in the state and across the country.

Conveniently located near tobacco farmers in Alamance and surrounding counties and to manufacturers of tobacco products in Durham, Winston-Salem, and other cities, Mebane became one of the leading North Carolina towns where tobacco growers and tobacco buyers came together in late summer and early fall. The first tobacco auction warehouse opened in Mebane in 1909 and was soon followed by two others. The three warehouses—Piedmont, Planter's, and Farmer's—stood on three corners in town, each one taking up a large part of a city block.

In the 1920s, the three warehouses were among the top-selling warehouses in the state and the Southeast. The peak year came in 1947, when their combined annual sales rose to about 10 million pounds of tobacco. In 1952, they were still selling close to six million pounds.

Tobacco farming was hard, backbreaking work. Men, women, and children labored in the fields during the day and sat up in the barns while wood or oil heaters cured the tobacco at night. When they drove into town for the tobacco auction each year, farmers found out if the months of hard labor had paid off. The price of their crop, and thus their yearly income, would be decided in just a few minutes, as buyers from the major tobacco manufacturers walked up and down the aisles examining the leaves and responding to the auctioneer's chant, which always upped the price.

The tobacco auctions were a boon to local merchants. When the farmers were paid for their tobacco, Mebane's downtown was crowded as tobacco families shopped for clothing, home appliances, grocery staples, school supplies for their children, and other necessities. Many used this time to pay for goods and services at local stores and doctors' and dentists' offices that they had charged throughout the year.

In the late 1940s and early 1950s, the Mebane tobacco market opened with a Tobacco Festival sponsored by the town's civic clubs and businesses. Merchants chose young women, most of them high school students, to represent them in the contest for Miss Tobacco Festival Queen. On the day of the parade, the contestants took their seats in convertibles or on floats pulled by trucks and joined bands and majorettes from surrounding towns in processions down Center and Clay Streets while large crowds—estimated at 4,000 in some years—lined the streets.

At the end of the parade, the contestants mounted a large stage set up on Third Street between Center and Clay Streets for the final events surrounding the crowning of the new Miss Tobacco Festival Queen. The crowning of the queen was followed by a dance held in the streets and warehouses that went on far into the night.

Tobacco was North Carolina's "golden leaf" from the late 19th century to the late 20th. It was the major cash crop for thousands and a major player in the state's economy until the last years of the 20th century, when antismoking campaigns, reduction in government price supports, higher taxes on tobacco products, foreign competition, and medical lawsuits brought hard times to tobacco farmers and cigarette manufacturing companies.

As early as 1919, local residents, along with newspapers, Four-County Fair brochures, and other publications, were calling Mebane "the biggest little town on earth" because it was growing so fast and had so many amenities. The description caught on, and the phrase is still frequently used today to describe the town that sprang up along the railroad in the 19th century, grew and prospered in the 20th, and now ranks among the fastest-growing towns in the state.

Although Mebane had a healthy downtown with many services and conveniences for its citizens as early as the 1920s, the height of downtown Mebane came in the 1940s, 1950s, and early 1960s. The main business district in the 1950s boasted one lawyer's office, three drugstores, one hotel, several small family-owned grocery stores, restaurants, a public library, a telephone company, a funeral home, a variety of retail stores, three barbershops and several beauty shops, several full-service gasoline stations (commonly called filling stations), a post office, two medical clinics, two dentists' offices, an optometrist's office, a photography studio, three auto dealerships and several repair shops, a bus station, three pool halls, a popular movie theater, and a weekly newspaper. If you could not find what you wanted in Mebane within a few blocks, you could easily travel by car, bus, or train to shop in Durham, Burlington, or Greensboro.

From the 1960s onward, Mebane was transformed by some of the changes sweeping other small communities across the nation. The construction of Interstate 85 in the late 1950s and Interstate 40 in the 1980s and 1990s linked Mebane more closely to the outside world and made it a more attractive place to work and live. New industries located just outside the city limits, and the town became an ideal bedroom community for people working in the Research Triangle and the Piedmont Triad, providing an escape from the congestion and expensive housing market of those areas while supplying access to jobs and recreational and cultural activities in the larger cities.

Unfortunately, many downtown merchants eventually closed or relocated after steadily losing customers to stores on the outskirts of town and to large retail stores and shopping malls in nearby towns. Several factories closed as the textile and furniture companies became victims of changing economic times in a global economy.

White Furniture Company was bought out by Hickory Furniture in 1985 and was renamed Hickory-White. In 1993, the 230,000-square-foot plant closed, ending the 112-year history of what is often regarded as the oldest furniture factory in the South. Today, years after the famous whistle fell silent, the huge downtown plant stands as an imposing reminder of the days when it was the cornerstone of the town's economy.

Unlike other small factory towns along the Interstate 85 corridor, Mebane has prospered during rapidly changing times. People are attracted by the cheap land, low taxes, the interstate and other good roads, and the airports in Raleigh and Greensboro. Aggressive recruitment campaigns by the City of Mebane, merchants associations, developers, and several industries and businesses located in outlying areas near the interstates also help to bring people to the area.

In the 1990s, the population increased by over 2,500 people, and by 2011, it had climbed to close to 12,000 as Mebane continued to be among the fastest-growing areas in North Carolina. New schools sprang up, along with apartments, condos, hotels, and upscale housing developments. Several physicians and clinics moved into town. Mebane acquired the same fast food places, big box stores, and strip shopping centers found in other towns across the nation. In 2011, Tanger Outlets built a huge shopping center on the outskirts of town, bringing jobs and tax income to the city.

Although many businesses have sprung up today on the outskirts of town to cater to the growing population, Mebane still has an attractive and thriving downtown, thanks to the efforts of city officials, local merchants, the Mebane Business Association, Destination Downtown, and other individuals and organizations. Many retailers still call their customers by name and provide old-fashioned service and unique merchandise.

Modern Mebane continues its long history of providing free or inexpensive services and entertainment to the community. The public library was relocated in 2005 to the renovated hosiery Dixie Yarns Mill, the recreation department offers a wide variety of athletic programs for people of all ages, and the spacious Mebane Arts and Community Center schedules concerts, plays, banquets, and other events. An annual Dogwood Festival, outdoor summer concerts on Clay Street, a unique nighttime Christmas parade, and other downtown events draw large crowds and remind many older citizens of what Mebane was like during the Tobacco Festival and other happenings from decades ago.

Although airlines, interstate highways, and automobiles have revolutionized the transportation industry, the train continues to be a central part of Mebane's life today. Amtrak passes through several times during the day, and freight trains can be heard rumbling through during the day and night. From the children in the library yelling "Train!" to pedestrians waving from the street whenever Amtrak passes by to the care with which people cross the tracks, citizens understand the opportunities and dangers that the railroad has brought to Mebane.

Mebane is not the same town today that it was in the 1950s, but most residents believe that it is a great place to live and is still "the biggest little town on earth."

One

The Railroad

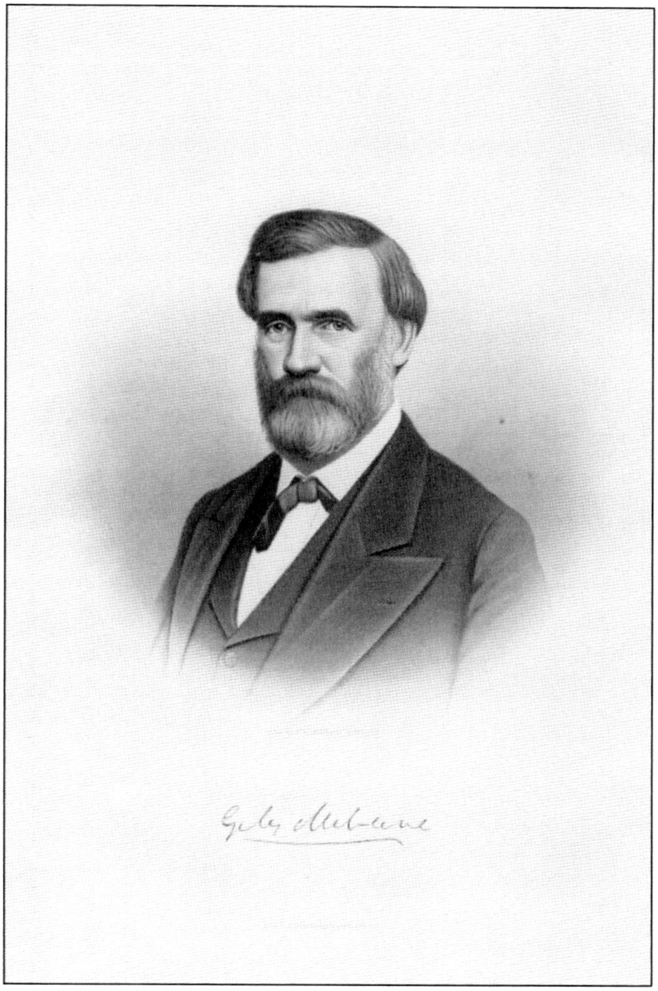

The most influential member of the family that gave Mebane its name, Giles Mebane was a lawyer and longtime member of the North Carolina legislature. He was the biggest promoter of the North Carolina Railroad and sponsored a bill to carve a new county, Alamance, out of Orange County in 1849. In 1855, when the railroad came through Alamance County, the first train to steam into Mason Hall was pulled by an engine bearing a sign that read "The Giles Mebane." It was met by close to 100 people. (Courtesy of William Giles Mebane.)

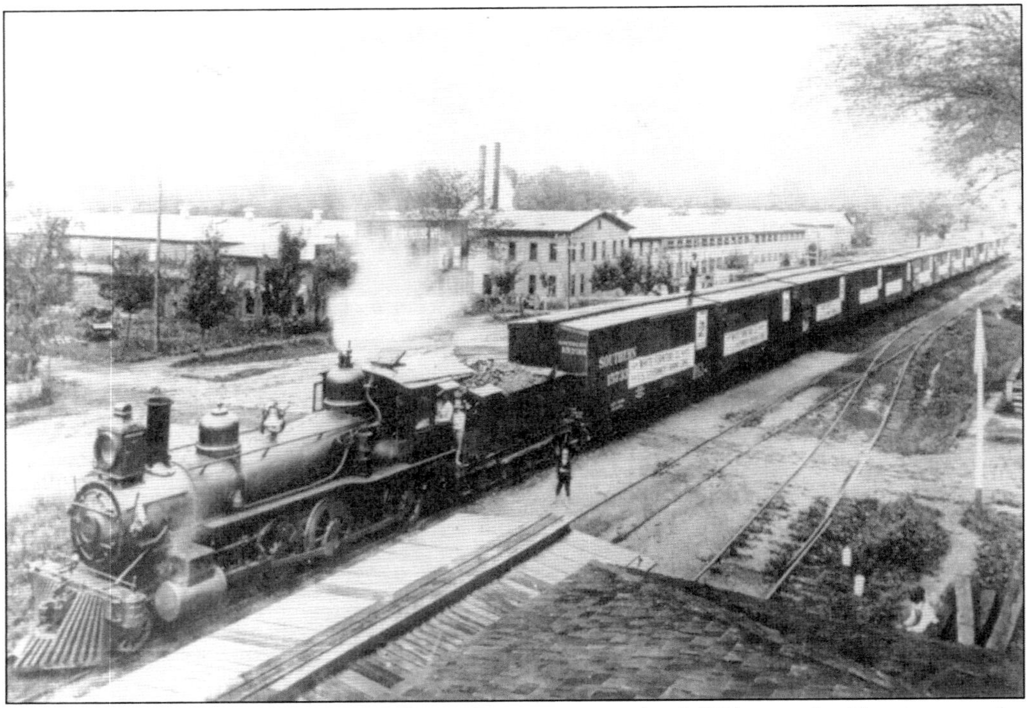

In 1906, White Furniture Company shipped an entire trainload (58 boxcars) of furniture to the Panama Canal Zone during its construction. It later provided most of the furniture for the new Grove Park Inn in Asheville. The plant burned in 1923 but was quickly rebuilt, bigger and better than ever. During World War II, White's made 50,000 bunk beds for the military. When the war ended, some 500 people were working at White Furniture Company in Mebane and its second plant in nearby Hillsborough. (Courtesy of Sam White.)

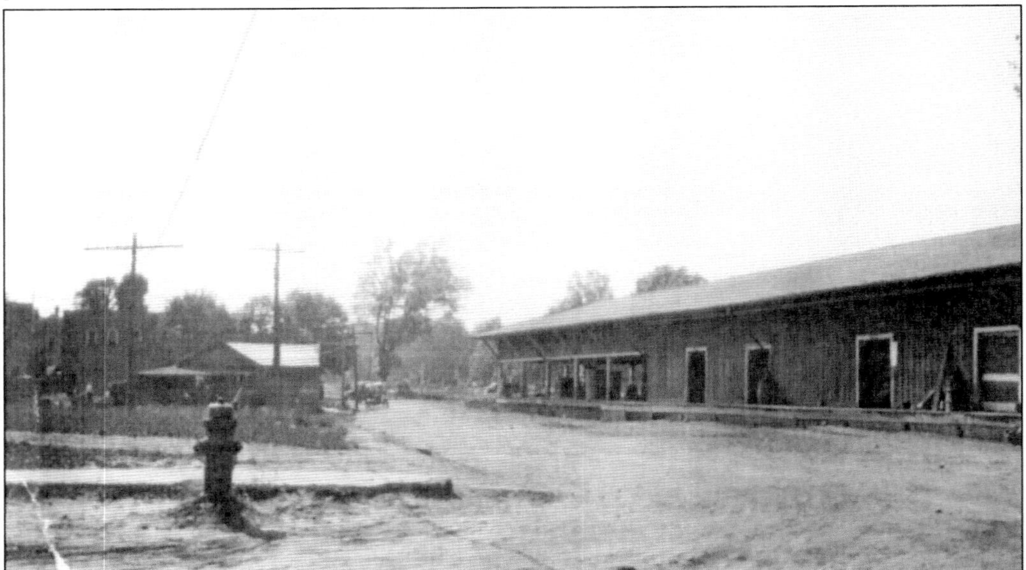

Pictured here is the railroad depot on Washington Street around 1910. Washington and other streets in Mebane would not be paved until the 1920s. (MHM.)

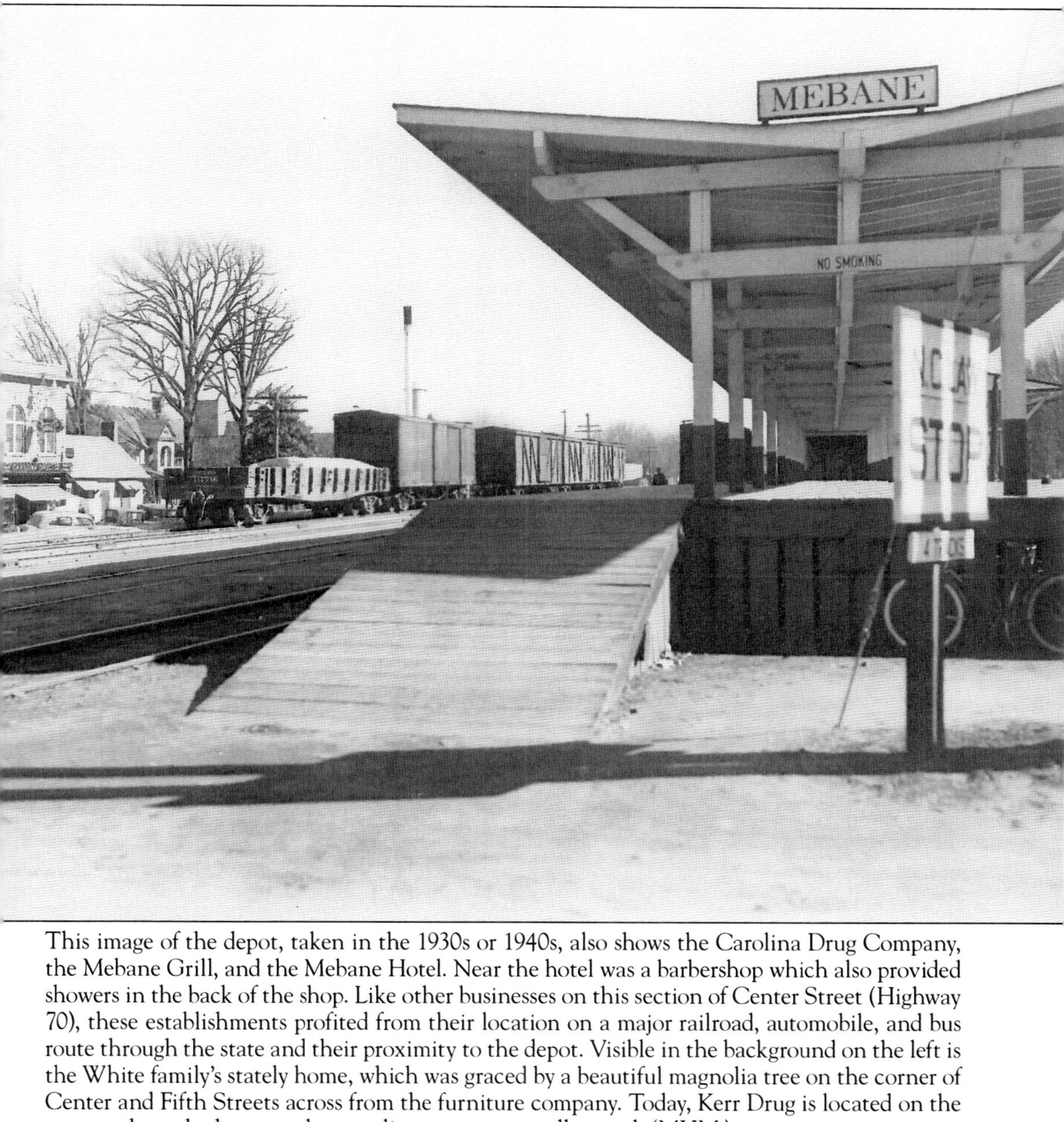

This image of the depot, taken in the 1930s or 1940s, also shows the Carolina Drug Company, the Mebane Grill, and the Mebane Hotel. Near the hotel was a barbershop which also provided showers in the back of the shop. Like other businesses on this section of Center Street (Highway 70), these establishments profited from their location on a major railroad, automobile, and bus route through the state and their proximity to the depot. Visible in the background on the left is the White family's stately home, which was graced by a beautiful magnolia tree on the corner of Center and Fifth Streets across from the furniture company. Today, Kerr Drug is located on the corner where the home and magnolia tree once proudly stood. (MHM.)

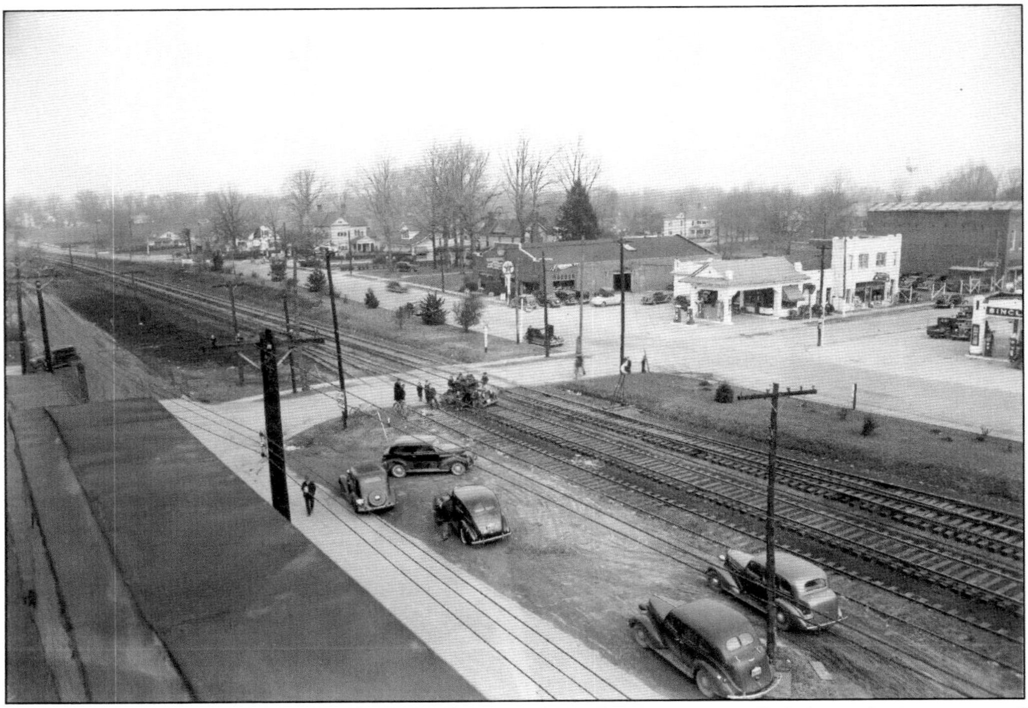

With the railroad tracks and Highway 70 (Center Street) running parallel through the center of town and several railroad crossings from side streets, train and car crashes were inevitable. This 1940 photograph shows a crash at the Third Street and Highway 70 crossing with a good view of a section of Center Street, which was changed dramatically in the late 20th century. (MHM.)

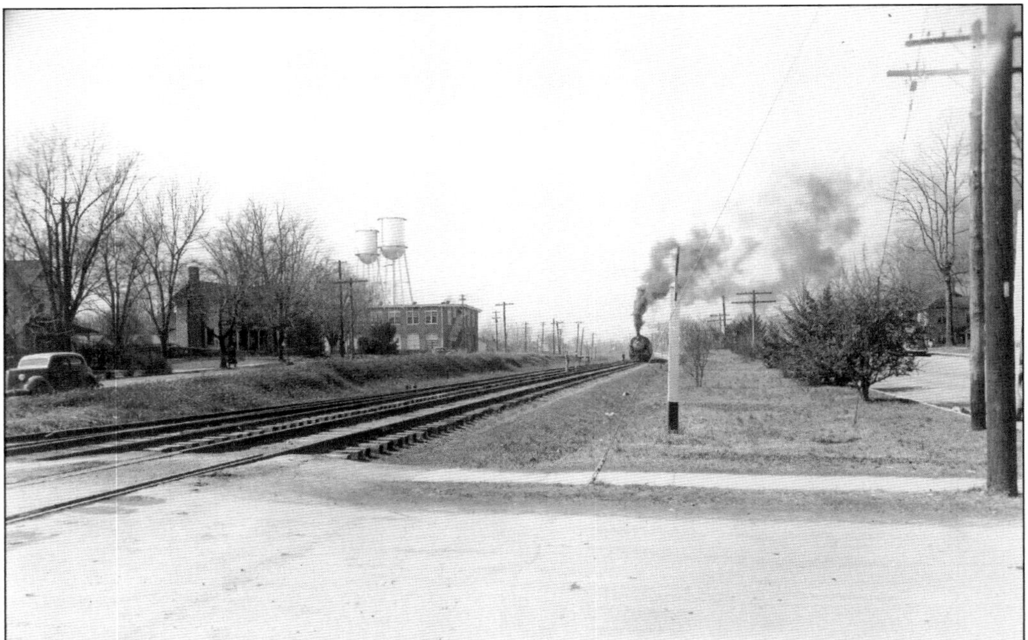

A steam train stopped near Dixie Yarn Mill after the crash waits patiently for the tracks ahead to be cleared before it resumes its journey. (MHM.)

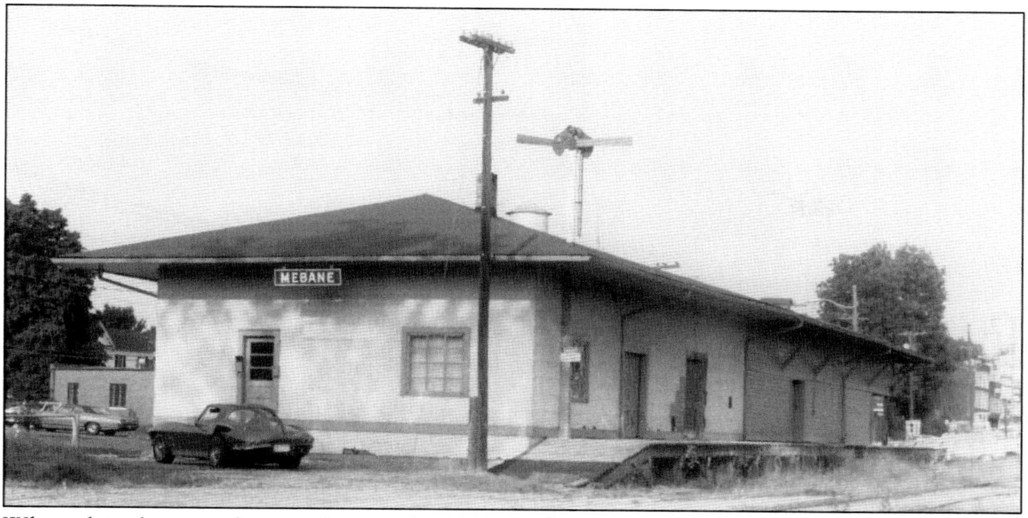

When this photograph was taken in the 1960s, railroad passenger travel was declining and the depot was becoming a lonely place. Like people all across the nation, Mebane residents were turning to faster and more convenient travel provided by the airlines, automobiles, and the interstate highway system. The depot soon closed and was demolished in the 1970s. (MHM.)

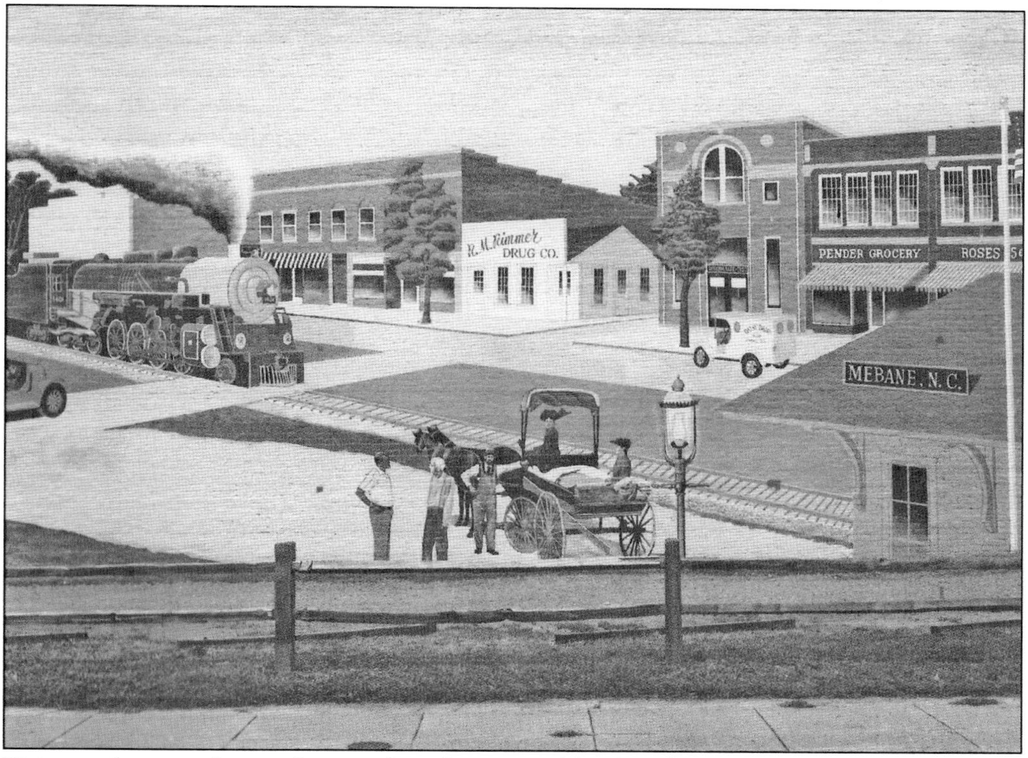

This is a close-up of a mural painted on the external brick wall of Rice's Jewelry by Gibsonville painter and sculptor Ogden Deal and his son Chuck in the early 1980s. Commissioned by James Rice to enhance downtown Mebane and honor Milton McDade, the town's historian, the mural portrays downtown Mebane in 1929. It depicts the old train depot, a train steaming through Mebane, a horse and carriage, Mebane's 1923 fire truck, McDade, Mebane artist Ceab Anderson, and several other people. (MHM.)

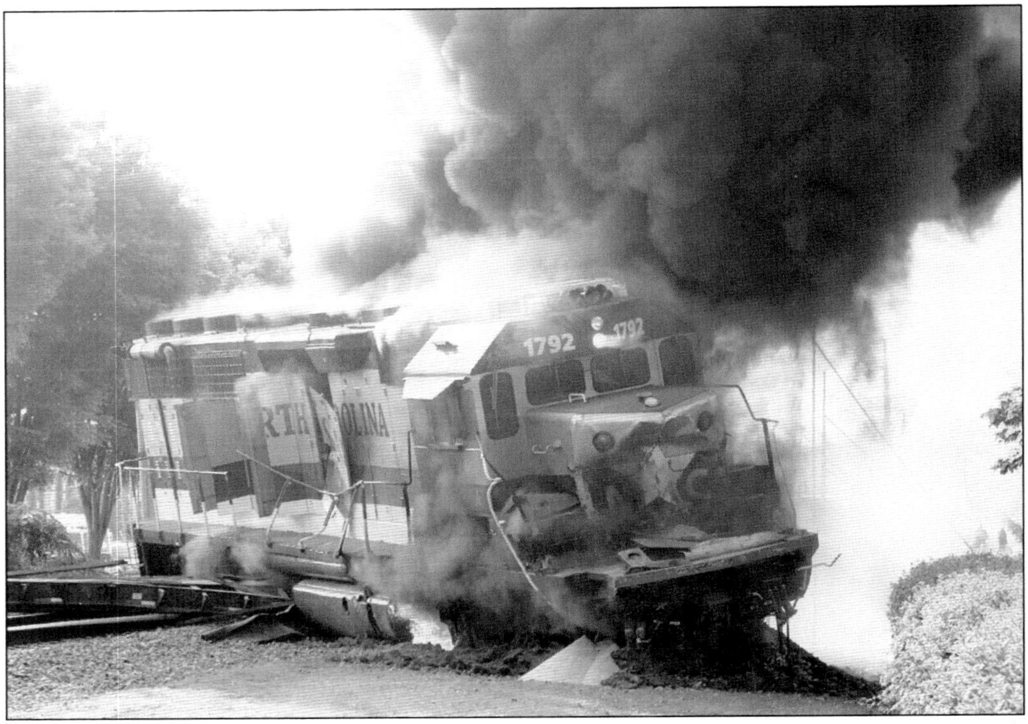

The 1940 crash was just one of many that have occurred over the decades. The above photograph shows the burning engine from an Amtrak-truck crash that occurred in 2010 at the Fifth Street crossing. The engine caught fire and jumped the tracks. The Mebane Fire Department and emergency services from surrounding areas rushed to contain the fire, attend to the injured passengers, and clean up the wreck. The Amtrak was carrying 36 passengers and three crewmen. Eleven passengers and one crewman were rushed to local hospitals for treatment, but none suffered serious injuries. Hundreds of spectators spent much of the day watching the cleanup. The dramatic photograph below shows firefighters trying to contain the fire. (Both, courtesy of the *Mebane Enterprise*.)

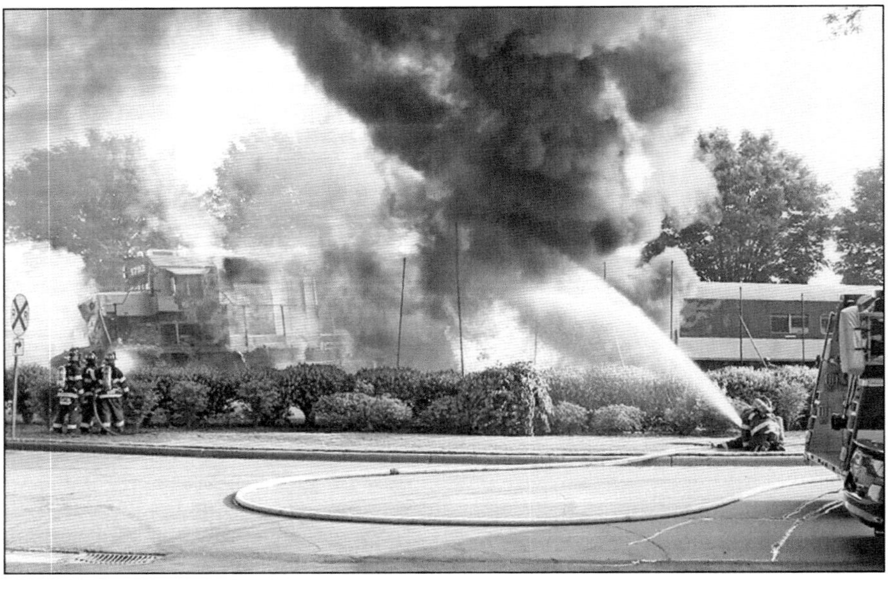

Two

Industries

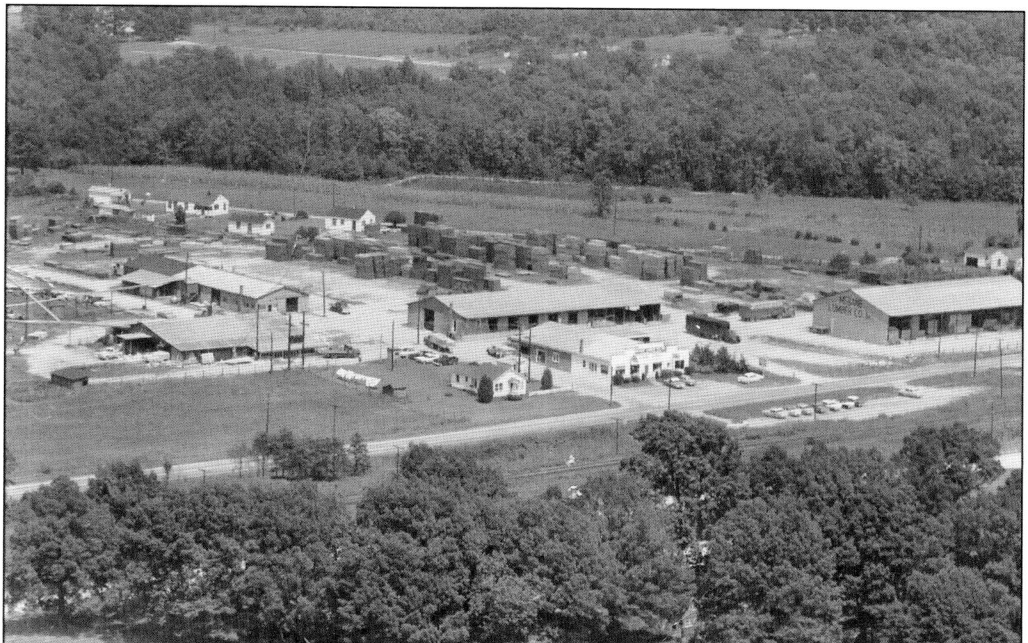

Originally founded on East Center Street in 1945 by Mebane lawyer June Crumpler, the Mebane Lumber Company is still operating today under different owners in the same location. Crumpler also started a construction firm that built several housing developments on the outskirts of town, providing affordable small homes for young married couples and others in the postwar period. These were Mebane's first suburbs. (MHM.)

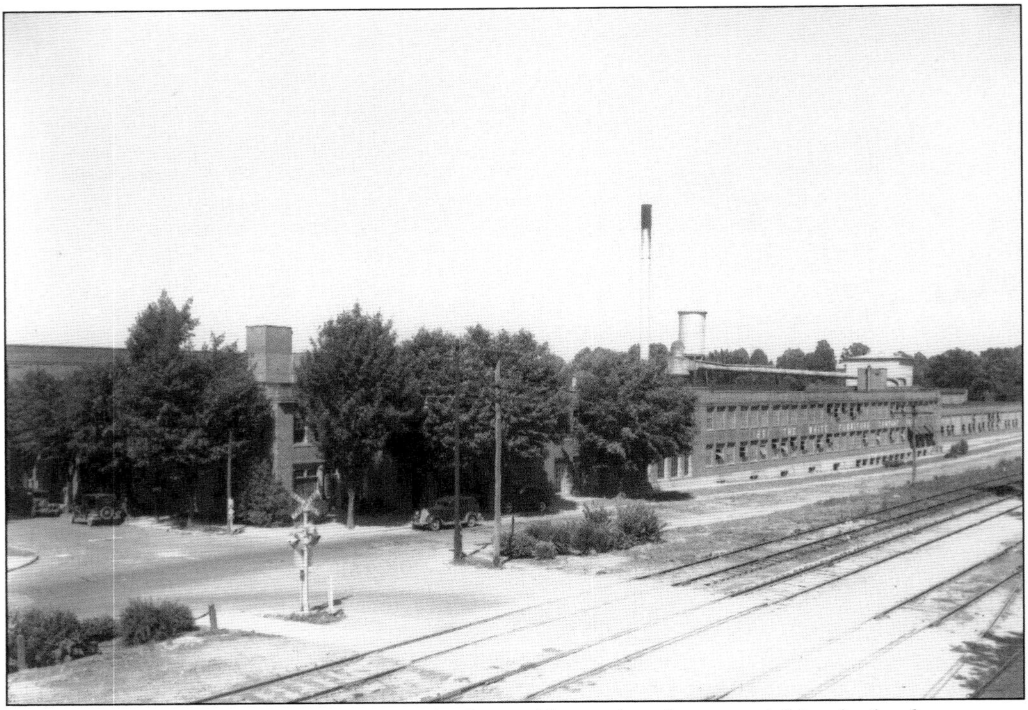

In 1923, White Furniture Company caught fire and burned to the ground. Hundreds of spectators gathered along the railroad and side streets to watch firefighters from the Mebane Fire Department and nearby towns fight the huge blaze. The company quickly rebuilt. Using bricks the second time around, the building still stands today. This image shows the factory around 1940 at the Fifth Street and Center Street crossing. (MHM.)

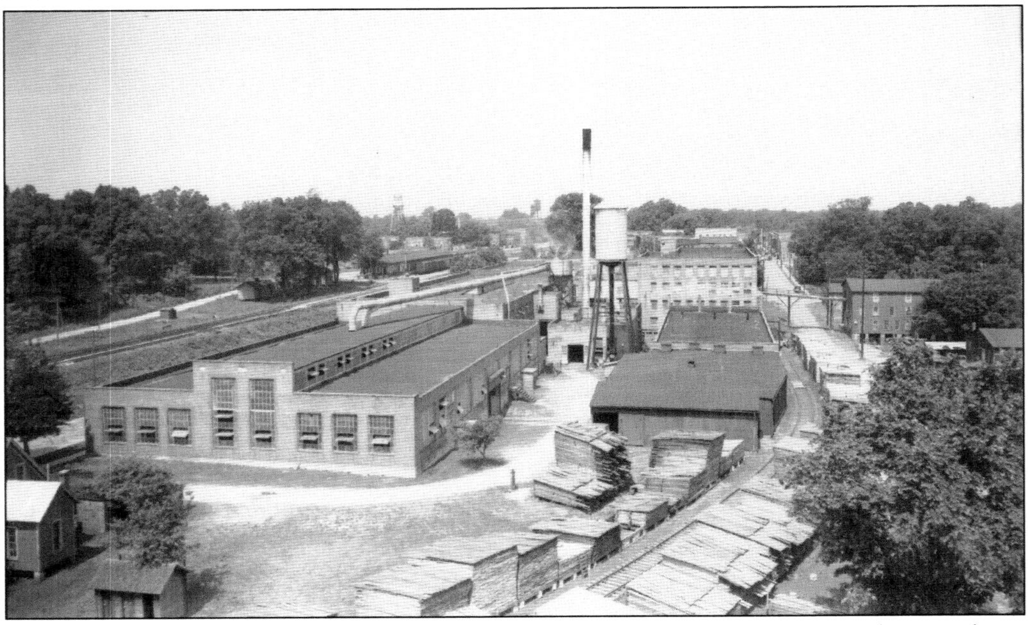

Taken from the top of a nearby building in the 1930s, this photograph looking to the west shows the huge company between the railroad and Clay Street. The depot can be seen in the upper left, and Clay Street is to the right. (MHM.)

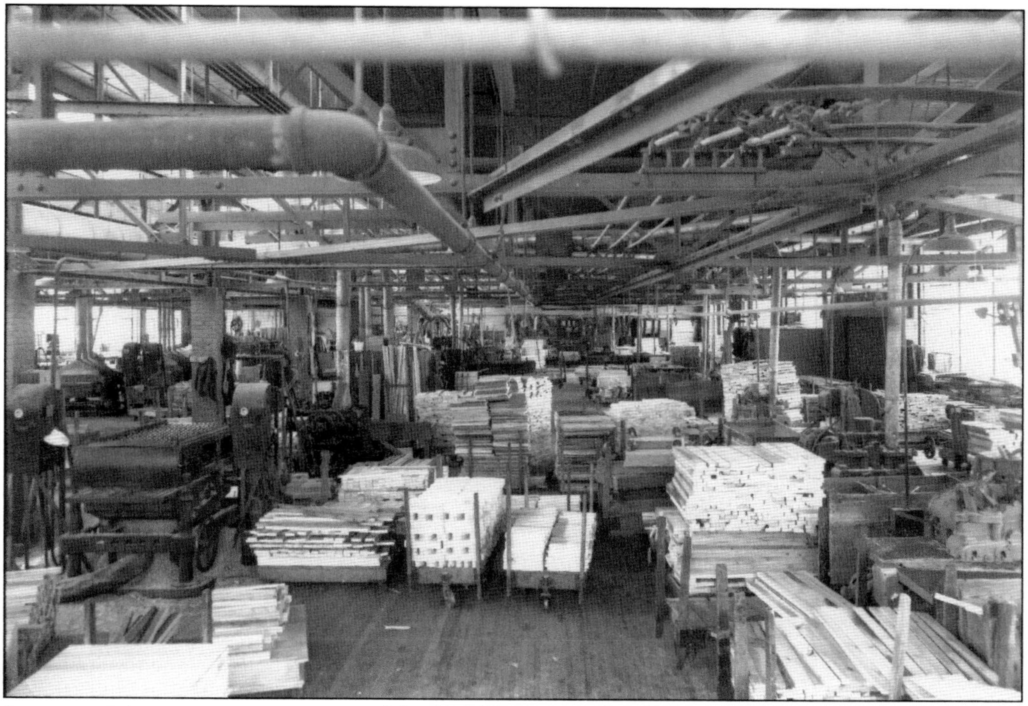

Just one of the many interior areas of the 200,000-square-foot factory, this huge room is filled with lumber that will be processed by several machines and skilled workers as it is transformed into high-quality furniture that will be shipped to buyers all across the United States. (MHM.)

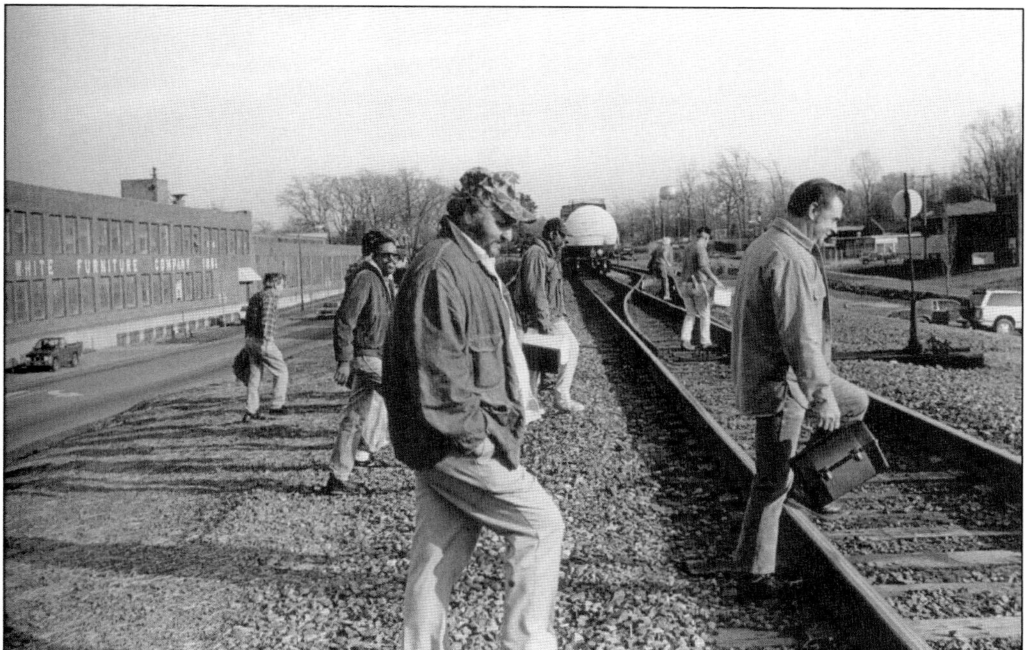

Here is the familiar sight of workers crossing Center Street and the railroad after the famous whistle signaled that it was quitting time at the White Furniture Company. This photograph was taken in 1992, one year before White's closed. (Courtesy of Bill Bamberger.)

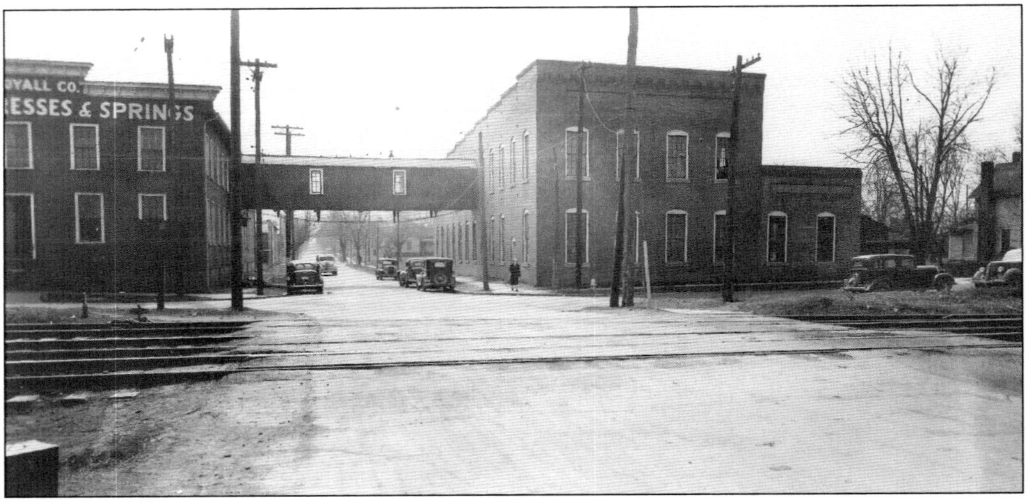

The Mebane Company was organized in 1904 as the Mebane Bedding Company by William Warren Corbett and several other investors with $3,300 in capital. Originally a maker of straw and cotton mattresses, it bought out several other manufacturing plants in North Carolina and added bedsprings, bed frames, sofas, studio beds, and other items over the years. It went through several name changes, becoming the Mebane Royall Company, the Mebane Company, and eventually Kingsdown, which continues operation in Mebane and in plants in several other cities today. This 1940 front view of the Mebane Company shows the overpass across Third Street that connected the two main areas of the plant on the corner of South Third and Washington Streets and beside the railroad. Apparently posing for an advertisement, Lucille Crabtree enjoys a Kingsdown mattress while, from left to right, Carl Crabtree, Griffin McClure, L.P. Best, Preacher Green of Green & McLure, and an unidentified Kingsdown salesman and nurse look on. (Both, MHM.)

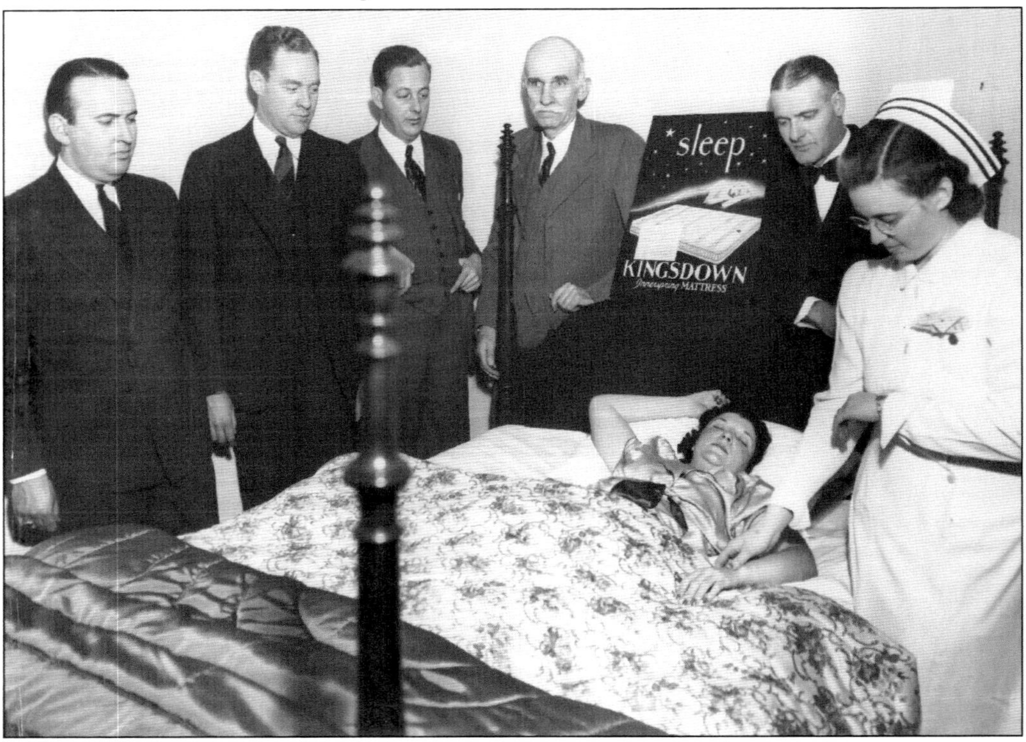

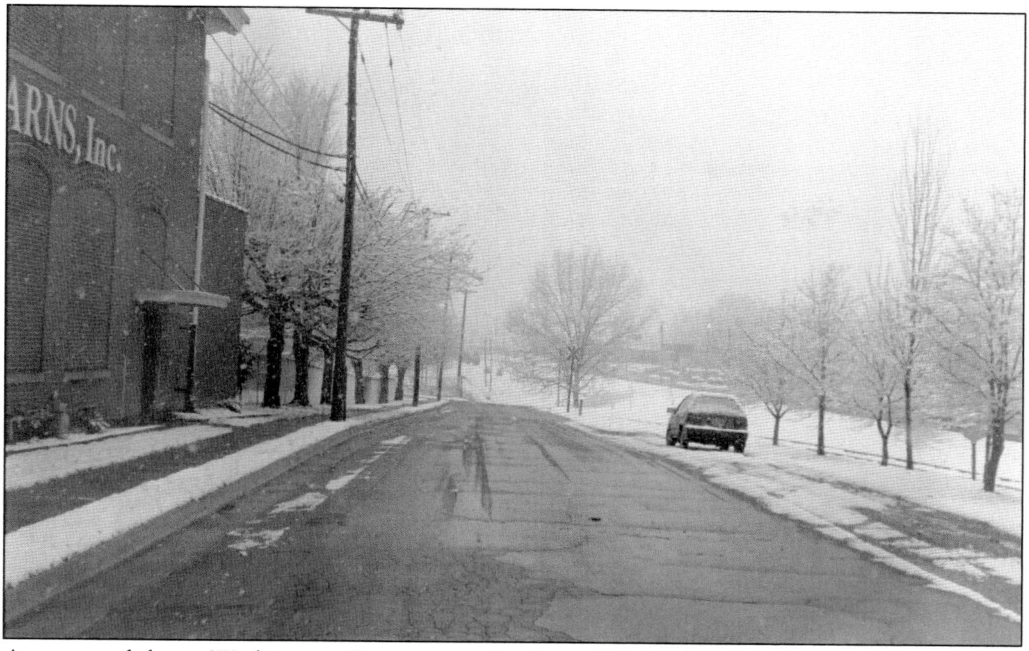

An automobile on Washington Street passes by Dixie Yarn Mill on a snowy day in the 1980s. The City of Mebane purchased this mill and transformed it into a beautiful public library in 2005. (MHM.)

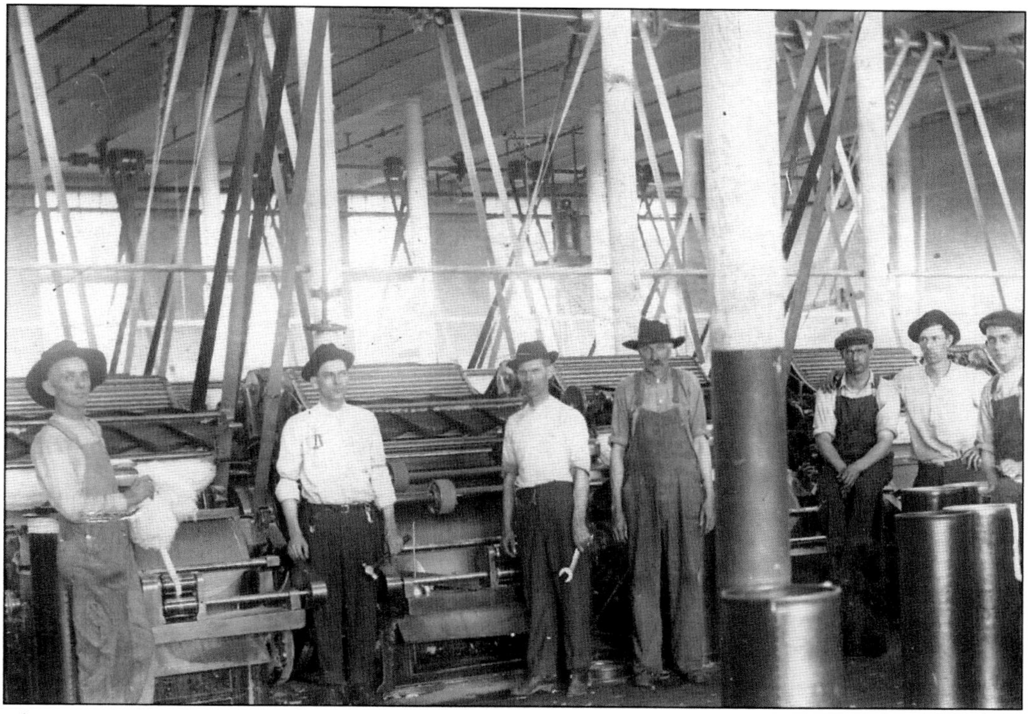

These men are working inside one of the mills in the 1920s. Like most textile mills, Dixie Yarn Mill was especially hot and humid during the summer months. Pictured from left to right are David Yancey, Weaver Tripp, unidentified, Bill Jones, Bud Horner, and two unidentified. (Courtesy of Betty Tripp.)

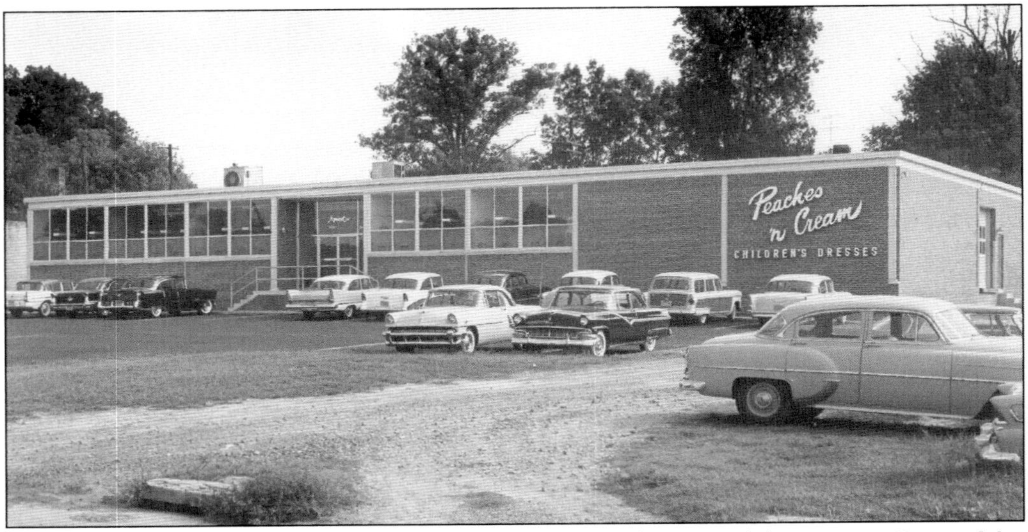

May Apparel was started in 1946 by brothers W.H. and Jack May and their cousin Garvin May as a manufacturer of quality children's clothing. It was originally marketed under the label of Peaches 'N Cream. First located on the corner of Fifth and Washington Streets, the plant moved in 1958 to a new facility where city hall is located now and to an even larger plant near Interstate 85 east of Mebane in 1969. Increasing competition from foreign companies led the company to cease operations in the United States in 2000. This photograph shows the firm at its second location. (MHM.)

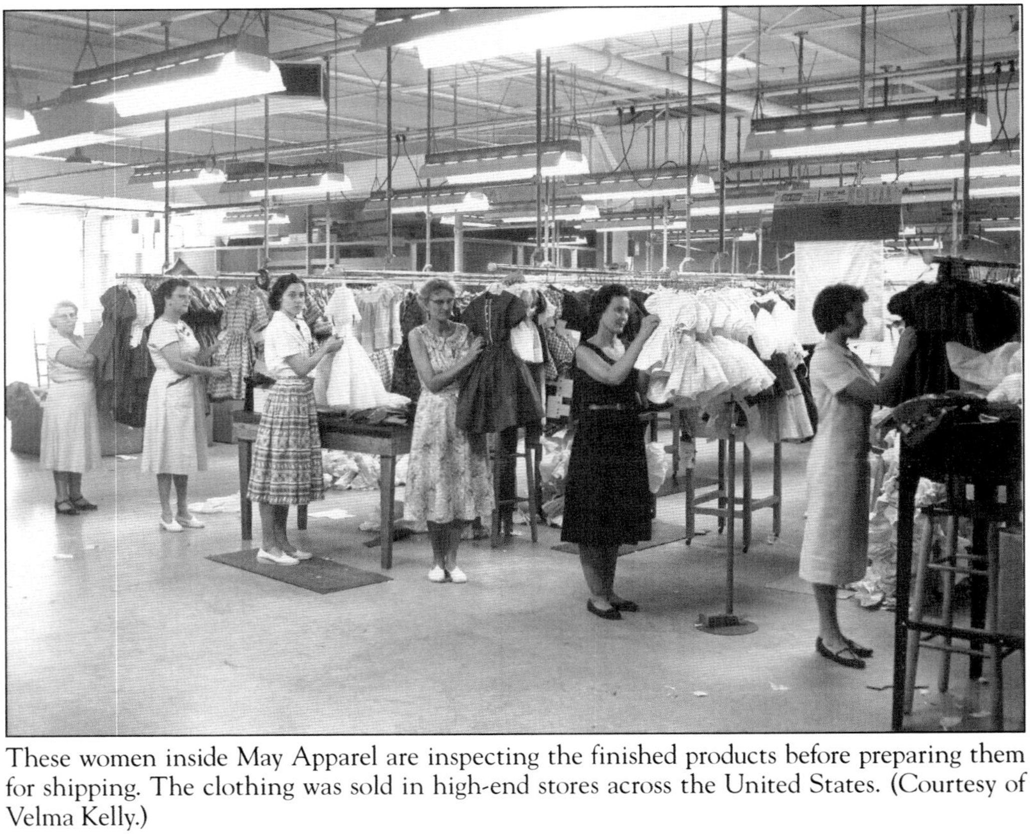

These women inside May Apparel are inspecting the finished products before preparing them for shipping. The clothing was sold in high-end stores across the United States. (Courtesy of Velma Kelly.)

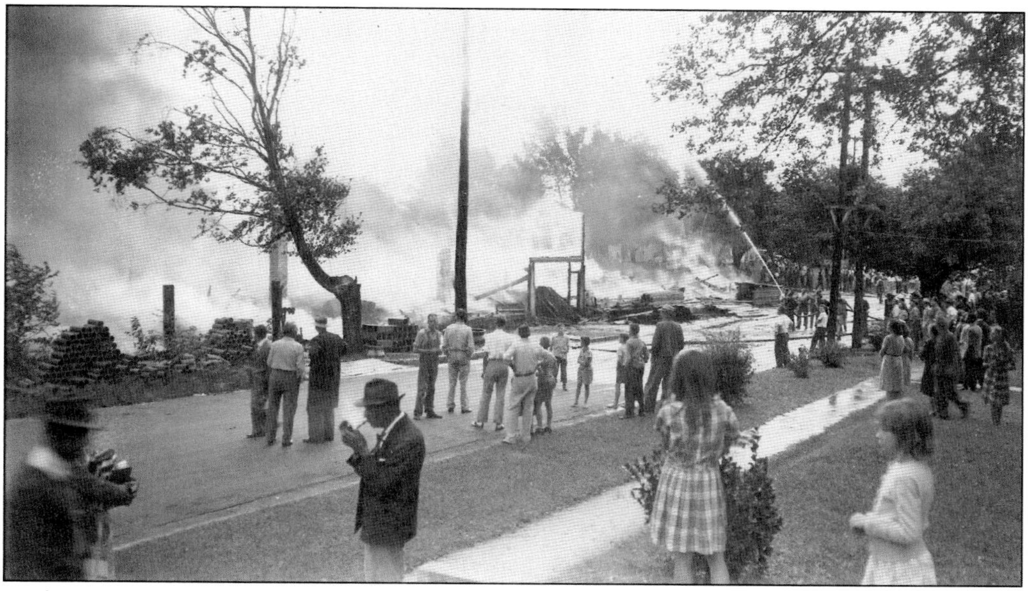

Professional photographers North and Grace Lynch took this photograph of the Mebane Fire Department battling a huge fire in 1945 on Fourth Street at Fitch-Riggs Lumber Company, owned by Abner B. Fitch and Will T. Riggs, while area residents looked on. This photograph was taken looking southwest toward what was the office and front of the building. The company was a total loss and was not rebuilt in Mebane. (MHM.)

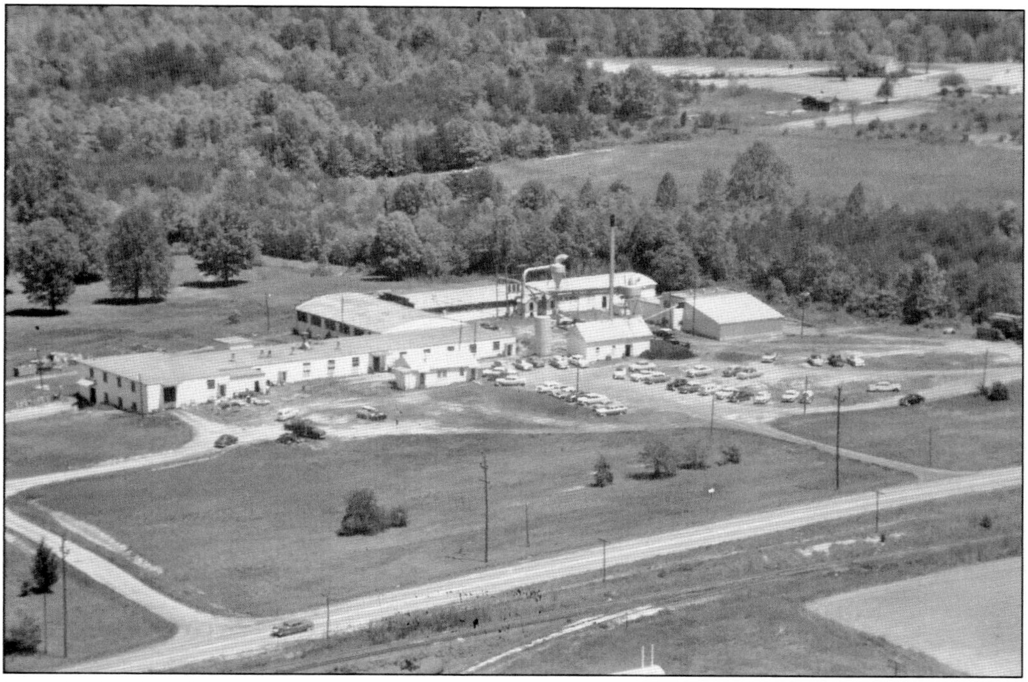

Founded by L.P. Best, Craftique began manufacturing its reproductions of antique Hepplewhite furniture in May 1946. Made of Honduras mahogany, the high-end furniture was soon selling all across the United States and in many foreign countries. In the late 1980s, the company was sold to Pulaski Furniture in Virginia. Pulaski operated the firm before selling the Craftique furniture line to John Erwin and Craig Shoemaker in 1997. (Courtesy of Craftique.)

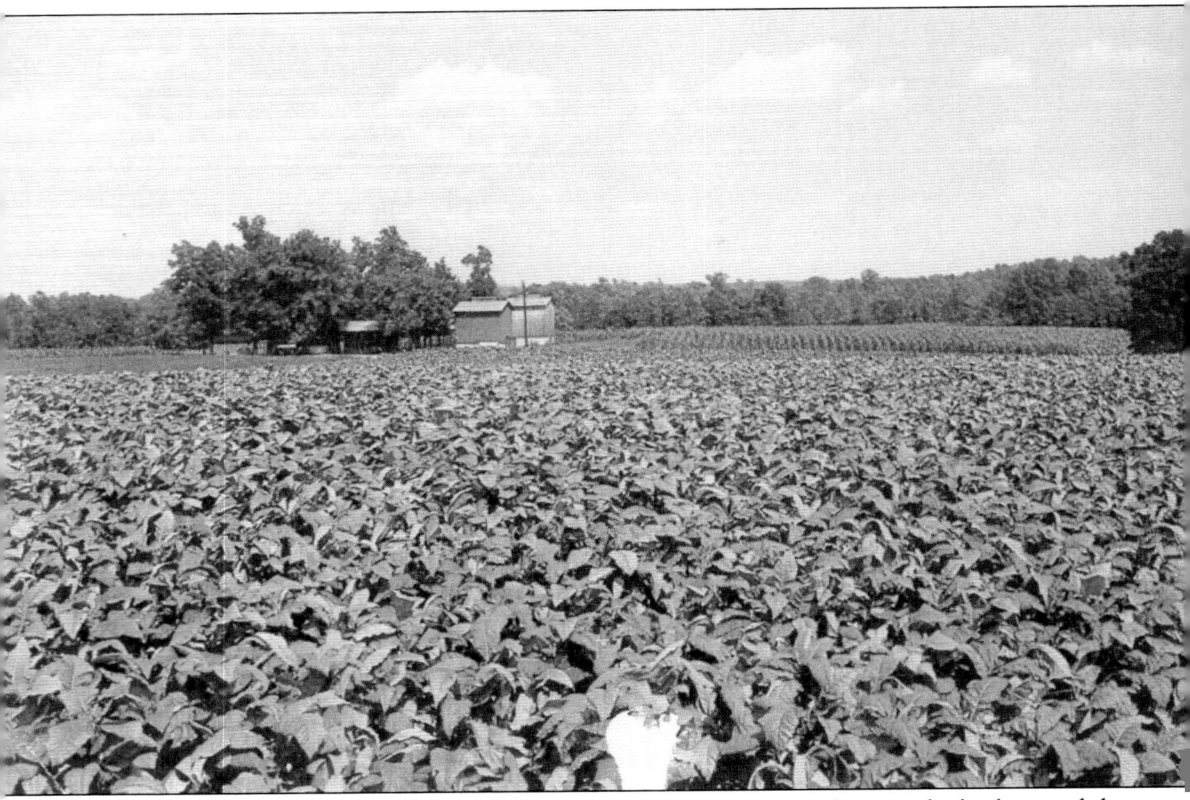

This photograph of a large tobacco field outside of Mebane shows a barn in the background that would be used to cure the tobacco when it had been harvested. The green, sticky leaves were tied to long tobacco sticks and placed on tiers inside the barn, where the leaves were dried by hot air passing through flues. The drying heat was produced by wood or oil burners. The curing process turned the leaves from green to a golden color and produced the flue-cured tobacco odor and flavor desired by tobacco factories and consumers. (MHM.)

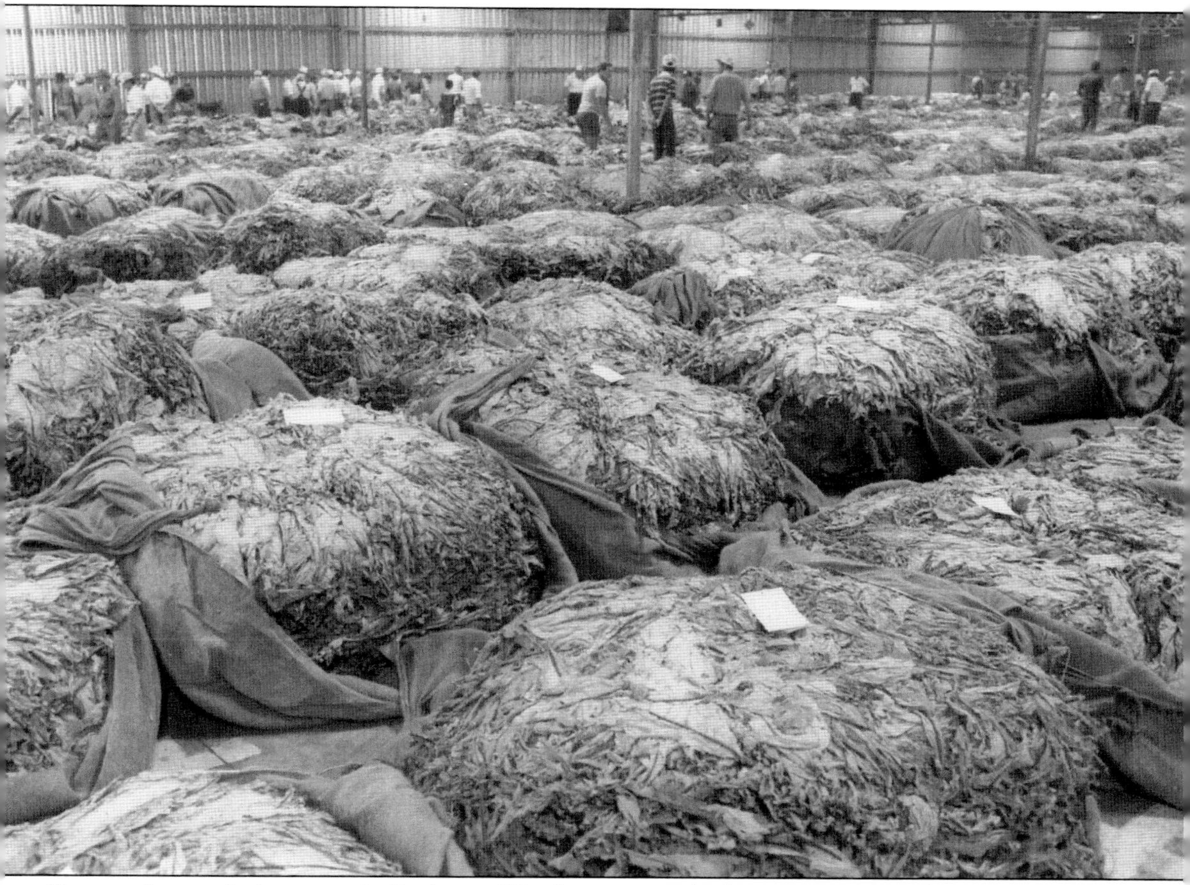

Rows and rows of tobacco in the Piedmont Warehouse await the beginning of the tobacco auction in 1982. For many farmers and their families in the 1980s, tobacco was still a way of making a living and a way of life, but profitable tobacco farming was in the midst of a long slow decline because of government regulations and changing attitudes toward tobacco consumption. Mebane was no longer known as a tobacco town. (MHM.)

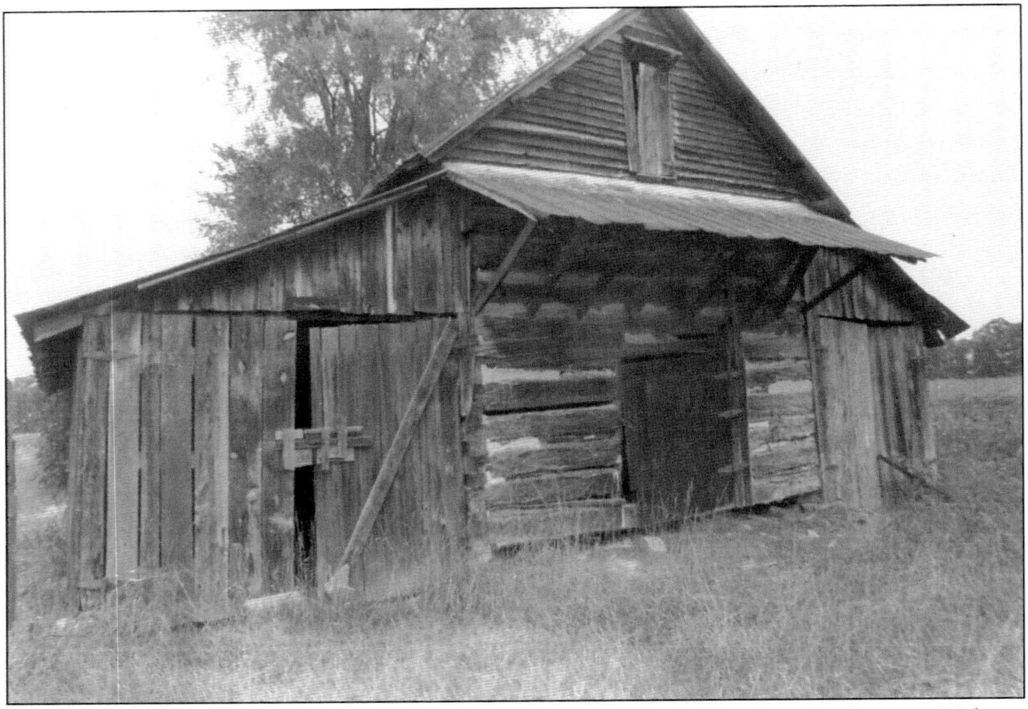

This undated photograph of an old abandoned tobacco barn on the Douglas farm on Mebane Rogers Road stands as a reminder of days past when tobacco was king. (MHM.)

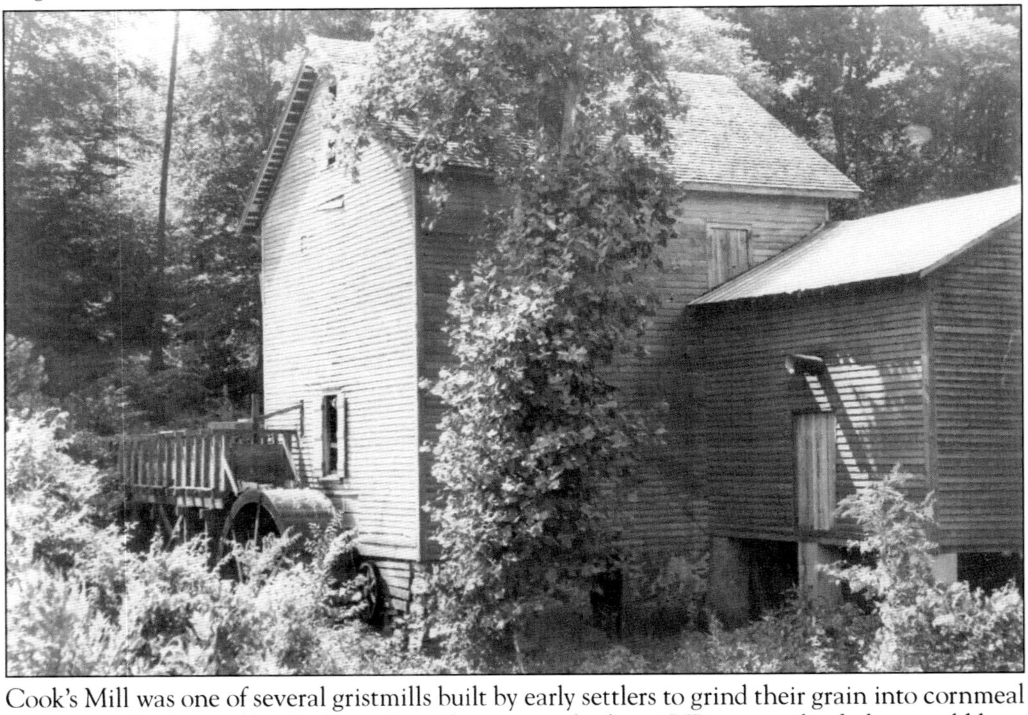

Cook's Mill was one of several gristmills built by early settlers to grind their grain into cornmeal and flour. The first mill to be located on this site was built in 1757 just north of what would later be called Mebane. The Cook's Mill in this photograph was the last of three mills that were built on this site. It closed in the second half of the 20th century. (MHM.)

Three

BUSINESSES

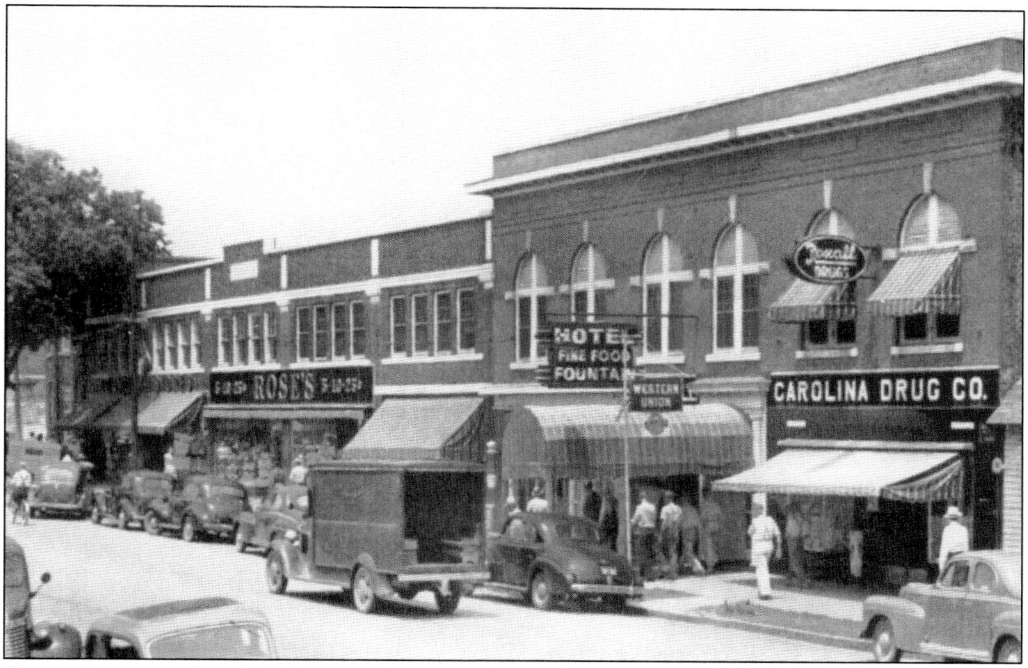

Shown here are the Center Street stores from Rose's 5, 10, and 25¢ store (commonly called Rose's Dime Store) to Carolina Drug on a busy day during the tobacco market in the 1930s. After being paid for their crops, tobacco farmers and their families crowded the streets and stores looking for bargains in clothing, school supplies, and other necessities. Rose's was one of the most popular stores in town during the market, with adults drawn to the inexpensive merchandise and children attracted by the large candy counter and wide array of toys and games. Parents also took advantage of the low prices and generous layaway plan to buy presents for their children's Christmas. (MHM.)

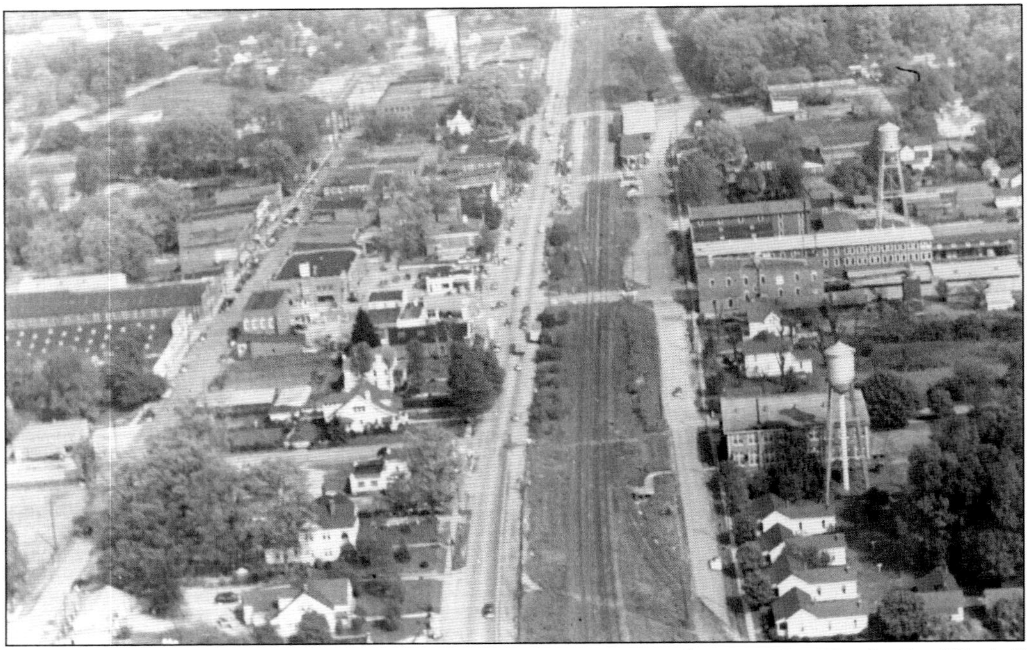

When these two aerial photographs of downtown Mebane were shot in 1951, Charles Jay "Shake" Harris was the pilot with J.C. Jordan as the photographer. Looking east, this image shows Dixie Yarn Mill, several mill houses, Kingsdown, and the depot. Center Street is shown on the left running down to the grain tower at the flour mill. (MHM.)

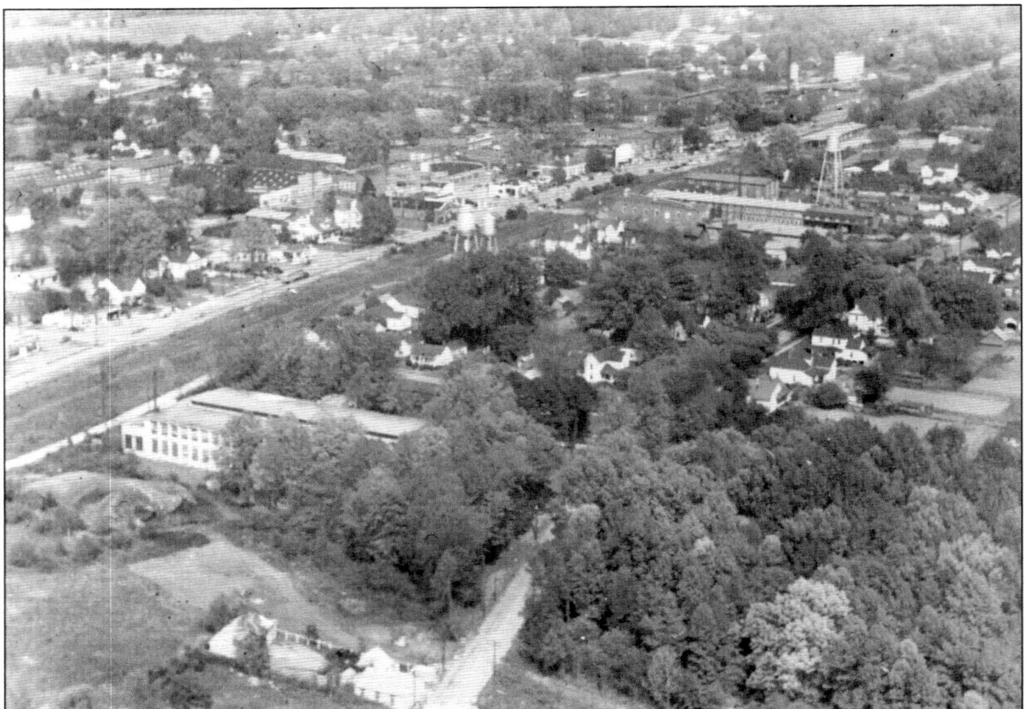

Shot on the same day in the same area, this photograph shows the other Dixie Yarn Mill and part of Holt Street. (MHM.)

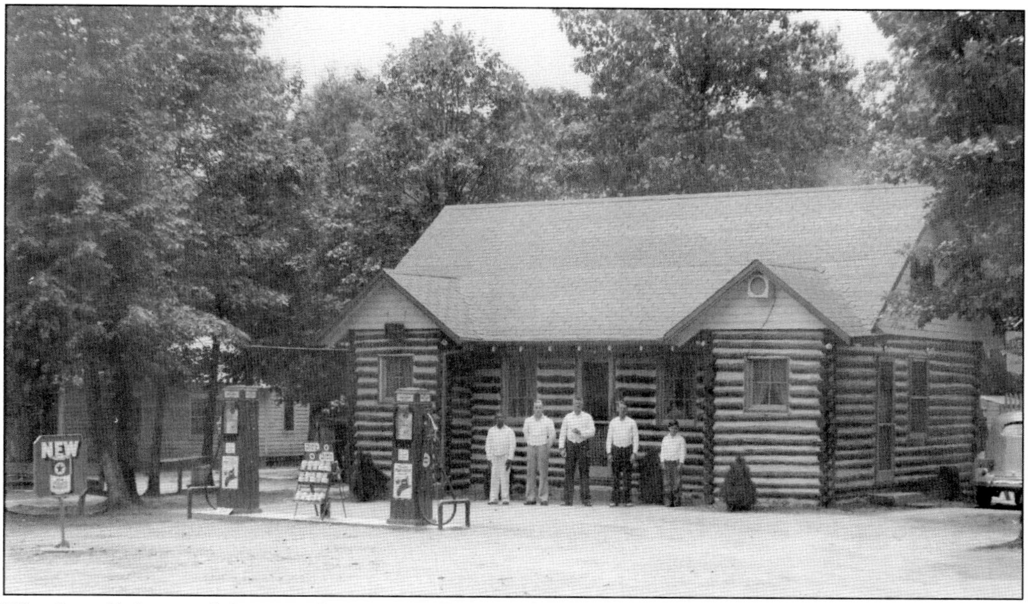

The Log Cabin and Service Station on East Highway 70 (Center Street) sold gasoline, but its main attraction in the two decades before World War II was its barbecue. In the photograph above, owner Gene Berry (center) and four of his employees pose outside, while the photograph below captures the look but not the aroma of barbecue cooking for hours inside the building in an open pit in the best North Carolina tradition. (Above, MHM; below, photograph by North and Grace Lynch, MHM.)

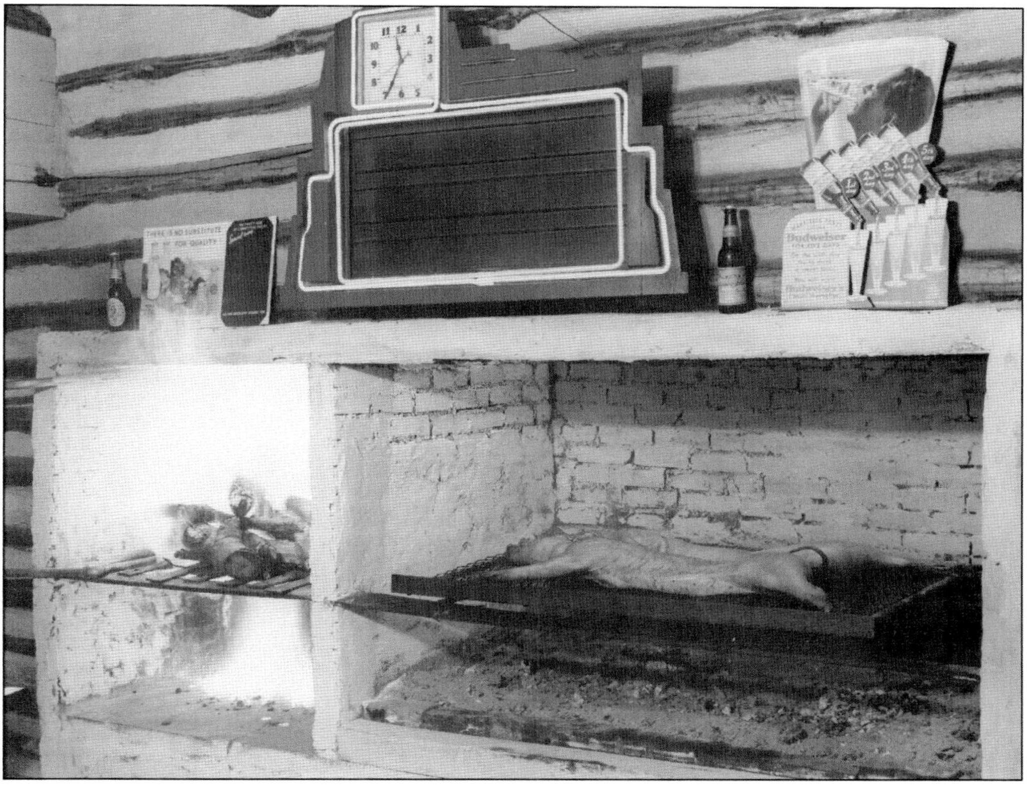

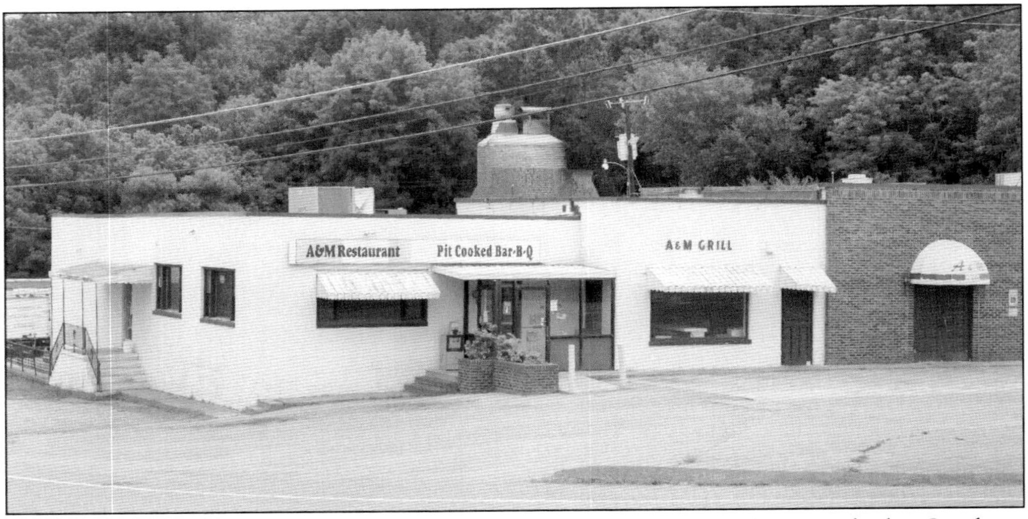

Many barbecue lovers in Mebane and surrounding areas favored the barbecue and other Southern delicacies served at the A&M Grill on East Highway 70. Charlie McAdams opened the little restaurant in 1947, and the McAdams family operated it until it closed in the summer of 2011. It was a popular spot for families, cruising high school students, reunions, and other events. (Courtesy of Kelly Gauldin.)

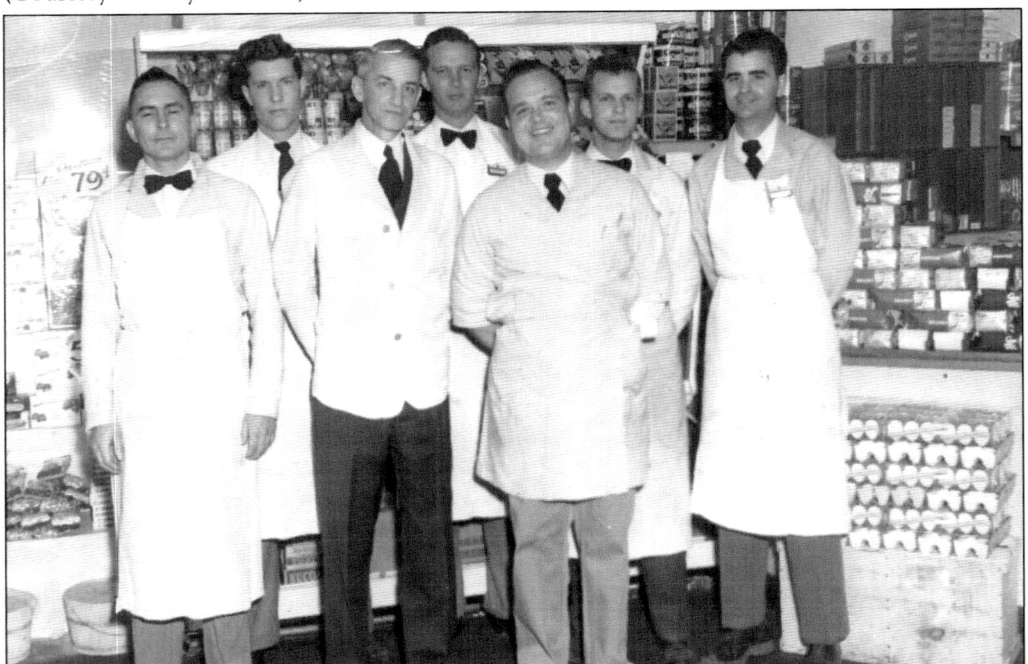

Pender's Store on Center Street was a popular downtown grocery for many years. In the early 1950s, several employees posed for this photograph. From left to right are Paul Lee, Garland Rook, John Lawrence, Kenneth Smith, Belton Brigman, Vernon Scott, and Jimmy Wilson. When the Colonial Store, Mebane's first "supermarket," opened in the mid-1950s, several of Pender's employees went to work there. The Colonial Store and other supermarkets that came to Mebane and nearby Burlington brought the demise of many of the small grocery stores around town. (Courtesy of Ellen Lawrence.)

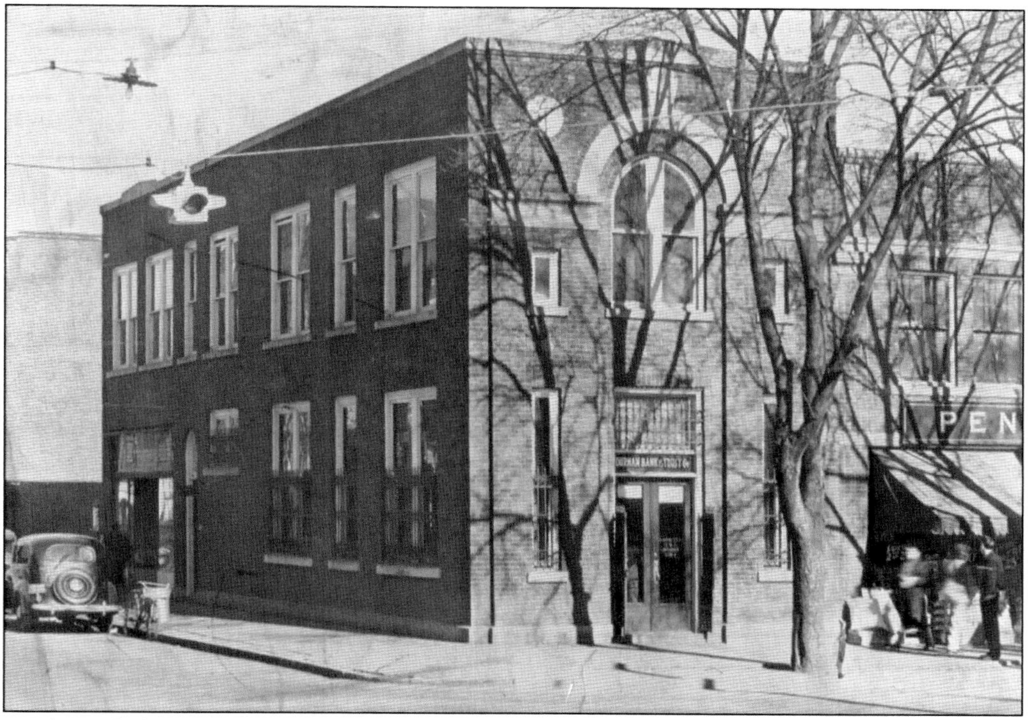

As the only bank in the small town of Mebane for many years, Durham Bank, shown here in the 1940s, gave personal and friendly service. As Mebane grew in the second half of the 20th century, the banking industry underwent a consolidation boom, other banks moved into town, and Durham Bank was transformed into Central Carolina Bank and then SunTrust. (MHM.)

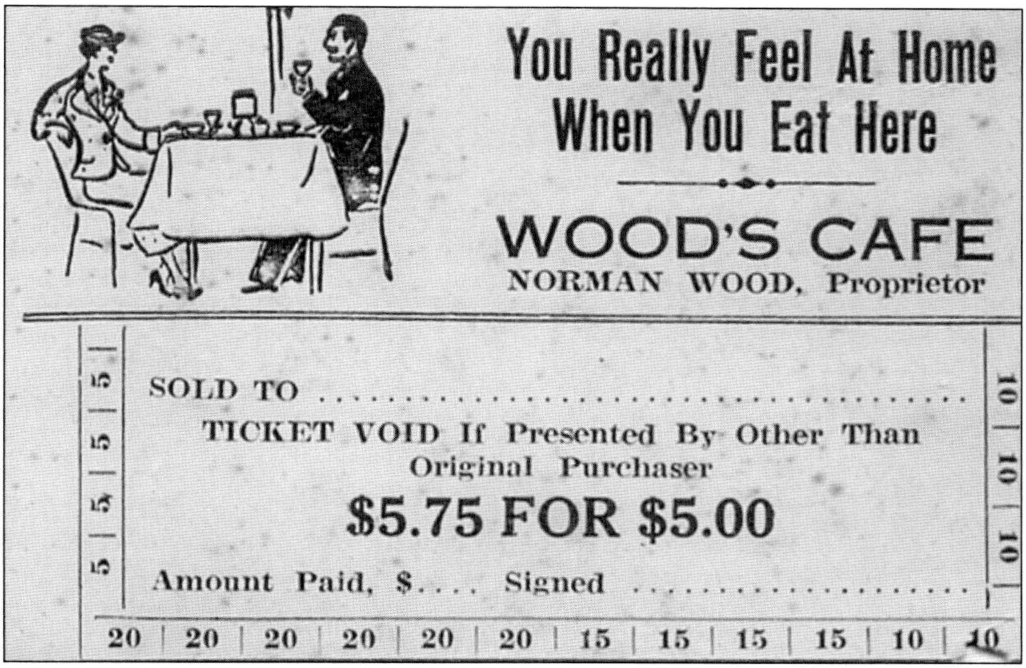

Normal Woods ran a popular café and hotel for many years on Center Street. This café meal ticket seemed to offer quite a bargain for people staying at the hotel (MHM.)

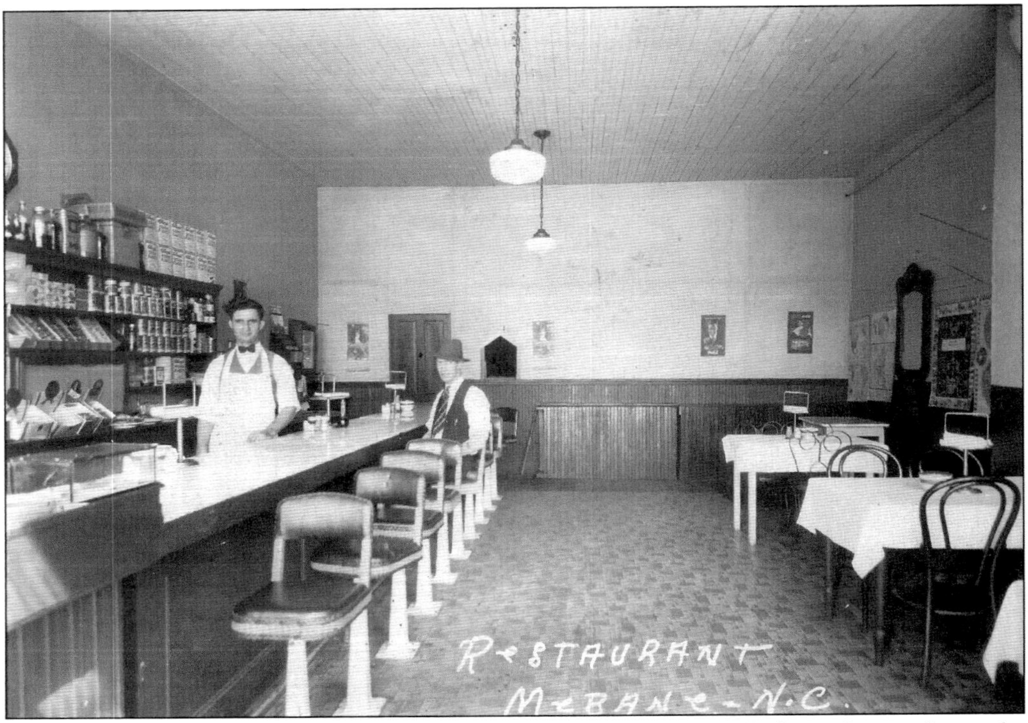

The Bartis family ran Gus Bartis's Café on Center Street for many years. At times, it also served as the Mebane bus station. Owner Gus Bartis is shown here with a lone customer sitting on a stool at the counter on a slow day. (Courtesy of Penny Bartis Butler.)

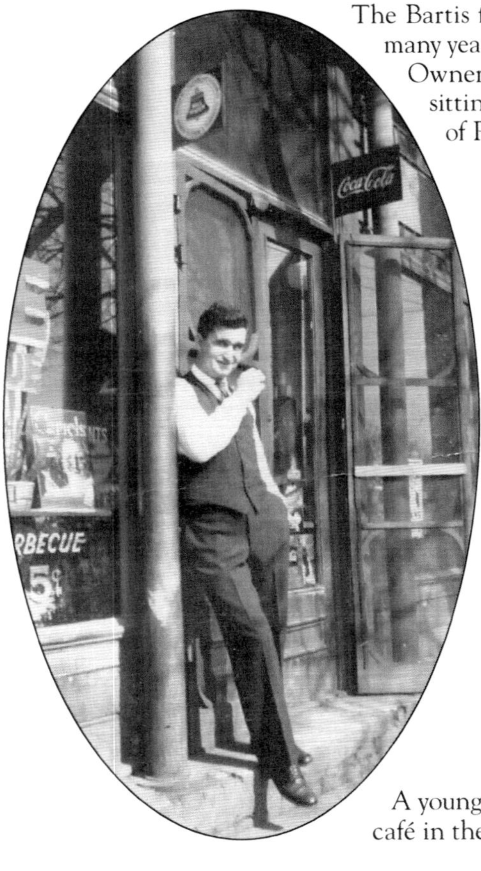

A young and dapperly dressed Gus Bartis stands outside the café in the 1930s. (Courtesy of Penny Bartis Butler.)

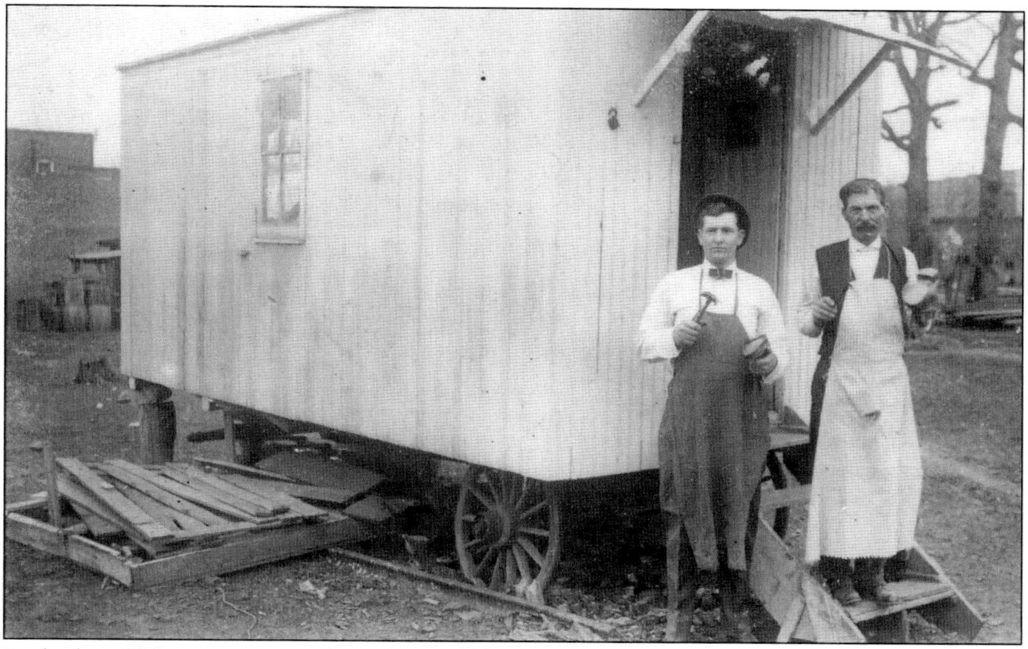

In the late 19th century, travelling shoe cobblers set up shop on Center Street. In the 1930s, the Works Progress Administration (WPA) built a post office on the site for $70,000. The Mebane Police Department occupies the building today. (MHM.)

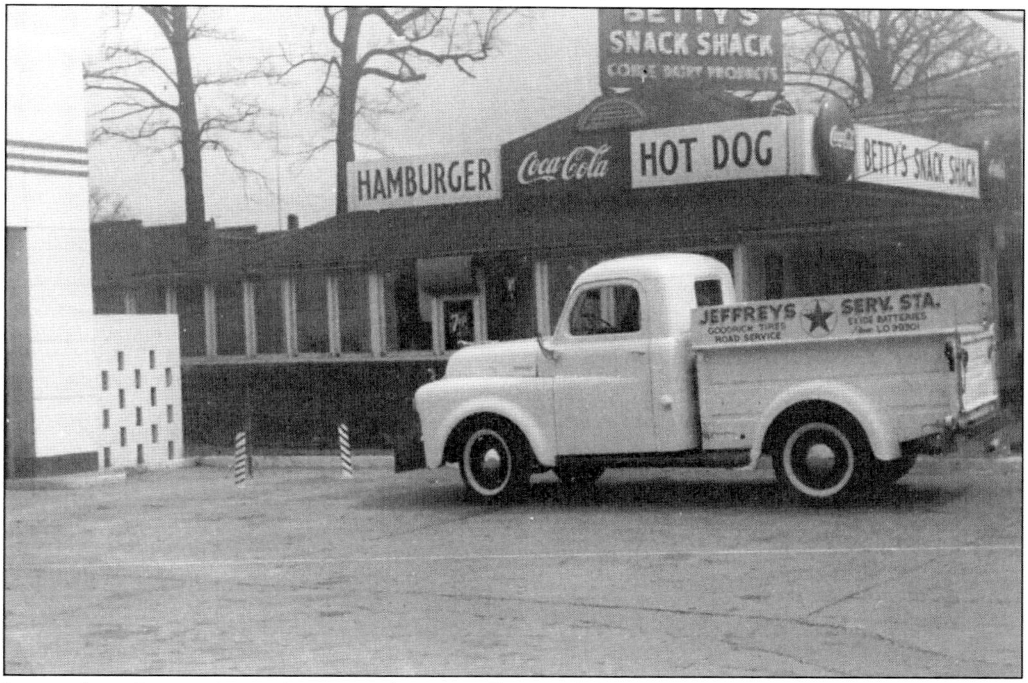

Located on Center Street between the post office and the Texaco service station, Betty's Snack Shack attracted patrons through its reputation and the smell of delicious hot dogs that traveled far down the street. It was impossible to walk by the little eatery without stopping for its famous hot dogs, hamburgers, and sandwiches. The popular diner closed in 1965 and was demolished to make room for an addition to the post office. (Courtesy of Nancy Lancaster.)

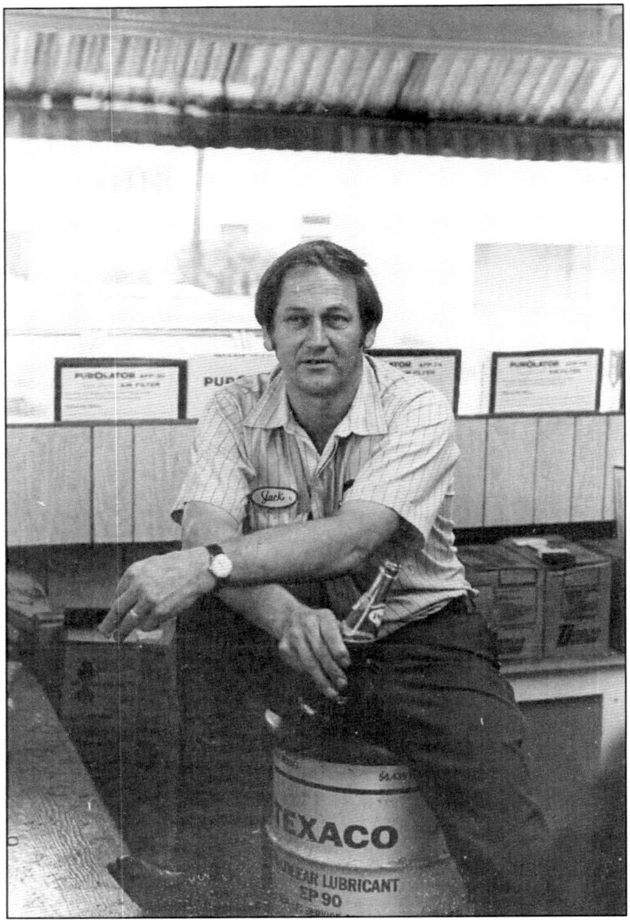

Jack Lancaster strikes a familiar pose inside the Texaco service station he and W.G. Jeffreys operated. Lancaster was also a volunteer fireman for 25 years. (Courtesy of Nancy Lancaster.)

The Superior service station on the corner of Center and Third Streets is shown here in the 1930s, during the early years of the automobile age. These were those golden years before self-service, when service station employees pumped gasoline into cars, checked the oil, washed the windows, took the money, and returned the change. (Courtesy of Rick Smith.)

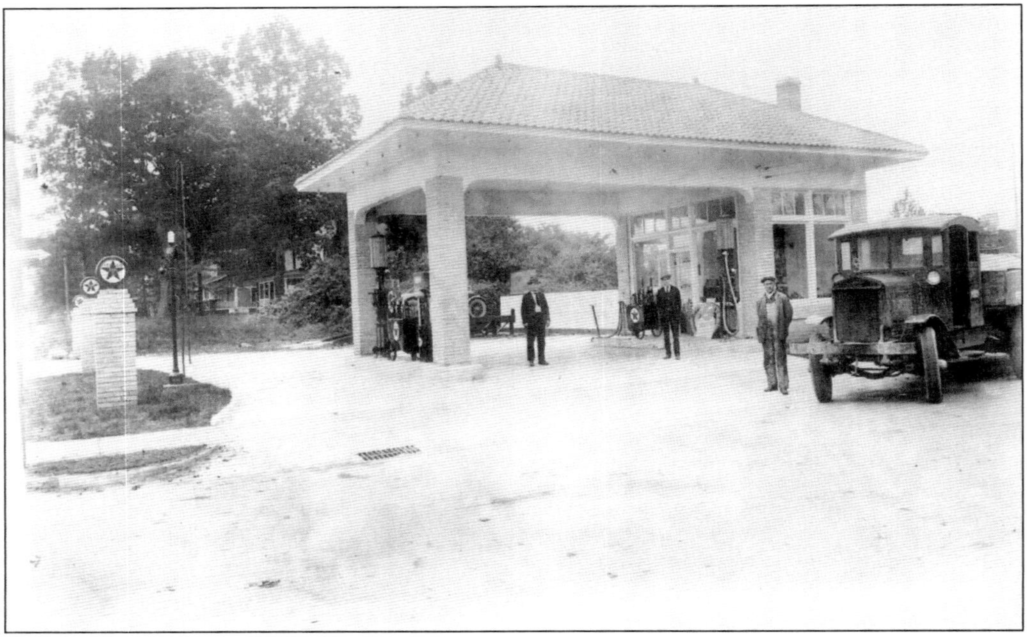

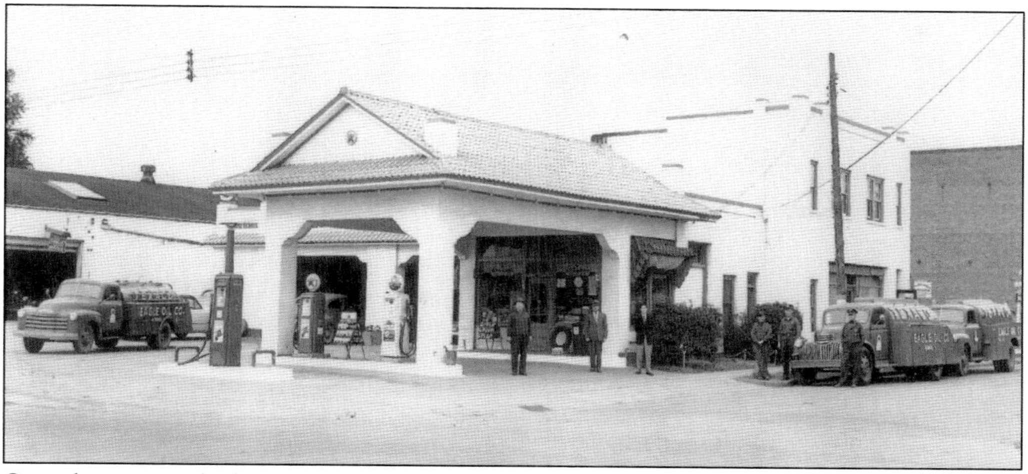

Over the course of a few years, the Superior service station on Center Street underwent several changes and eventually became a Texaco station. The Melville Chevrolet garage was also built next door, and the Eagle Oil Company was constructed behind the service station on Third Street. (Courtesy of Rick Smith.)

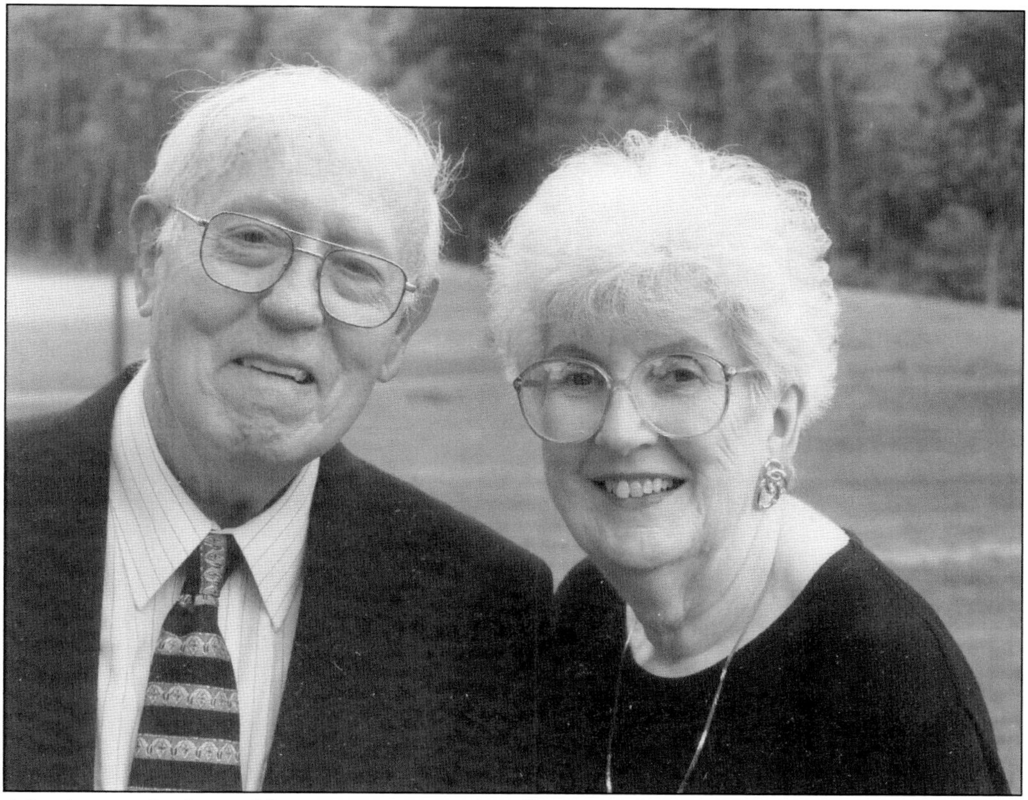

After he was discharged from service in 1945, William Lynch, shown around 2005 with his wife, Harriette, ran a photography studio in downtown Mebane and then Burlington before moving his studio to the back of his home on South Fifth Street where he and his wife, a painter, worked together for many years. He became the premier photographer of Mebane's people and events, and many townspeople believe that his photographs were so good that captions were not needed. (Courtesy of Debbi Lynch.)

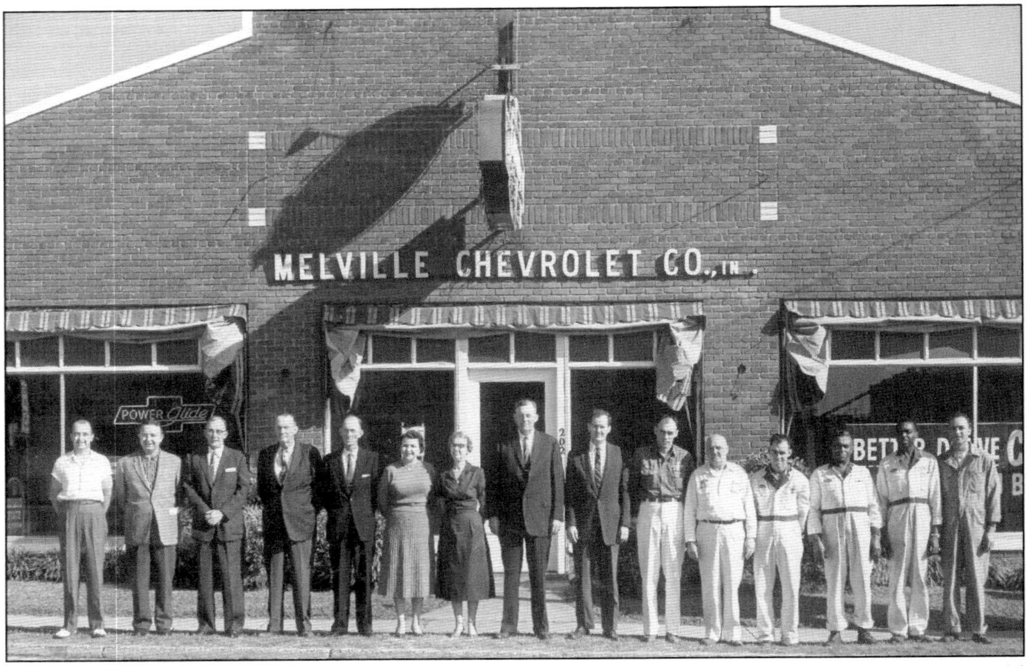

In the 1950s, Mebane citizens did not have to drive out of town to buy automobiles but could browse the new and used car lots of local Chevrolet, Ford, and Chrysler dealers. This 1957 photograph show the employees of Melville Chevrolet celebrating the 25th anniversary of the company established by C.M. Ray. (MHM.)

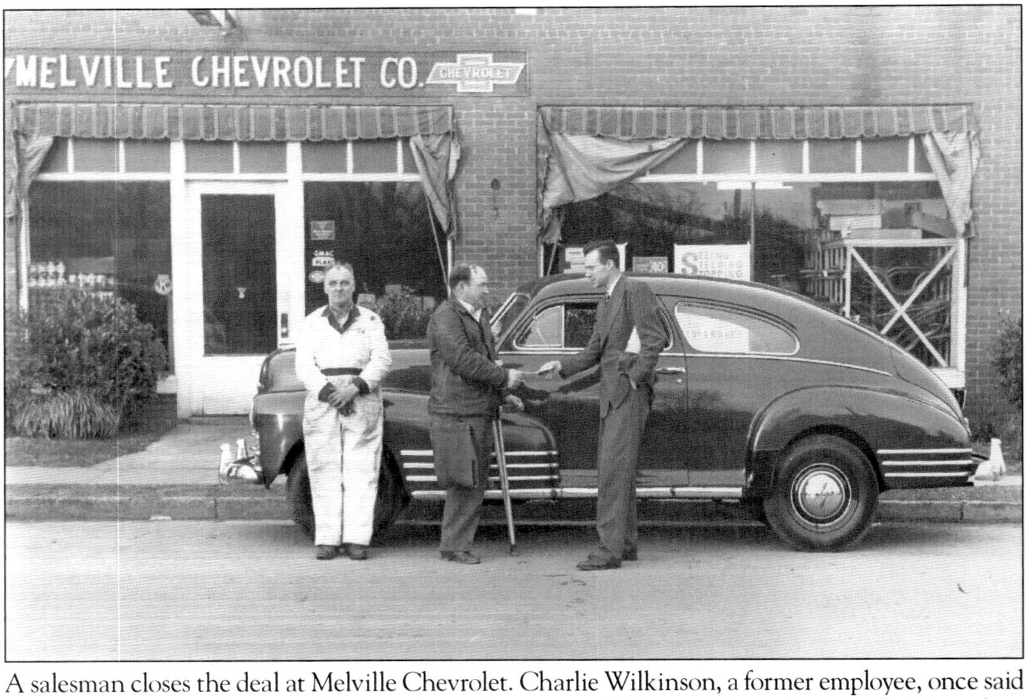

A salesman closes the deal at Melville Chevrolet. Charlie Wilkinson, a former employee, once said that Ray "loved to sell cars and he loved to make cars available to working class people. More than once I remember him taking a chattel mortgage on a mule as a trade-in on a new car sale." In its later years, other family members operated the company until it closed in the 1990s. (MHM.)

Neither rain, sleet, nor snow kept postman Johnny Lankford from his appointed rounds near Christmas in 1988. (Courtesy Johnny Lankford.)

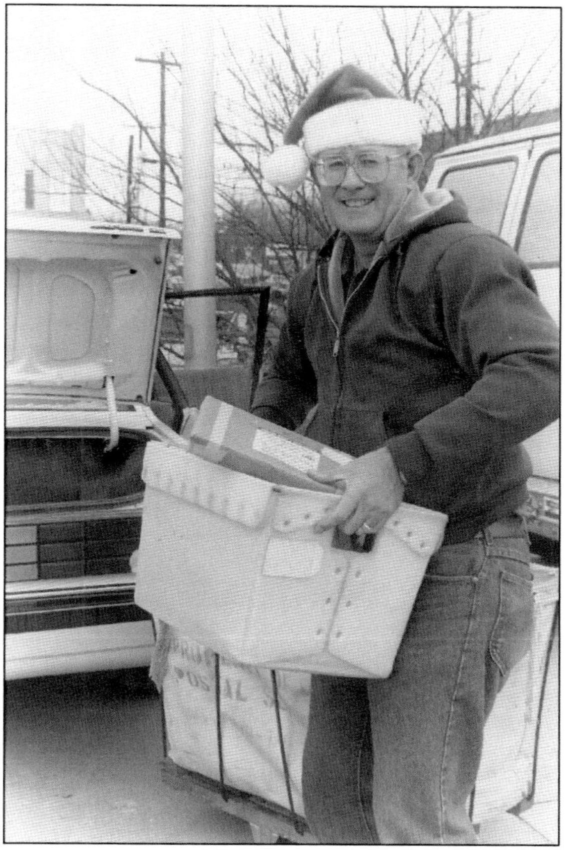

This 1938 photograph shows some of the businesses on Clay Street. A crowd is gathered in front of the Quality Store, a furniture store that is having a going-out-of-business sale. Also visible are the Mebane Clinic, a dress shop, the Commercial and Farmer's Bank Building on the corner of Clay Street and Fourth Street, a livery stable operated by W.T. Dillard, and the White Furniture Company. (MHM.)

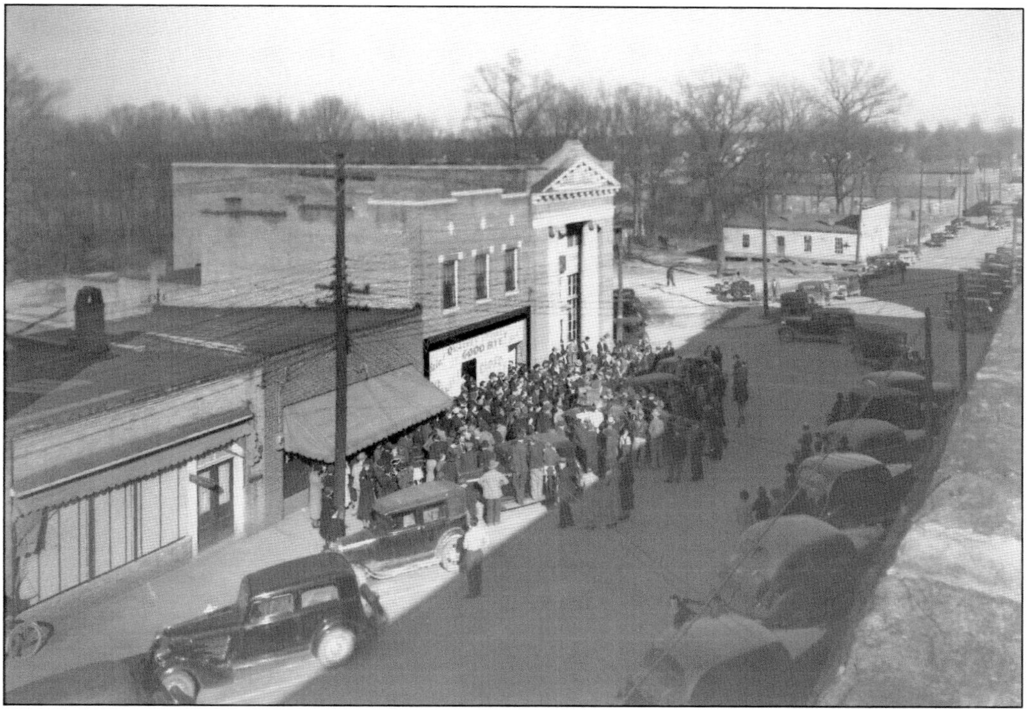

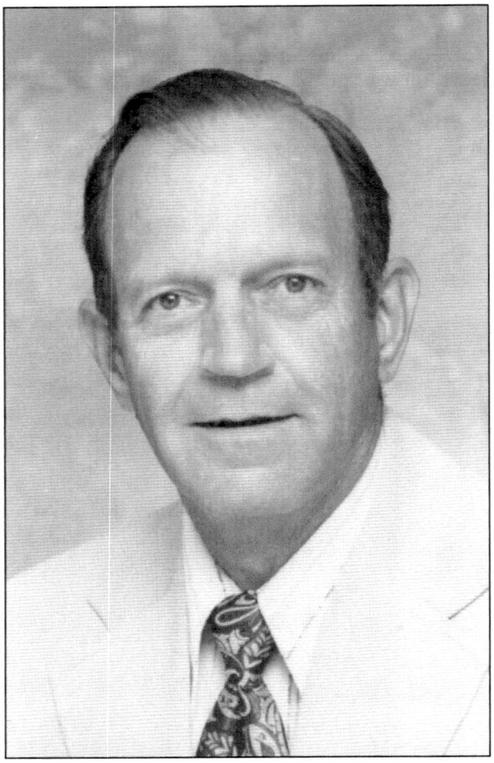

For close to 50 years, many Mebane residents received medical care in a clinic established on Clay Street in 1935 by Dr. Woodrow Tyson. Tyson eventually sold the clinic, and by the early 1950s, it was renamed the Mebane Clinic and was operated by Dr. George Bullard, Dr. George McLamb, and Dr. Clara Jones. The clinic served as a mini-hospital, staffed by nurses 24 hours a day and seeing an average of 60 patients a day, with some receiving overnight care. Dr. Bullard, shown here, worked at the clinic until his death in 1973. (MHM.)

George McLamb served as a physician at the clinic until his death in 1962. His wife, Beulah, worked as a nurse at the clinic for many years. (Courtesy of Martha Ann McLamb.)

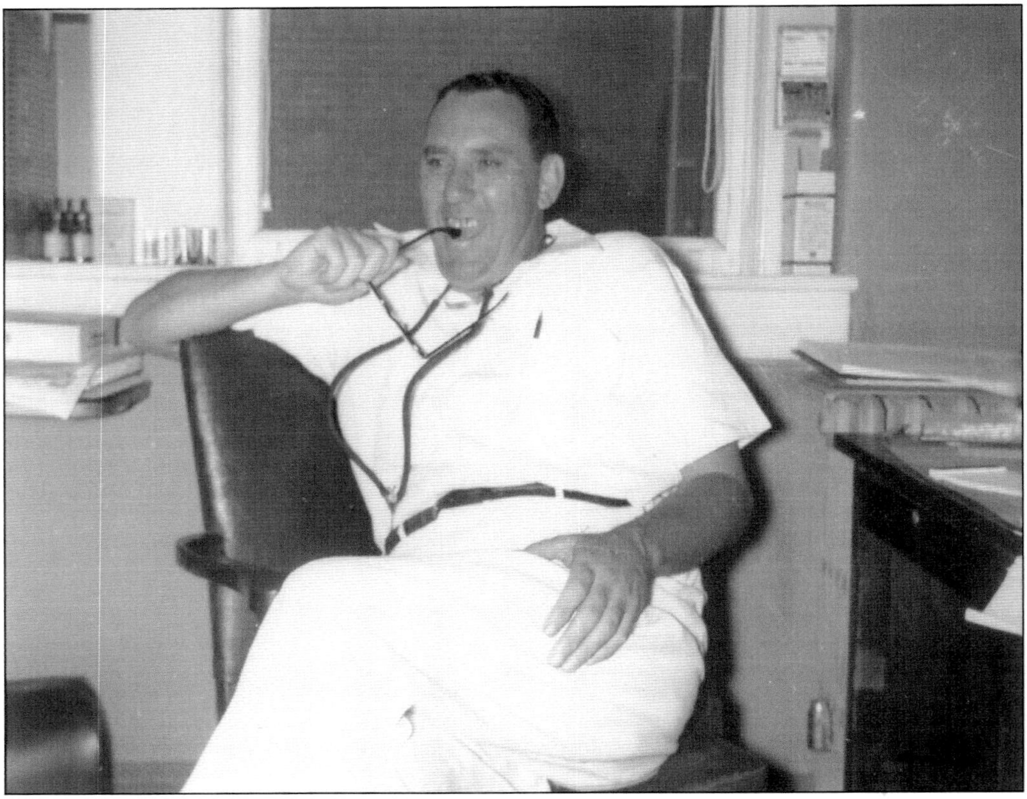

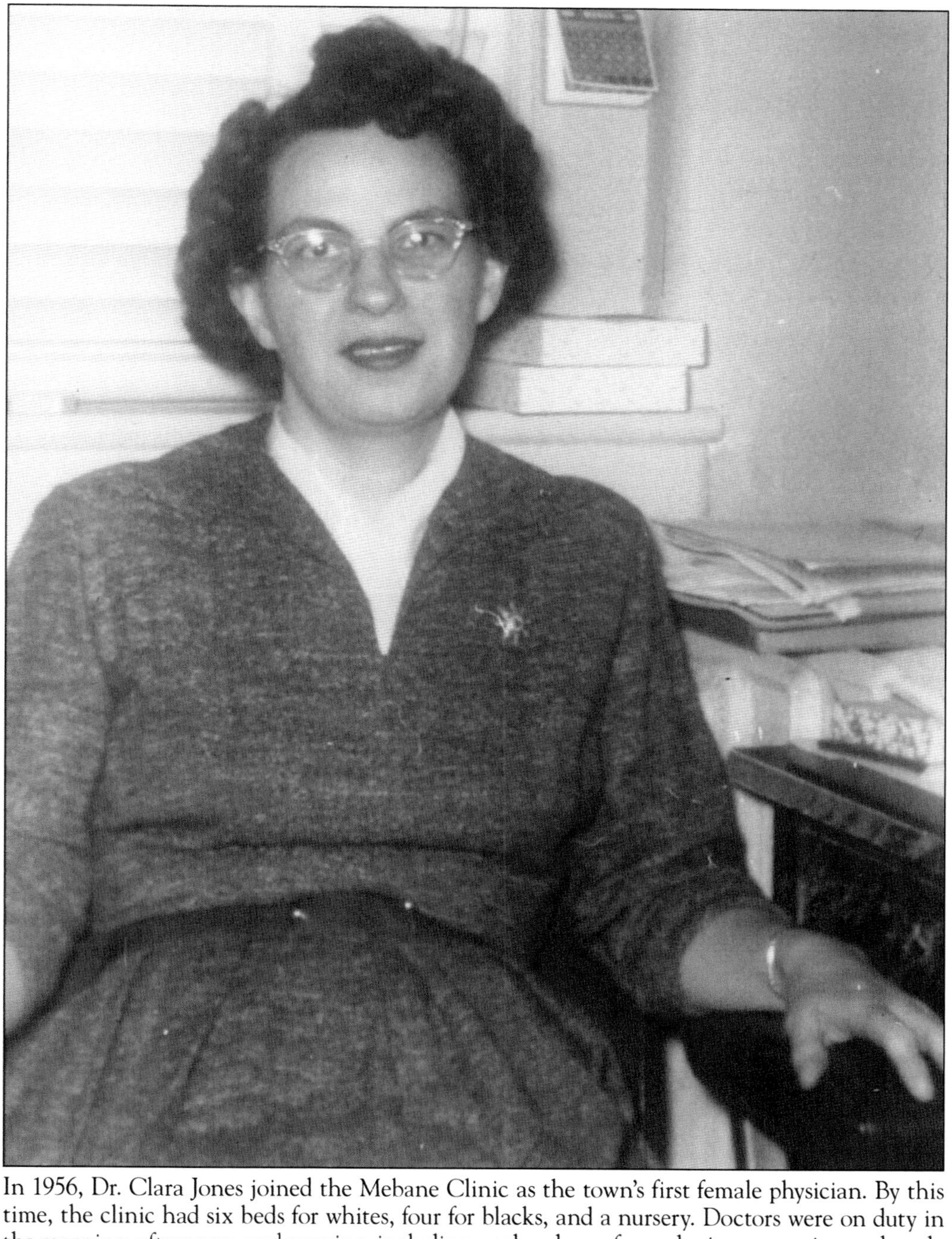

In 1956, Dr. Clara Jones joined the Mebane Clinic as the town's first female physician. By this time, the clinic had six beds for whites, four for blacks, and a nursery. Doctors were on duty in the morning, afternoon, and evening, including weekends, performed minor surgeries, and made house calls. Over the years, the clinic's physicians delivered thousands of babies, and women who gave birth there stayed several days until they and the child were ready to go home. Dr. Jones said in the 1980s that "some of the nurses who had been here a long time were delivering their second generation of babies" to the same families. After Dr. Bullard's death, Dr. Jones continued to operate the clinic until she retired and closed it in 1986, ending its long history. "If you could remember all of it," she said at the time, "you could make a good book out of it." The clinic's building is now occupied by Martinho's Bakery and Deli. (Courtesy of Margaret Bullard.)

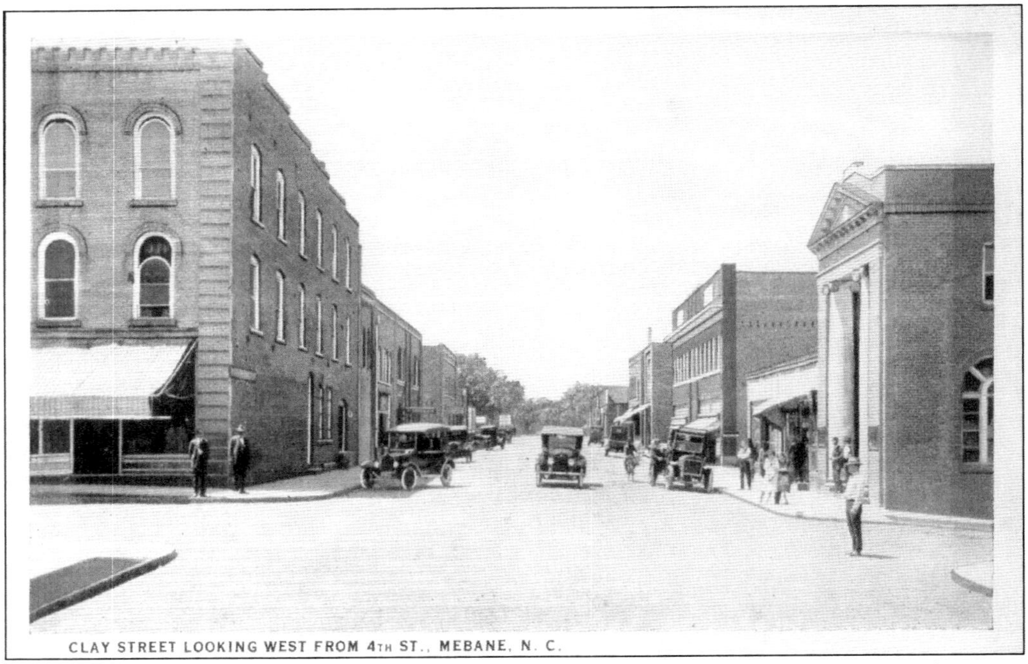

This photograph shows Clay Street looking west from Fourth Street in the 1920s. Over the years, the downstairs of the corner building on the left was occupied by a series of department stores, most notably Jones Department Store. The upstairs housed several inexpensive rental apartments and rooms that were accessible by stairs from a Clay Street entrance. The corner building on the right was the site of Commercial and Farmer's Bank. Clay Street was Mebane's main retail area for much of the 20th century. (MHM.)

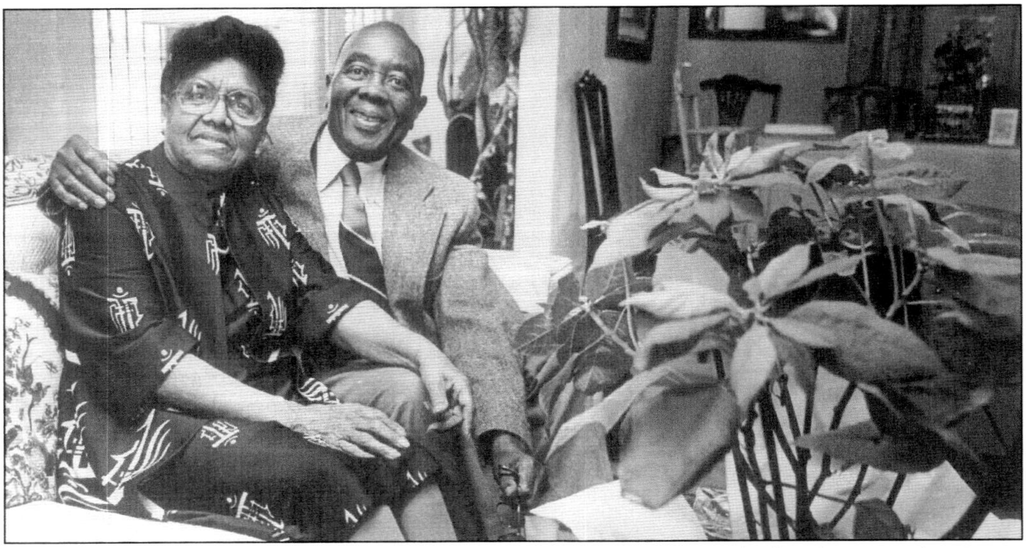

Tom Holt was a successful minority business owner who operated a barbershop on Clay Street beside Jones Department Store for many years in the middle decades of the 20th century. He employed two other black barbers and a shoeshine boy. The shop catered only to whites, as did another black barbershop located in the basement of a building across the street. A barbershop near Carolina Drug was operated by white barbers and catered only to white customers. (Courtesy of Iris Chapman.)

Two little girls are enjoying playing on the Clay Street sidewalk while their parents shop inside the Village Store. A popular store for over 50 years, it was the last of the old retail stores in downtown Mebane in the 1950s to close. (Courtesy of Ellen Lawrence.)

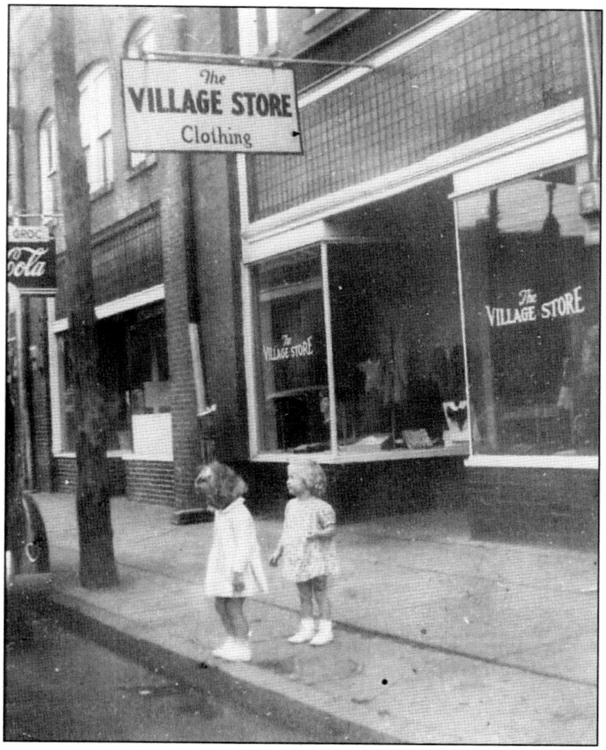

Keith Truitt (left) and Pete Bradley clean up after Hurricane Hazel struck Mebane on October 15, 1954. Mebane suffered minor flooding, downed trees, damaged roofs, broken windows, and damaged storefronts, but rain from the storm ended a major drought. Hurricane Hazel was the only category four hurricane to strike North Carolina in the 20th century and is forever etched in the memories of those who experienced it. (MHM.)

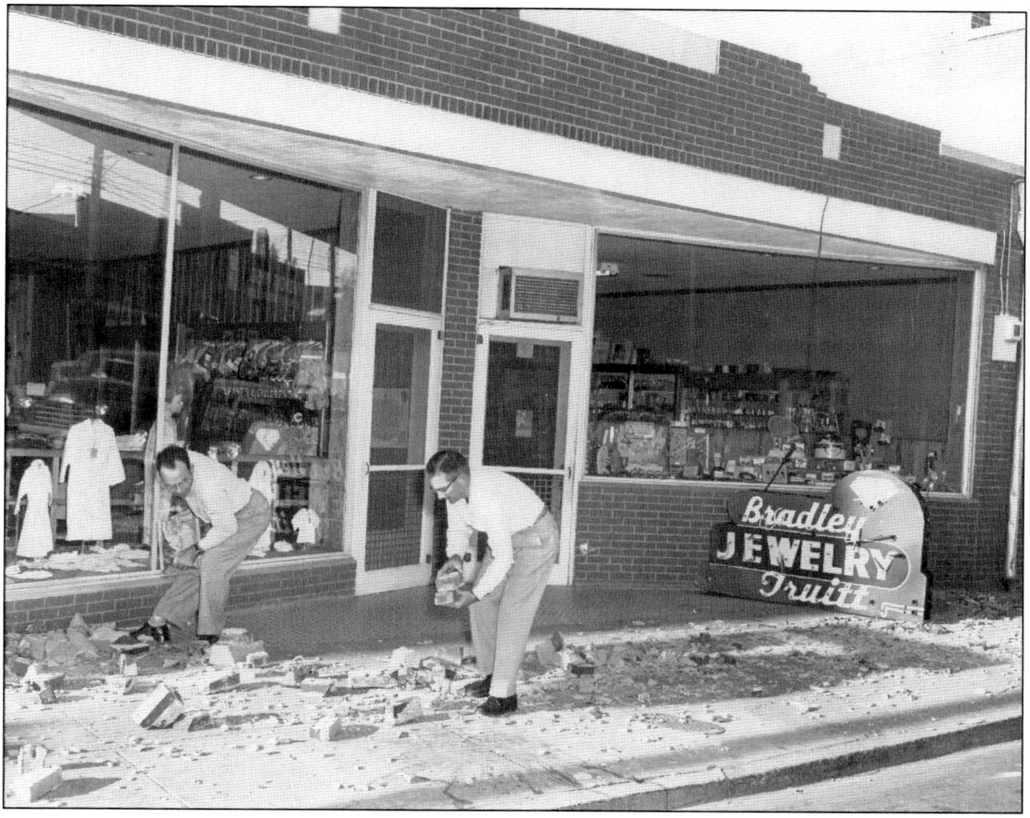

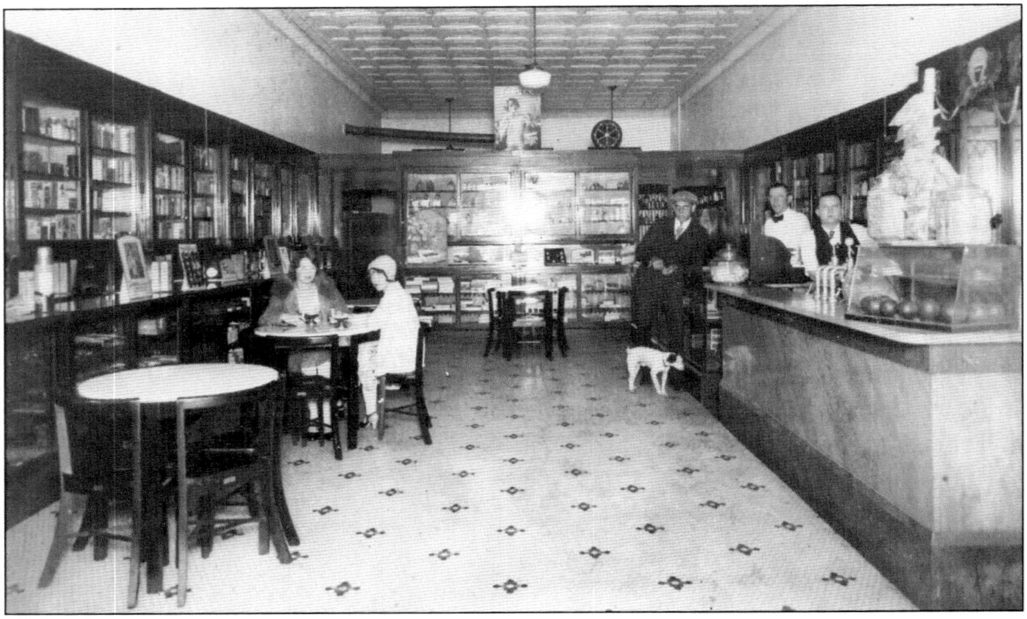

In the 1920s, two young women are relaxing near the soda fountain at Pickard's Drug Store on Clay Street. Pickard's was purchased by Virgil Warren in the 1920s or 1930s, and for decades, Warren's Drug Store, the Carolina Drug and Soda Shop on Center Street, and the Mebane Drug Company (commonly called Delmar White's) on Fourth Street were popular centers for residents wanting to meet with friends and enjoy a quick snack, soft drink, ice cream, or milk shake. (MHM.)

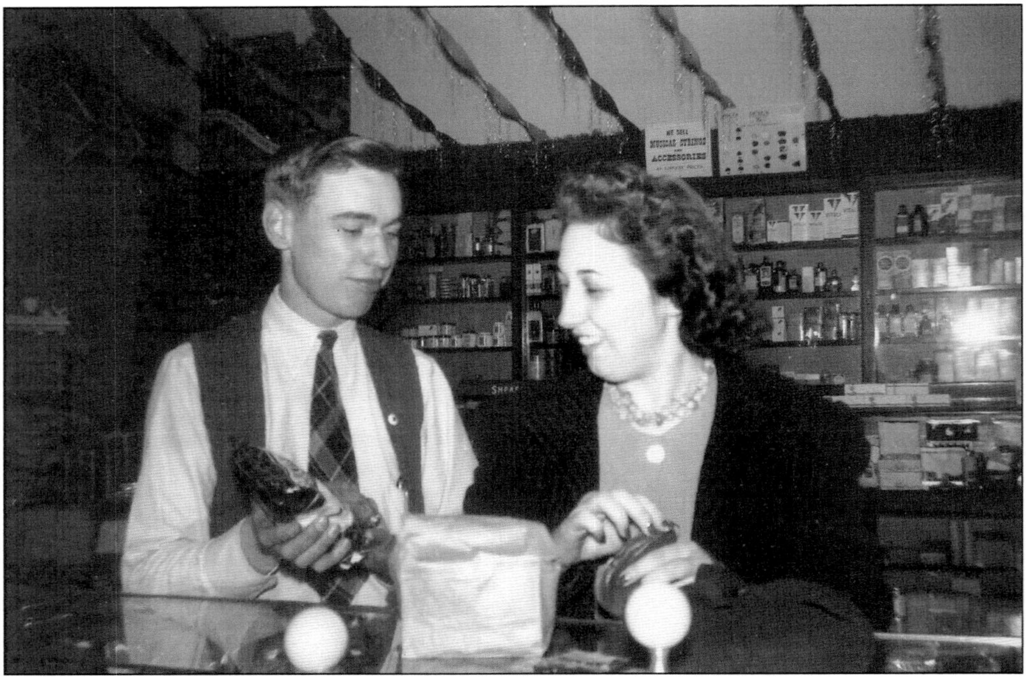

In the 1940s, pharmacist Calvin Oakley helps a customer with her order. Oakley was an employee of Virgil Warren for many years. Eventually, Oakley became the owner of the store in its original location beside Malone Crawford Clothing and then later on the corner of Clay and Fourth Streets. He worked at the store for over 50 years. (Courtesy of Bill Sykes Jr.)

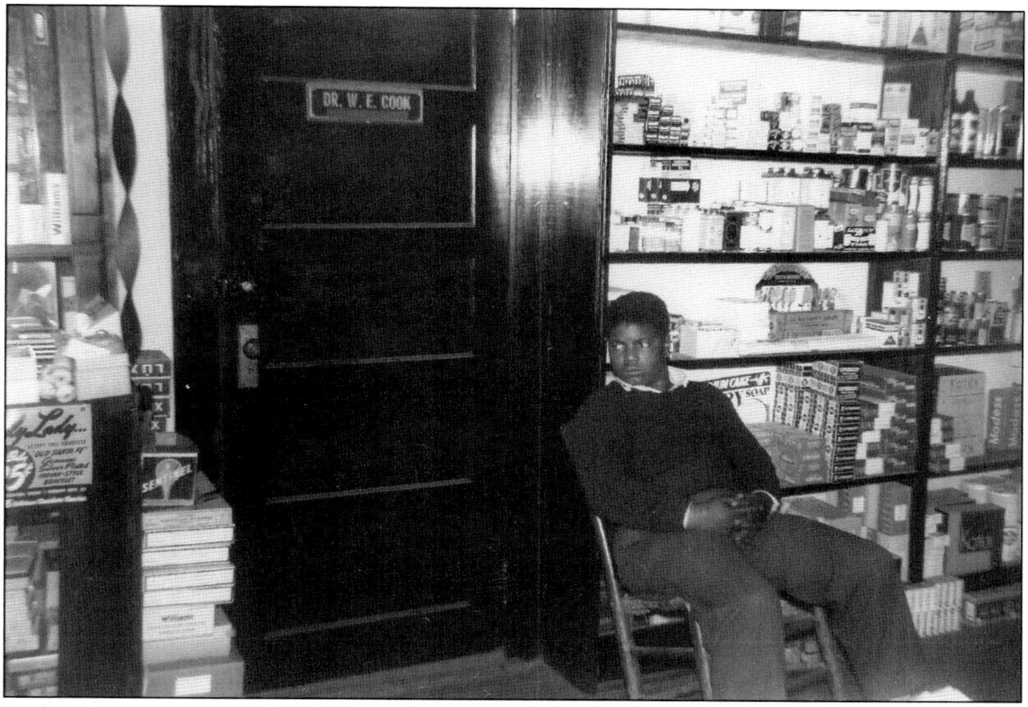

In the 1940s, an unidentified delivery boy sits in the back of Warren's Drug outside the door that led into Dr. W.E. Cook's office. This close relationship between physicians and pharmacists was not unusual during this time. (Courtesy of Bill Sykes Jr.)

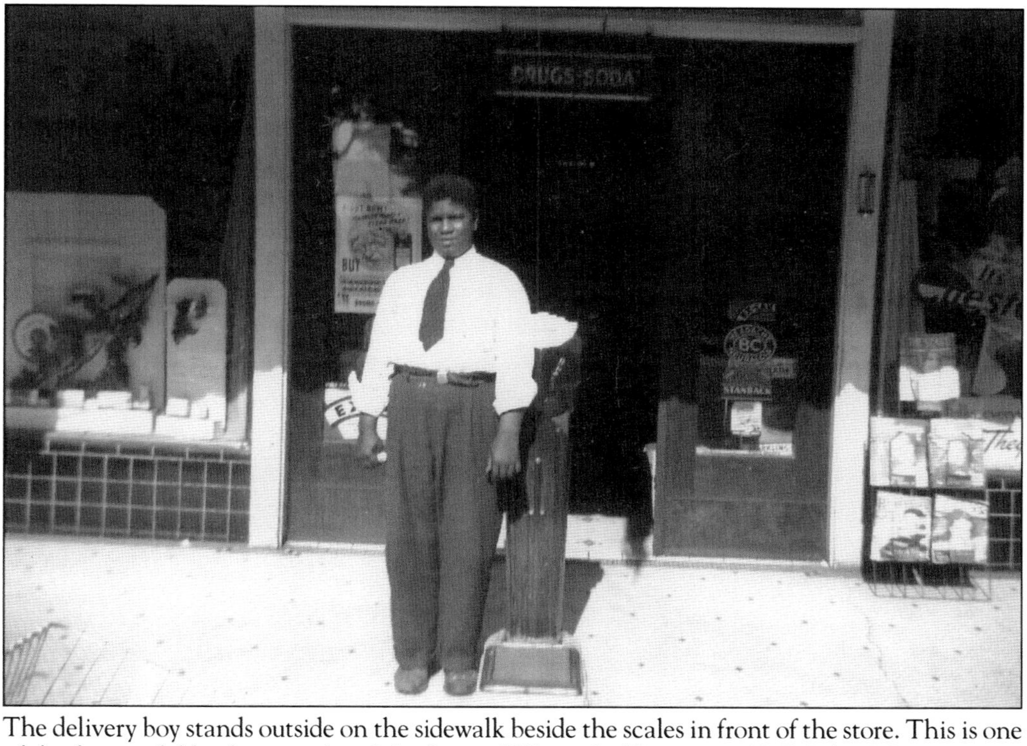

The delivery boy stands outside on the sidewalk beside the scales in front of the store. This is one of the few available photographs of the front of Warren's. (Courtesy of Bill Sykes Jr.)

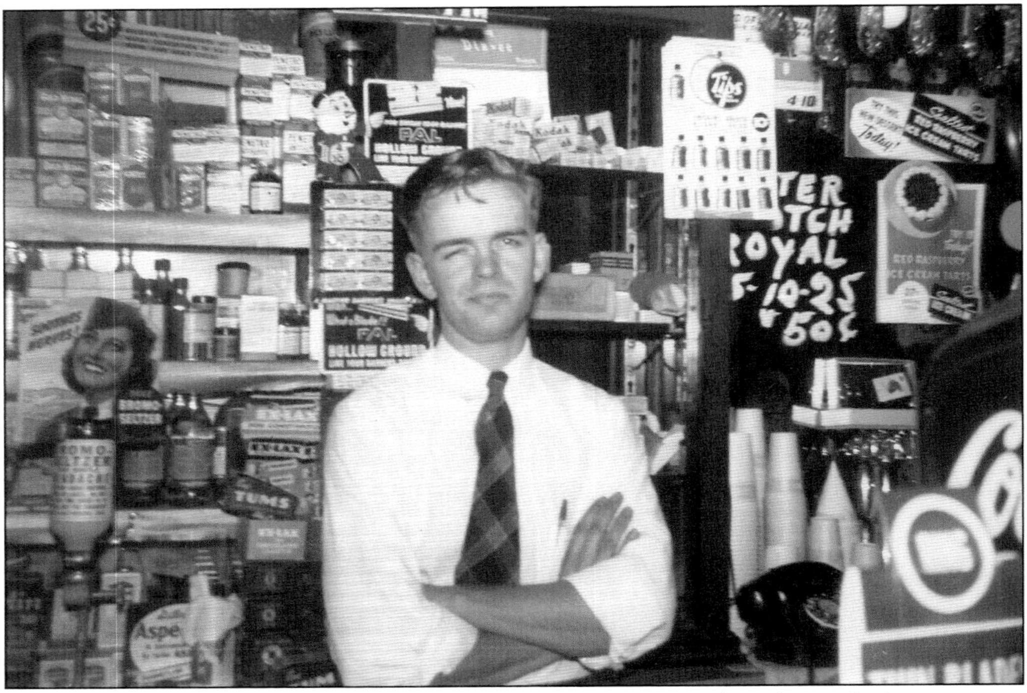

Ernest Richmond had a long career at White Furniture Company but also worked part-time at night and on Saturdays at Warren's Drug for many years. (Courtesy of Bill Sykes Jr.)

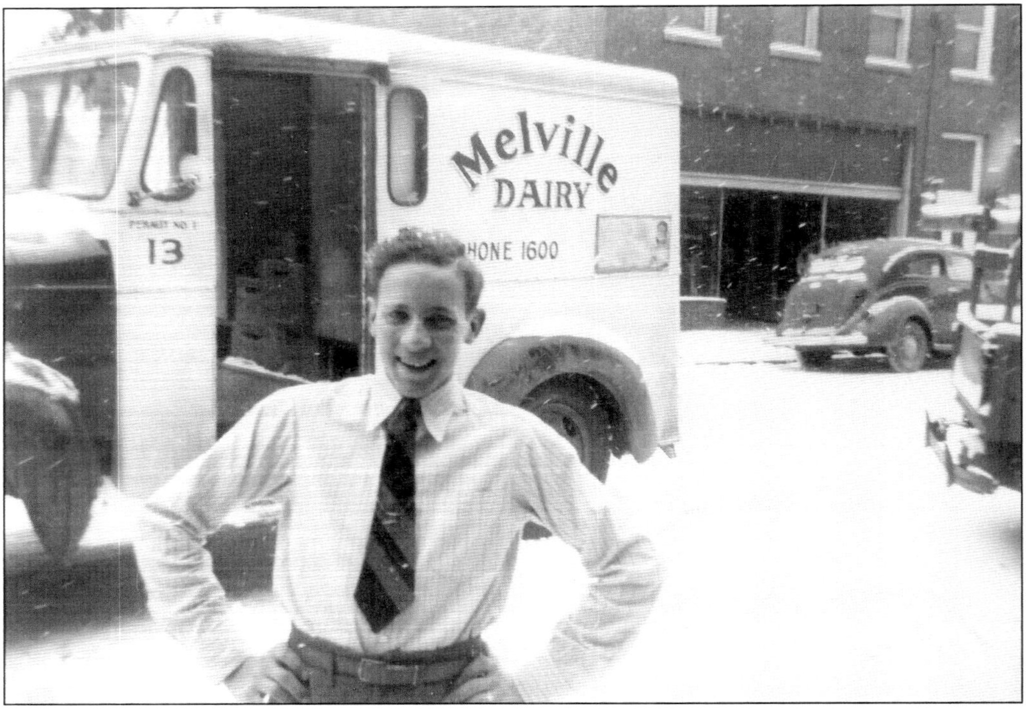

Bill Sykes Sr. stands on Clay Street in front of a Melville Dairy truck delivering ice cream to Warren's Drug. Based in Burlington, Melville was the major dairy in the area, distributing milk and other products to homes and businesses. (Courtesy of Bill Sykes Jr.)

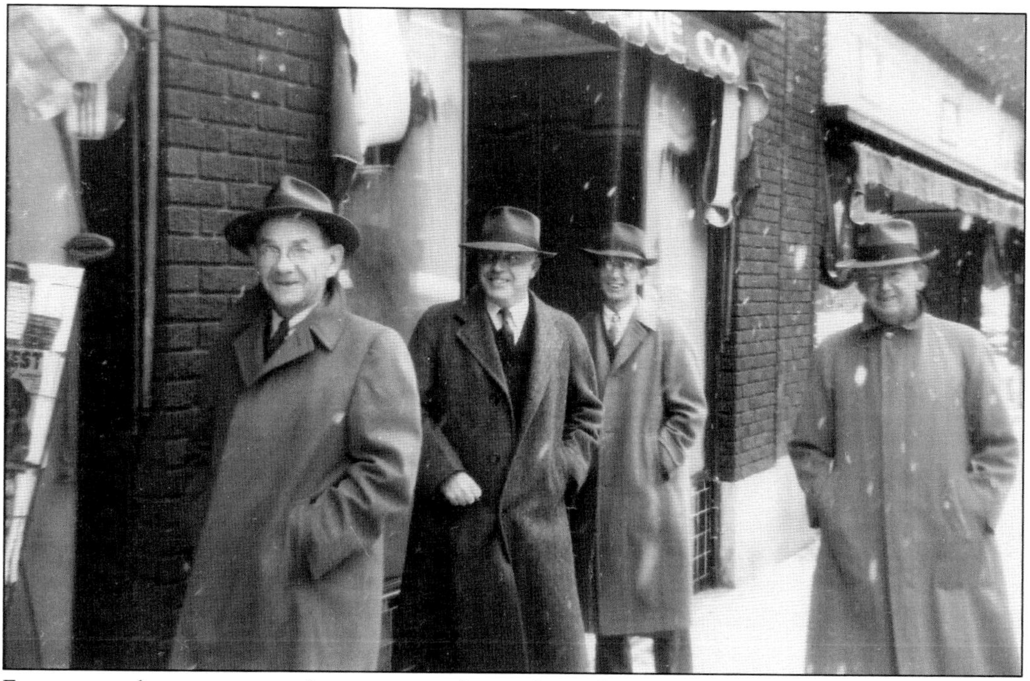

For some unknown reason, four men stand outside in the snow in front of a clothing store on Clay Street. (Courtesy of Bill Sykes Jr.)

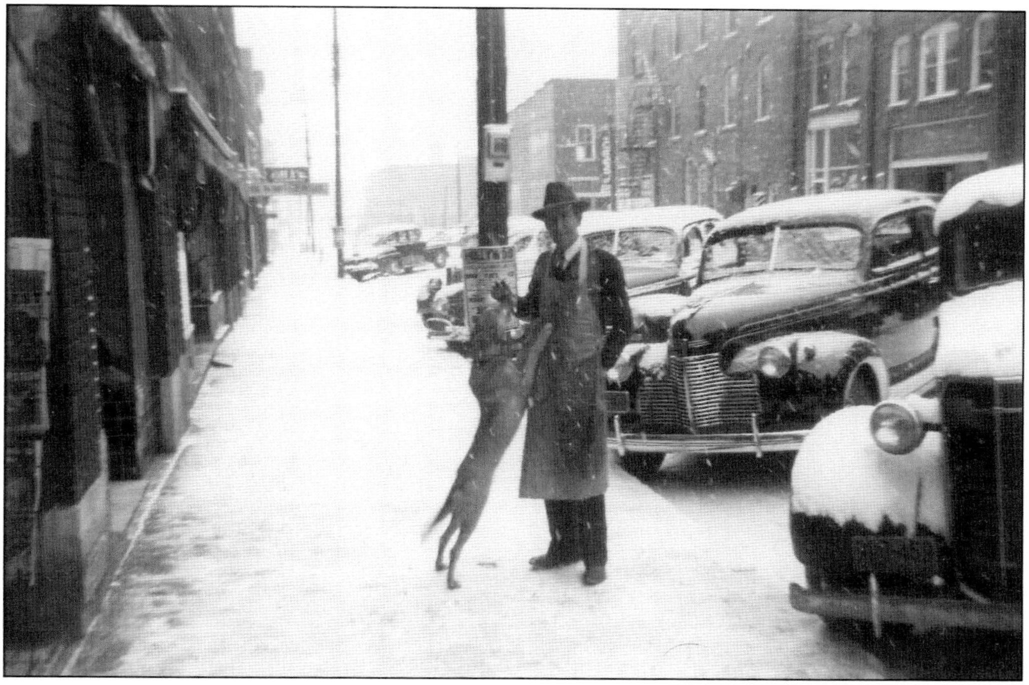

Thomas Mayes Sr. and his dog Topsy were familiar sights on downtown Clay Street in the 1940s. Trained as a cobbler's apprentice while growing up in a South Carolina orphanage, Mayes ran a shoe repair shop on Clay Street. (Courtesy of Bill Sykes Jr. and Judy Rembert.)

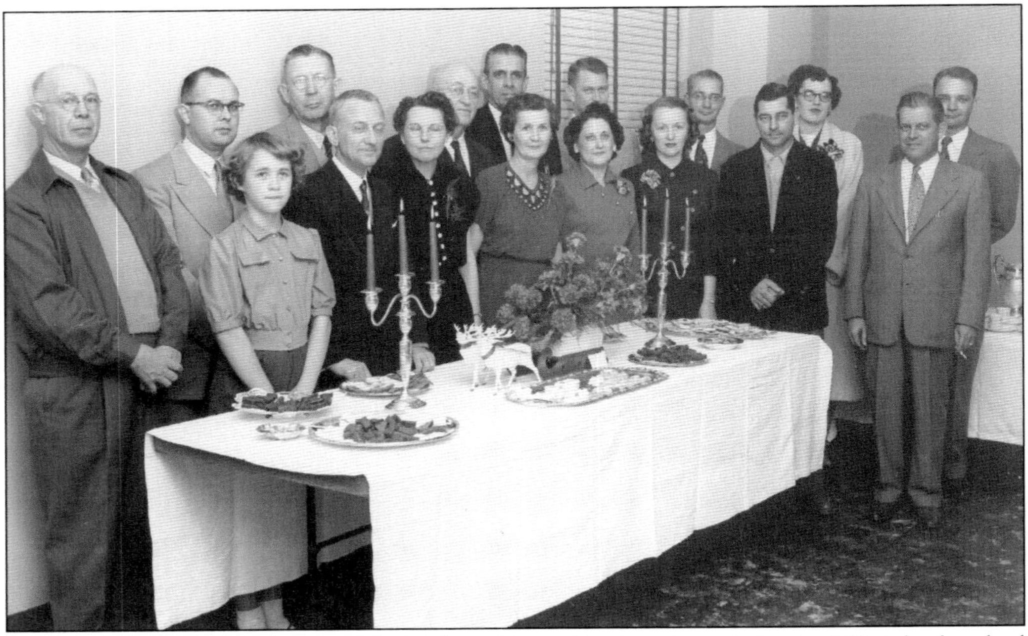

Several local businessmen started the Mebane Home Builders Association in 1909. The firm had no permanent home for years but met most often at the Reliable Furniture Company on Clay Street. In 1950, the firm changed its name to First Savings and Loan and constructed its first permanent office on Clay Street. This photograph shows an open house for the grand opening in 1952. (Courtesy of Rick Smith.)

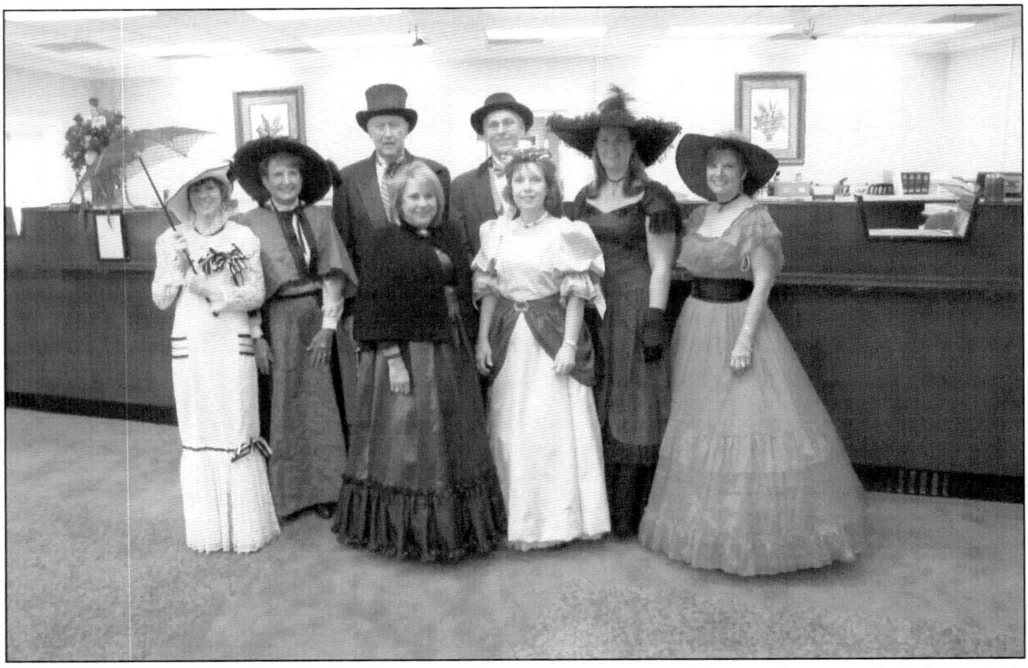

In 1959–1960, First Savings built its present office on the corner of Center Street and Highway 119. The employees dressed up in vintage clothing during the firm's centennial celebration in 2009. From left to right are (first row) Rhonda Bowling and Denise Snead; (second row) Jamie Park, Gail Jordan, Neal Smith, Rick Smith, Amy Canady, and Janis Murray. (Courtesy of Rick Smith.)

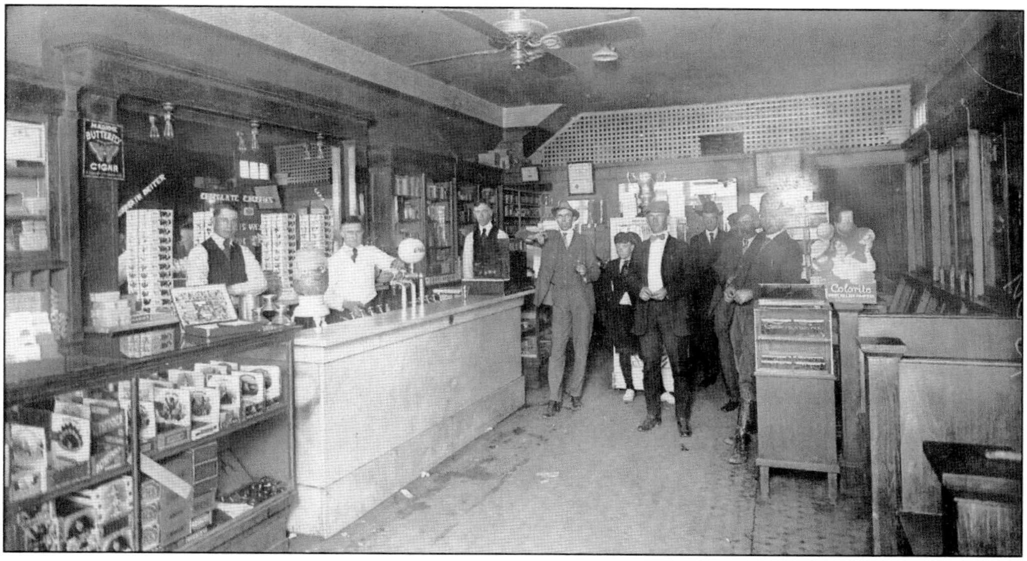

Rimmer Drugstore opened on the corner of Fourth and Center Streets in the early 20th century. Shown here in 1917 are, from left to right, Sam Ham, Ralph Stewart, Clydre Rimmer (owner and druggist), R.L. Fuller, an unidentified boy, A.H. Jobe, unidentified, W.L. Lineberry, and unidentified. (MHM.)

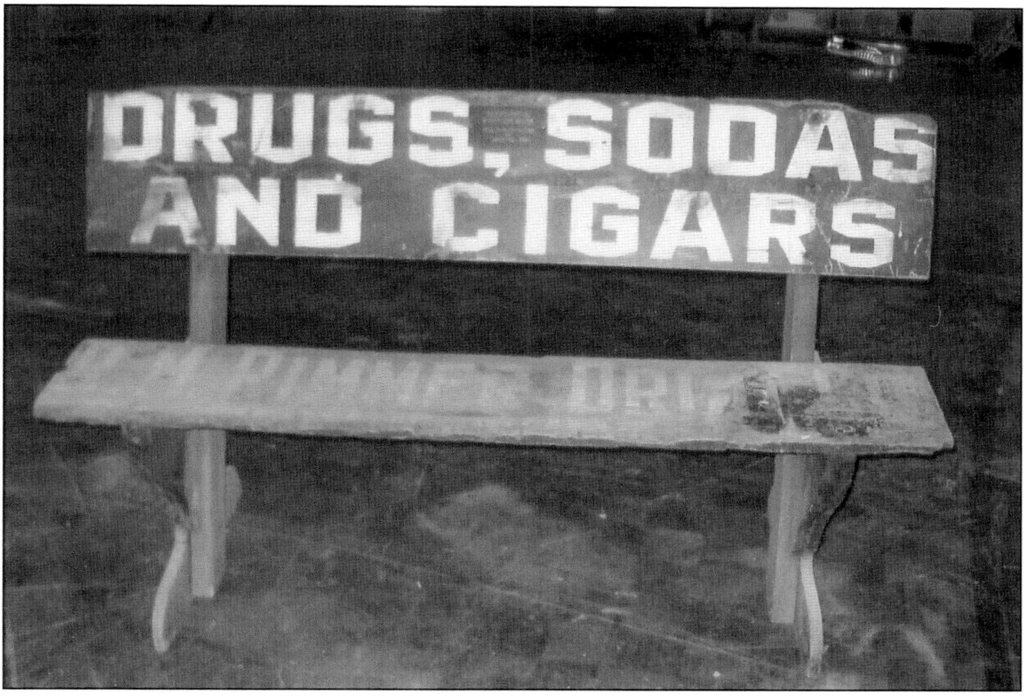

The Rimmer Drugstore bench sat in front of the store on the street for many years. The bench was popularly called the "whittling bench," because men with time on their hands would sit talking and whittling on the wooden bench with pocketknives. Today, the bench is prominently displayed in the Mebane Historical Museum. (MHM.)

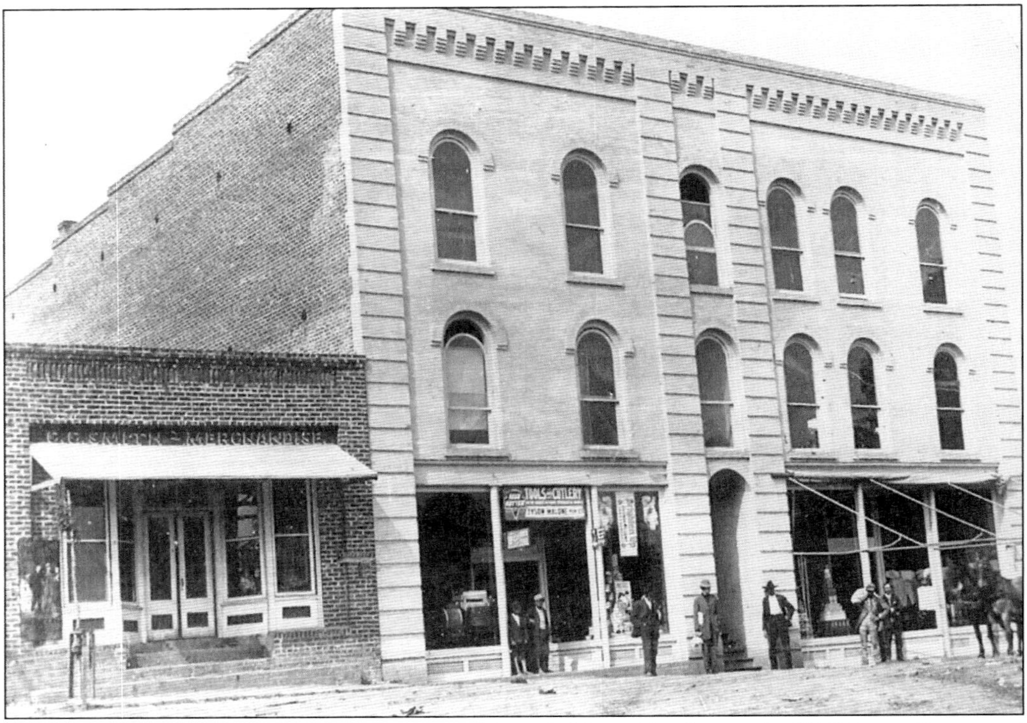

This 1909 photograph shows the exteriors of Tyson-Malone Hardware, the Wilkinson Store, and the C.G. Smith store on Fourth Street. (Courtesy of Tal Jobe.)

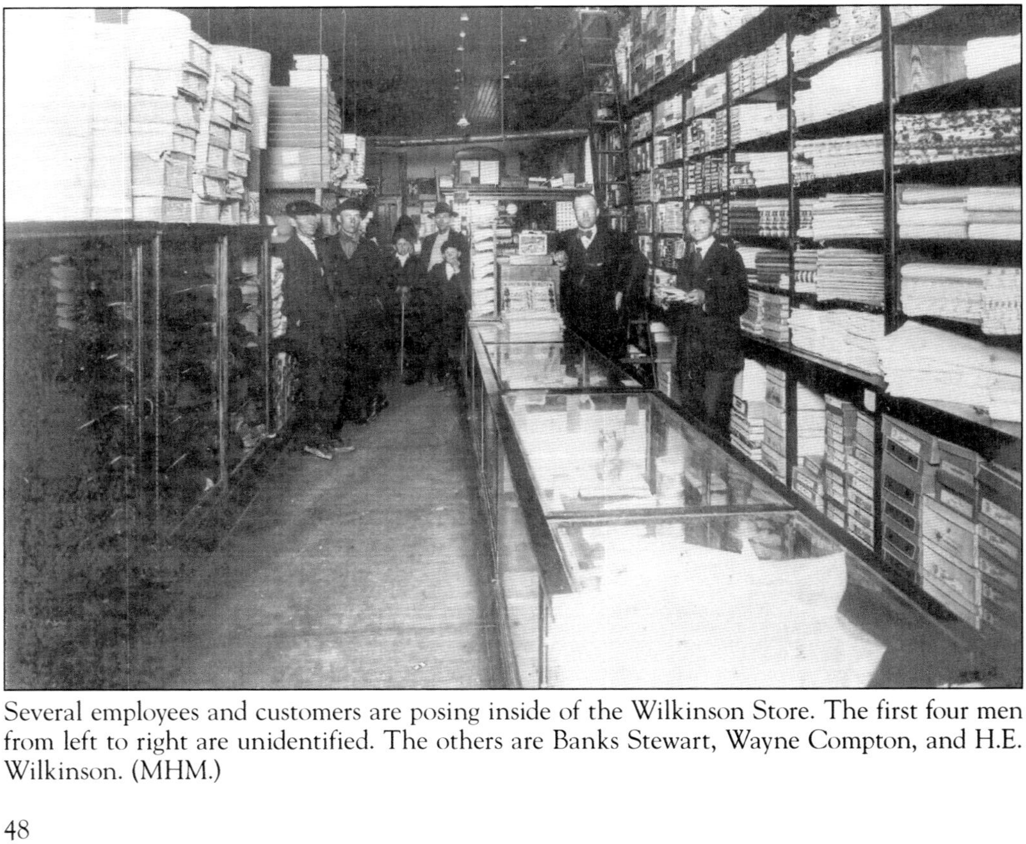

Several employees and customers are posing inside of the Wilkinson Store. The first four men from left to right are unidentified. The others are Banks Stewart, Wayne Compton, and H.E. Wilkinson. (MHM.)

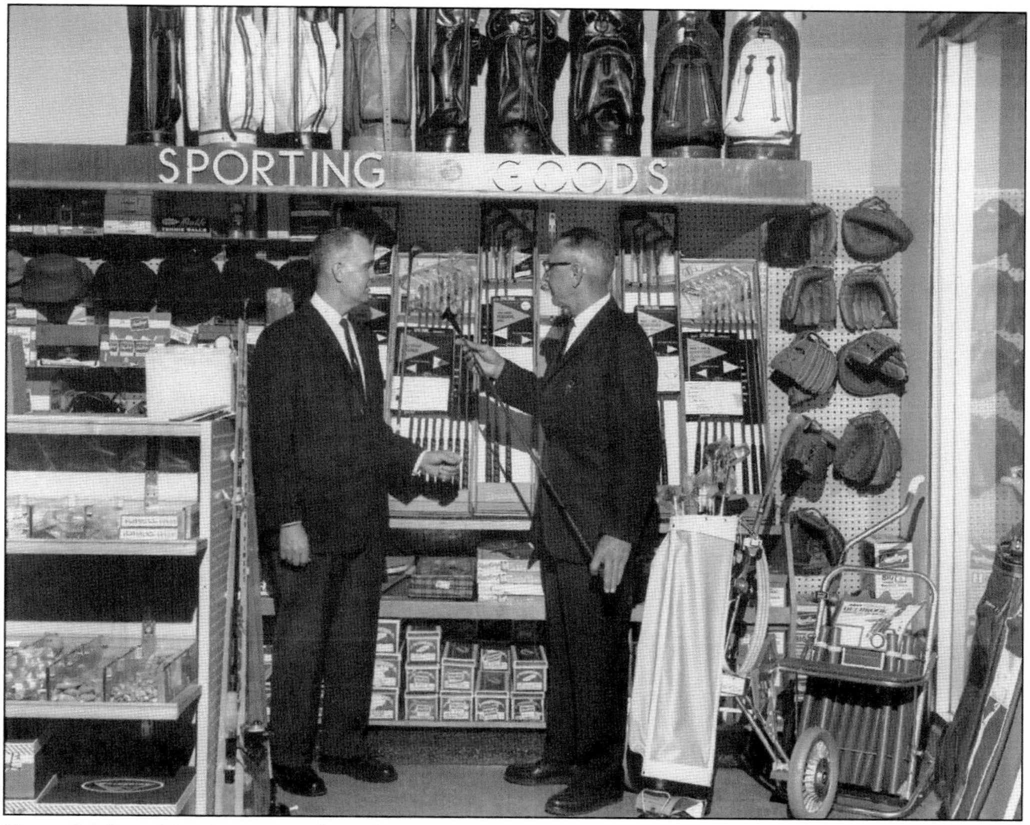

Tyson-Malone Hardware was founded as a partnership of R.H. Tyson and Walter Yancey Malone, one of the founders of the Mebane Tobacco Market. Initially located on Center Street, it later moved to the corner of Fourth and Clay Streets, where it spent most of its existence. In this photograph from the 1960s, Talmadge Jobe is helping former major-league baseball player Lew Riggs choose a golf club. (Courtesy of Tal Jobe.)

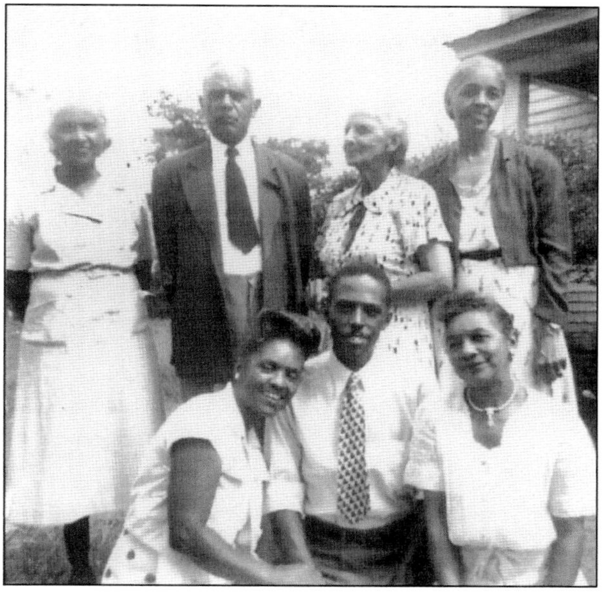

The Whitted family owned and operated Whitted's Store, a popular grocery on Holt Street in Mebane's West End community, where many of the town's African Americans lived. The community purchased produce, bread, meats, and other groceries from this store. (Courtesy of Iris Chapman.)

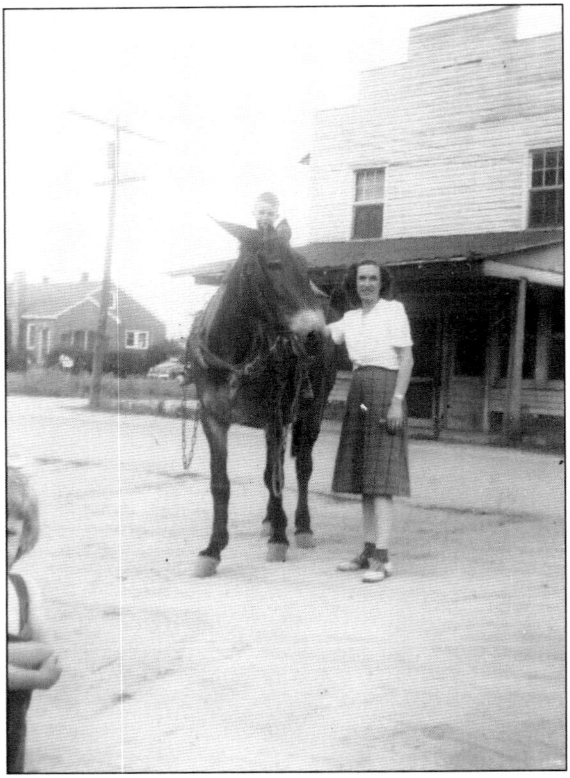

Eleanor Harris watches her son Jay struggle to ride Lady on Highway 119 North near Freshwater's Store in the late 1940s. (Courtesy of Lennie Harris Stout.)

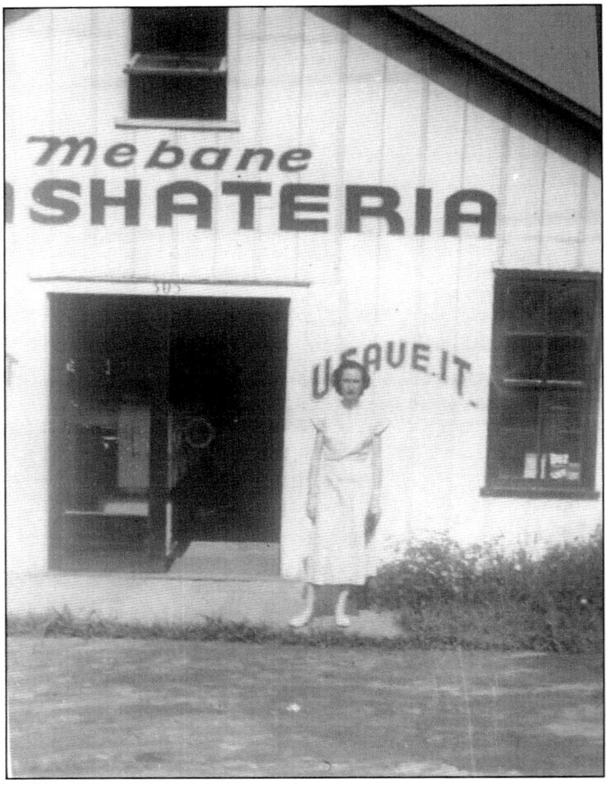

Eleanor Harris stands in front of the Mebane Washateria, an operation her family began on Highway 119 in 1947–1948. One of the first businesses in town to provide automatic washing machines, it was a popular place for women in the neighborhood and across town who were tired of washing clothes in tubs at home and then hanging them on a clothesline to dry. (Courtesy of Lennie Harris Stout.)

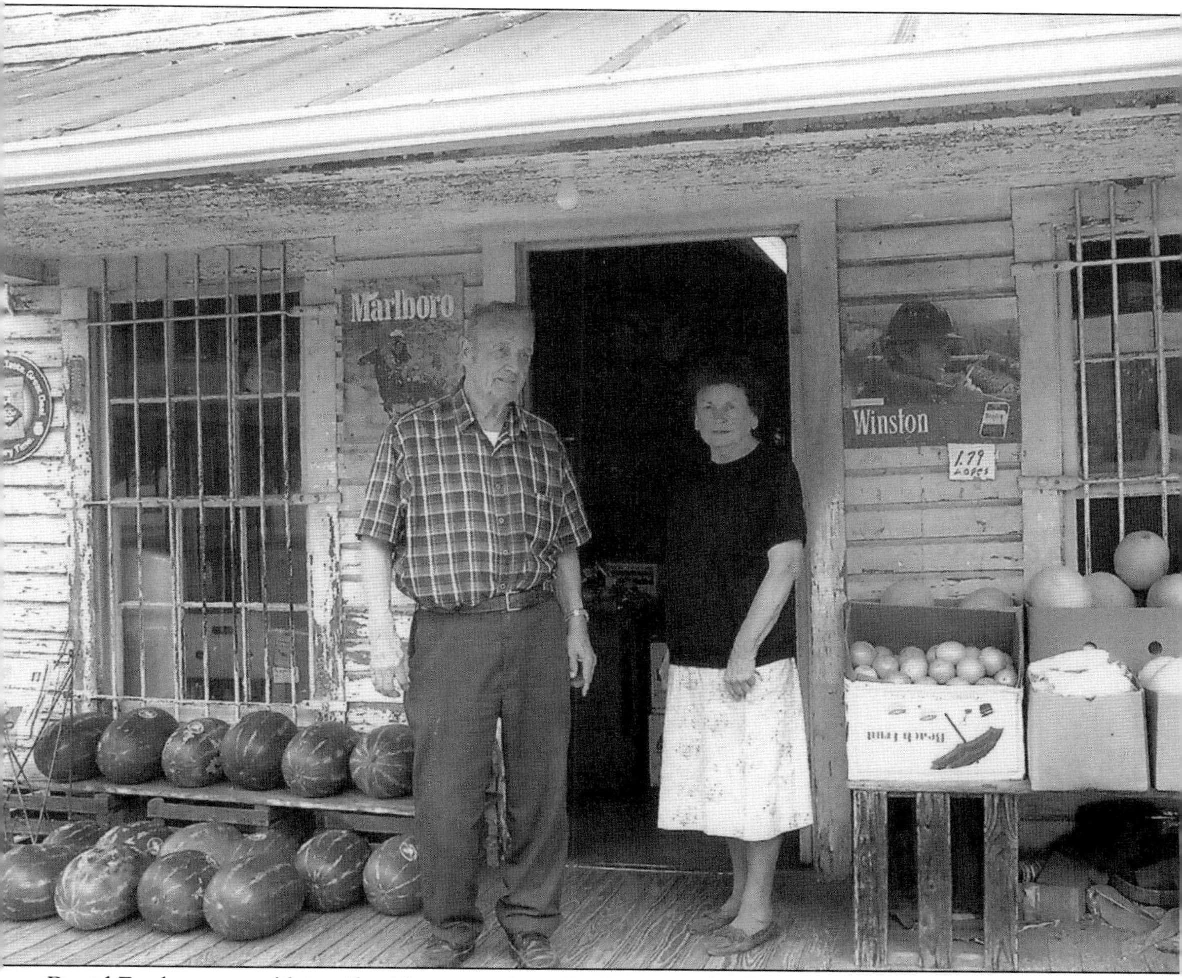

David Freshwater and his wife, Alma, stand on the front porch of D.L. Freshwater Grocery, the oldest and most popular of the many small grocery stores that thrived in Mebane for decades before the coming of supermarkets. David inherited the store in the late 1940s from his father, Thad Freshwater, who opened the store in 1914 on the outskirts of town on a dirt road and old stagecoach trail that later became North Highway 119. David's customers were mostly townspeople and black and white farmers from outlying areas. It was a very democratic place to visit—when customers entered the store, they rubbed elbows with people from all classes and all parts of town. Neighbors and friends came to buy groceries and to exchange jokes, to unwind with a bottle of Coke after work, to catch up on the news about neighbors who were sick or down on their luck, and to argue about politics or their favorite sports teams. David ran the store until he died inside the store in 2002, and soon the little store that had become an institution closed its doors. (MHM.)

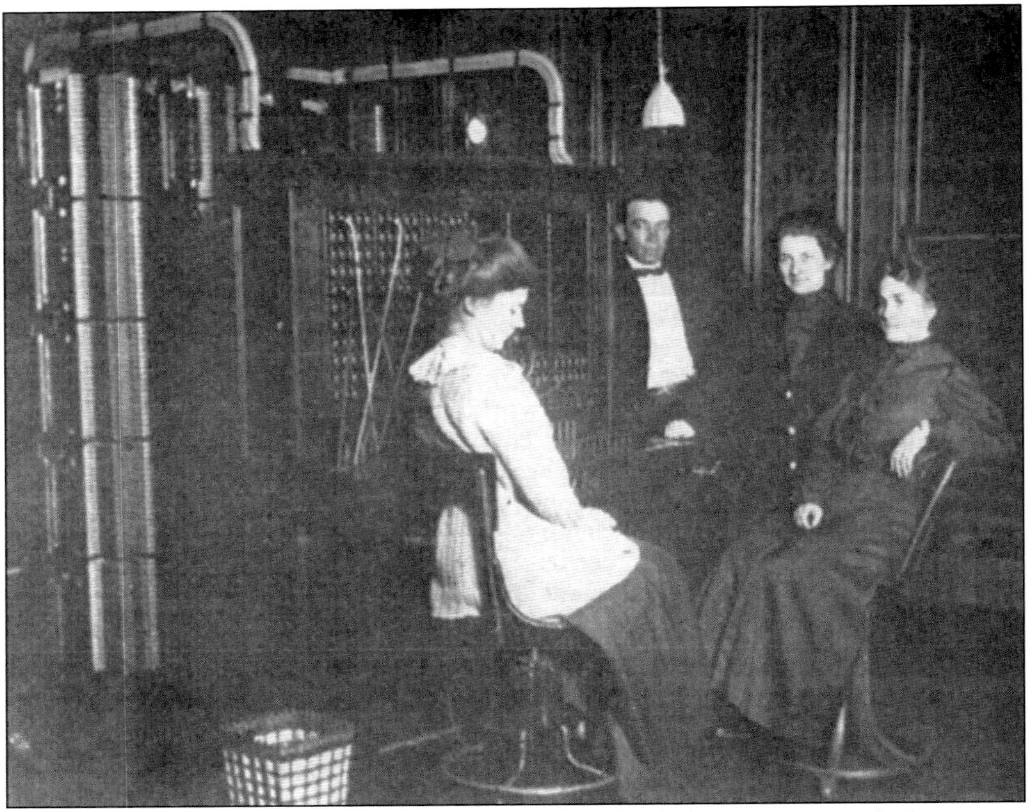

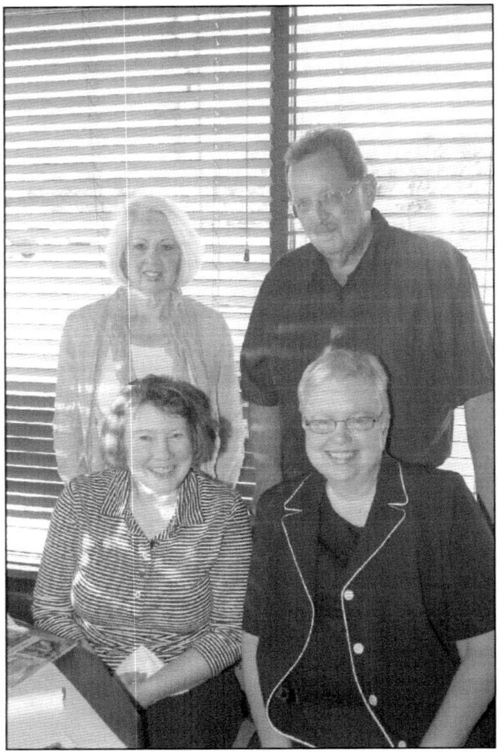

Although telephone service reached Mebane in the early 20th century, it grew slowly until Sam Hupman Sr. purchased the Home Telephone Company in 1922. Three employees, including two switchboard operators, are shown here with Hupman. The Hupman family ran the company for 76 years before selling it to Madison River Communications in 1998. Today, after passing through several owners, the company is known as Century Link. (MHM.)

Established as the *Mebane Leader* in 1909, the *Mebane Enterprise* has survived over a century of name changes, owners, and revolutionary technological advancements in news gathering and reporting. Pictured are, from left to right, (first row) Michelle Ozment (office manager) and Karen Carter (editor); (second row) Jackie Brown (general manager) and Stephen Mills (staff writer and photographer). (Courtesy of the *Mebane Enterprise*.)

Four

DEPRESSION AND WAR

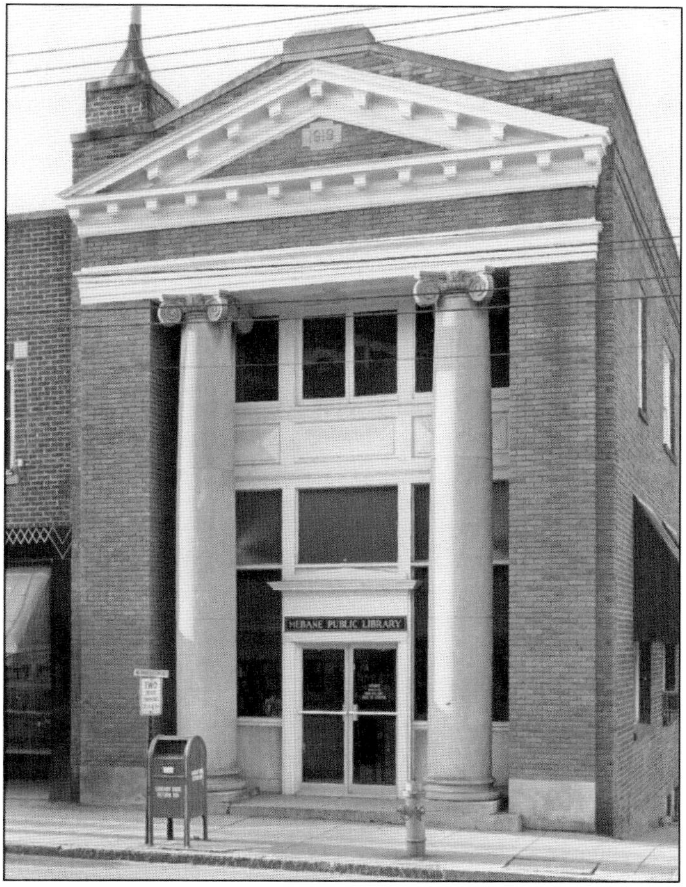

Several Mebane businesses failed during the Great Depression and the Second World War. Some, like the White Furniture Company, survived by reducing workers' wages or hours, while others, like the Commercial and Farmer's Bank, were forced to close. After meeting for several months in one room in the local high school, the Mebane Public Library gained its first permanent home when it rented a space in the failed bank building. Led by Eunice Harris and J.M. McIntyre, a local committee raised $3,000 in two weeks to purchase the entire building, then deeded it to the City of Mebane. This photograph shows the library in 1958. The exterior of the building has changed little since its days as a financial institution. (Courtesy of Mebane Public Library.)

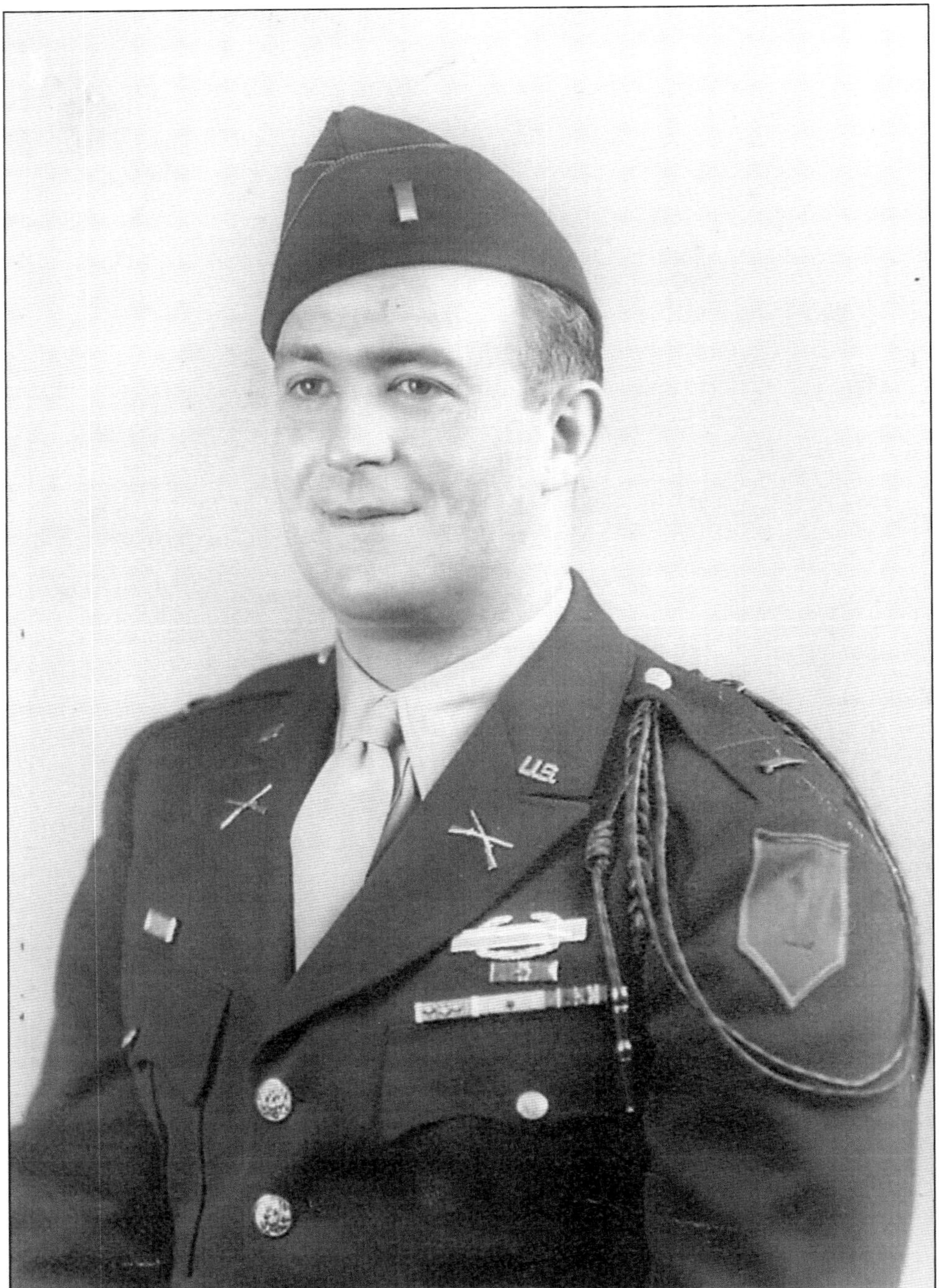

A native of Michigan, Lt. Lloyd Gettig was a highly decorated soldier who fought in North Africa, Italy, the D-Day invasion, and the Battle of the Bulge. After his feet were frozen during the Battle of the Bulge, he developed gangrene in his feet and legs and was flown for treatment to a hospital in France and then to Camp Butner in North Carolina. While he was recovering at Camp Butner, Zelma Clayton of Mebane read an article about him in the newspaper and decided to visit him They soon married. After the war he settled in Mebane and spent many years with the Nello Teer Construction Company. (Courtesy of the Gettig family.)

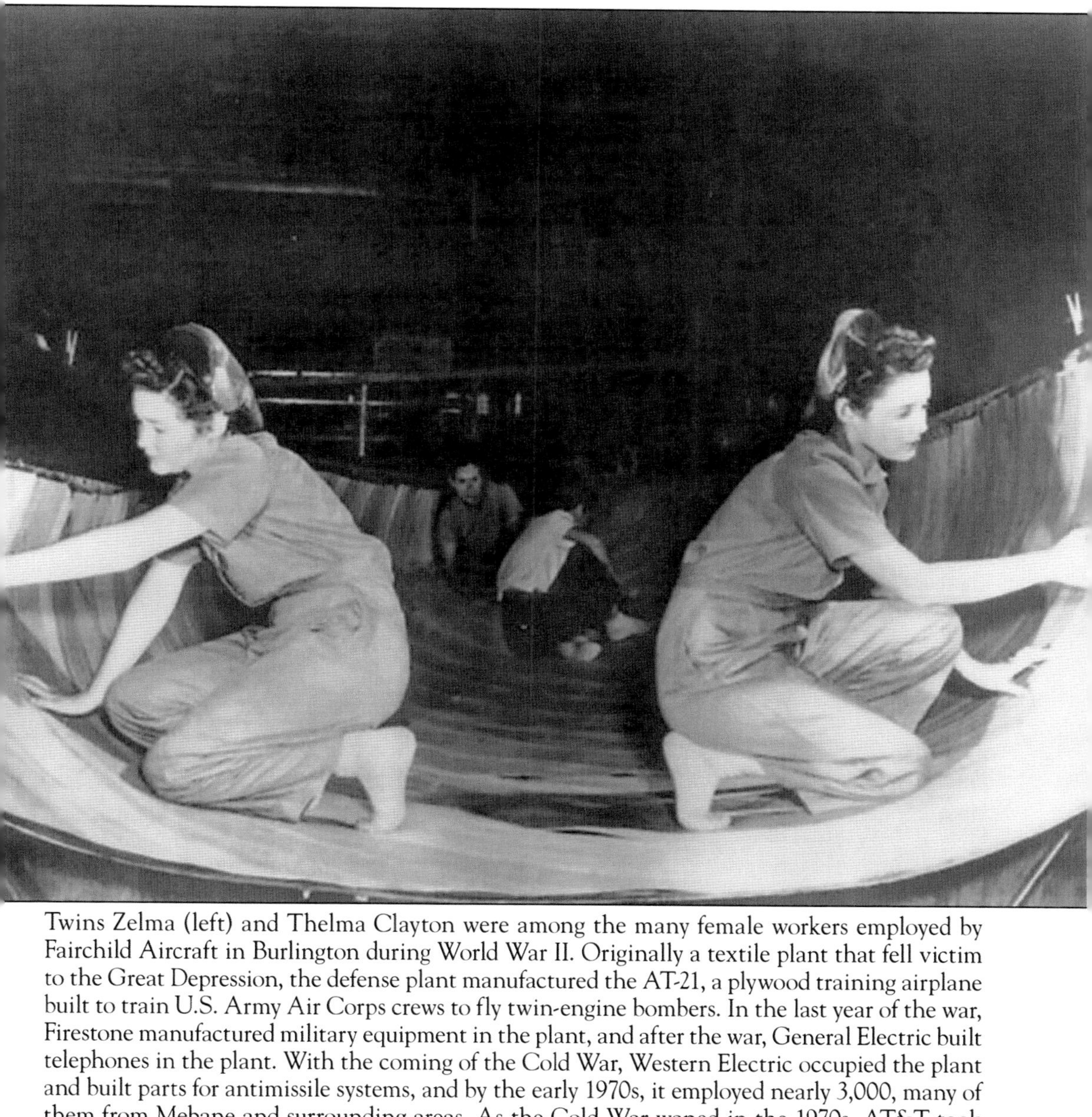

Twins Zelma (left) and Thelma Clayton were among the many female workers employed by Fairchild Aircraft in Burlington during World War II. Originally a textile plant that fell victim to the Great Depression, the defense plant manufactured the AT-21, a plywood training airplane built to train U.S. Army Air Corps crews to fly twin-engine bombers. In the last year of the war, Firestone manufactured military equipment in the plant, and after the war, General Electric built telephones in the plant. With the coming of the Cold War, Western Electric occupied the plant and built parts for antimissile systems, and by the early 1970s, it employed nearly 3,000, many of them from Mebane and surrounding areas. As the Cold War waned in the 1970s, AT&T took over the plant, operating it for several years before shutting down in the early 1990s and dealing a major blow to the local economy. (Courtesy of the Gettig family.)

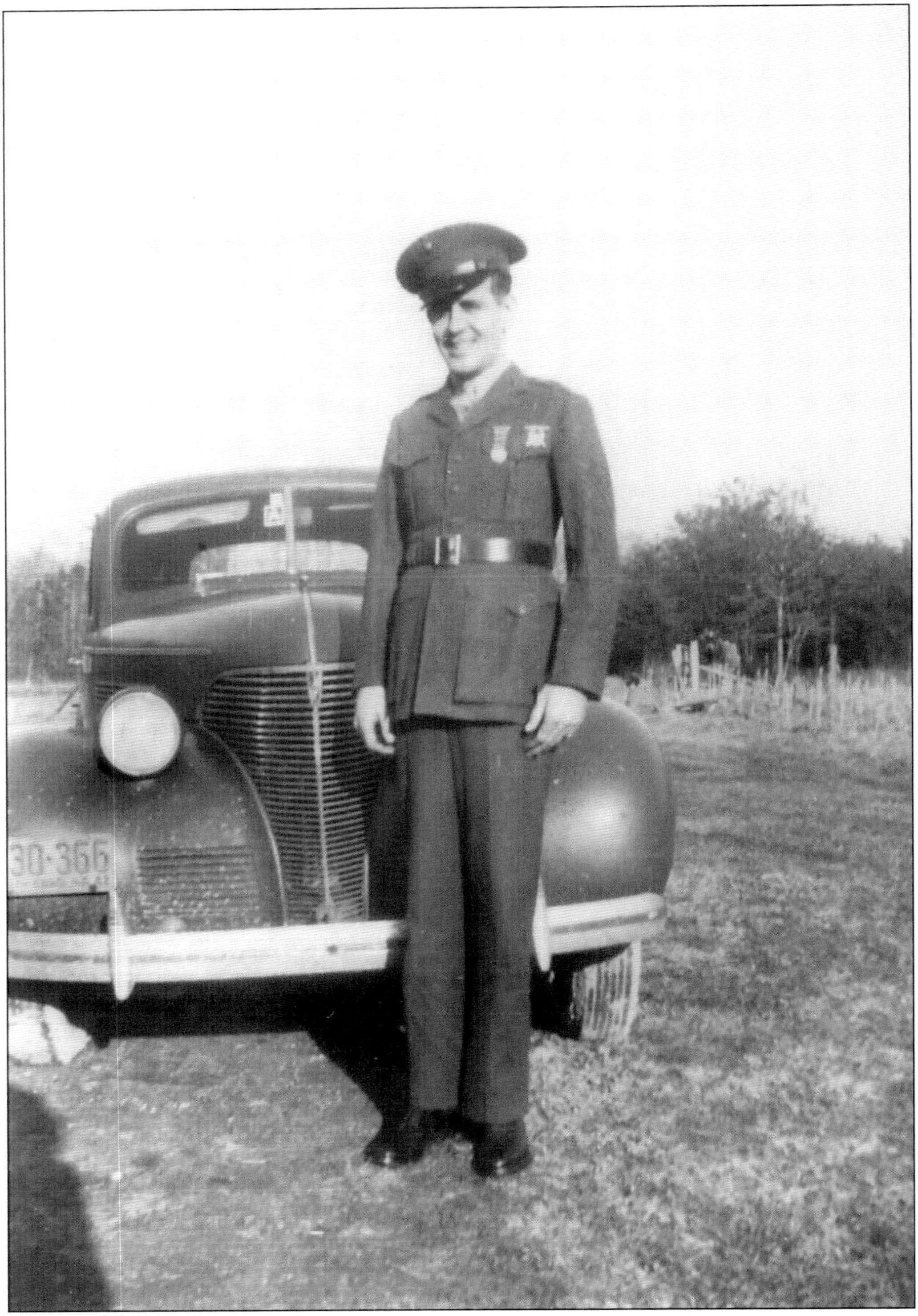

After serving in the Marine Corps in World War II, Thomas Mayes ("Brochie") Rembert Jr. returned to Mebane to operate a shoe repair shop on Clay Street and run a construction company that installed aluminum siding, doors, and windows. (Courtesy of Judy Rembert.)

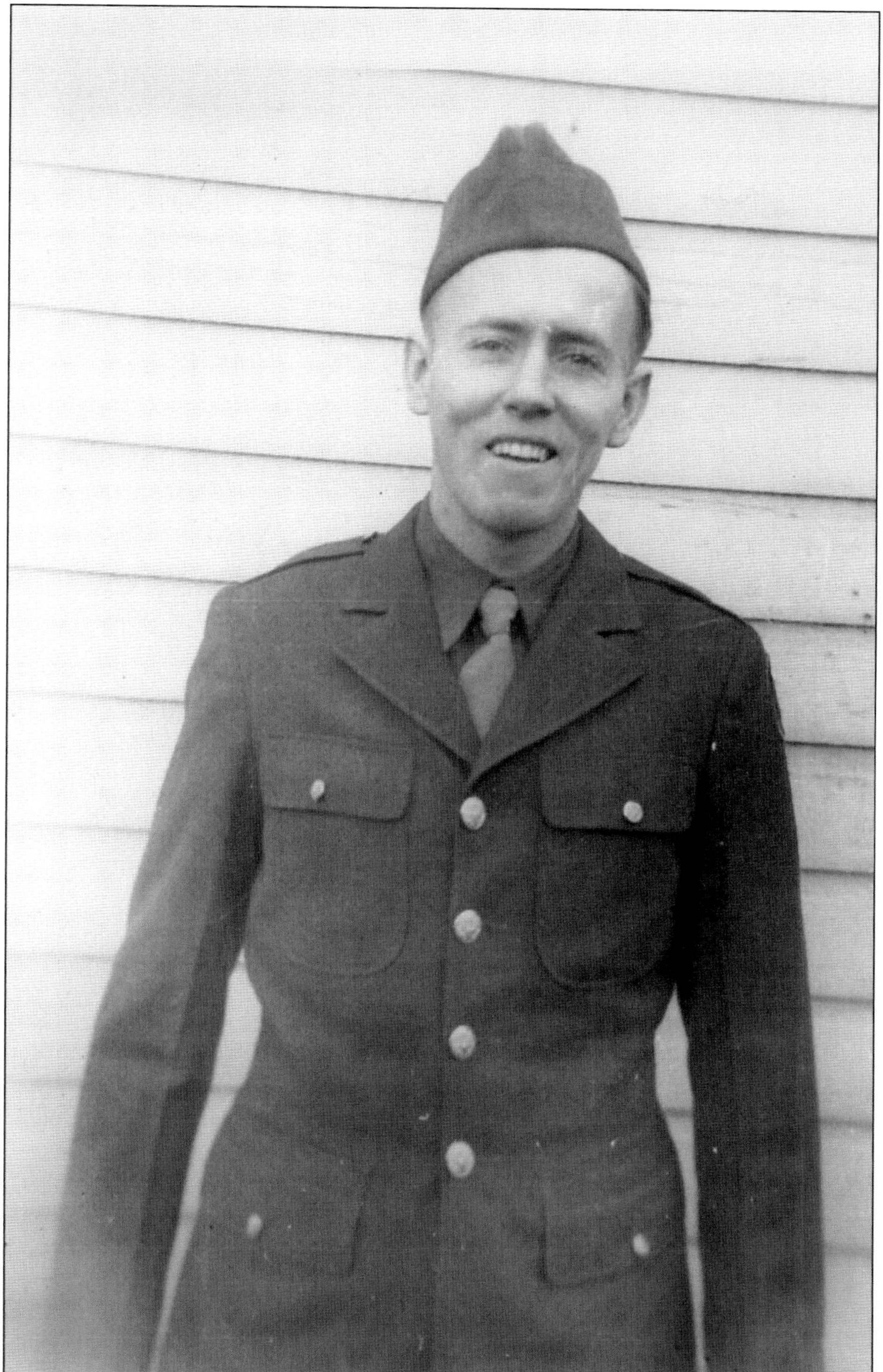

During World War II, William Lynch served as a topographical photographer making military maps for the Army in the South Pacific. After the war, he returned to Mebane and pursued a distinguished career as a commercial photographer. (Courtesy of Debbi Lynch.)

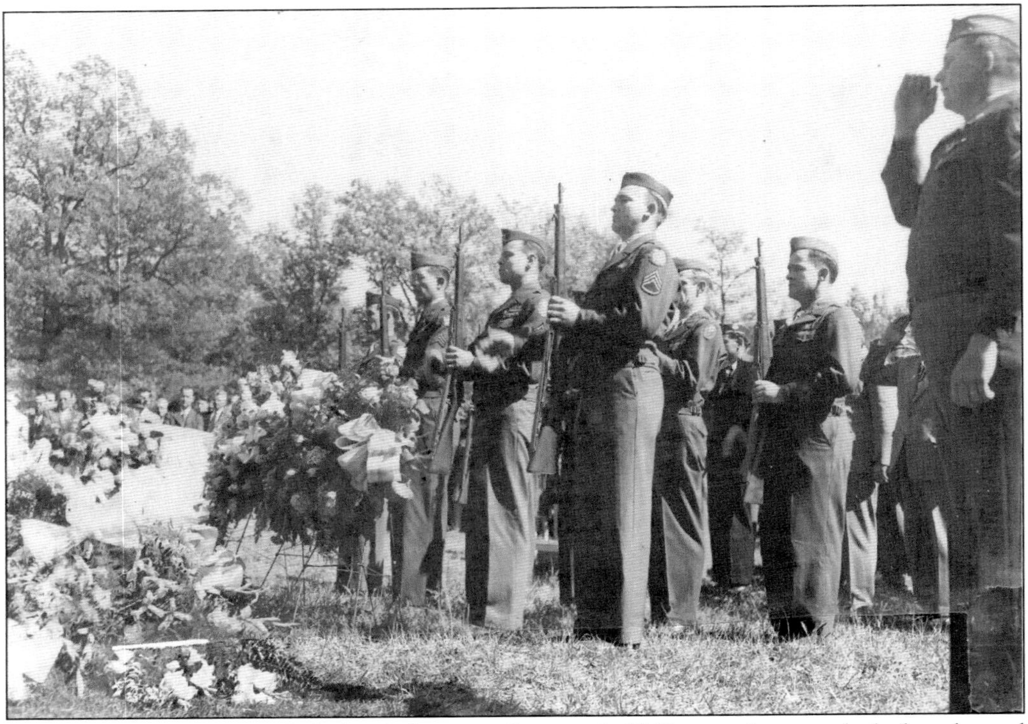

Sgt. Bernard McDade was killed in Belgium on January 8, 1945, just a few months before the end of the European theater of the war. Of the 65 veterans from the Mebane Presbyterian Church who served in the conflict, he was the only one killed in action. McDade was honored with a full military funeral. (MHM.)

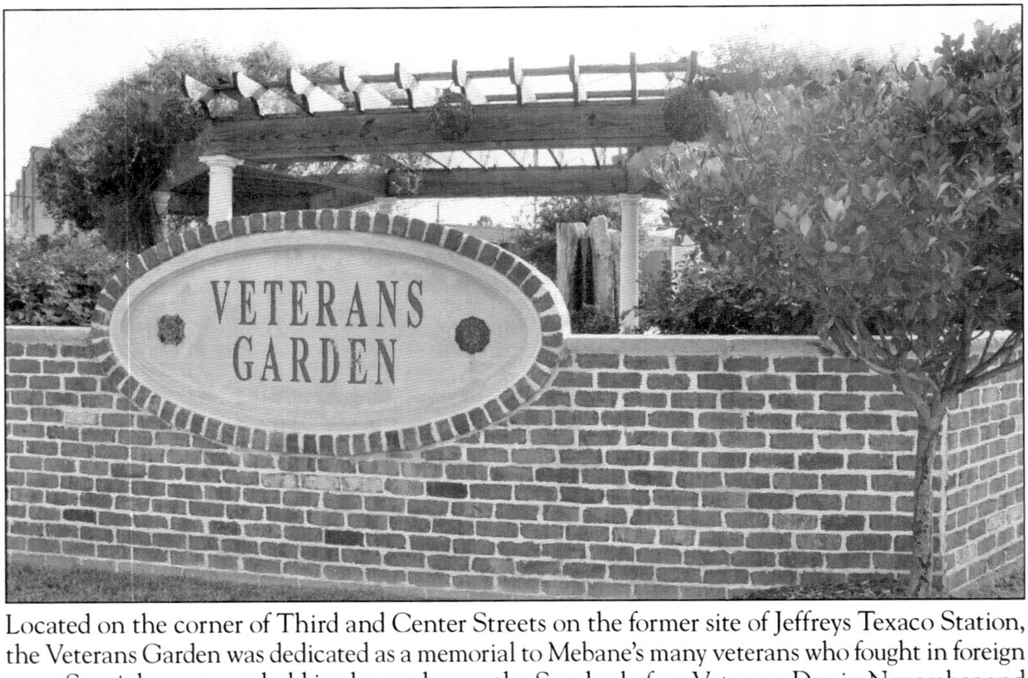

Located on the corner of Third and Center Streets on the former site of Jeffreys Texaco Station, the Veterans Garden was dedicated as a memorial to Mebane's many veterans who fought in foreign wars. Special events are held in the garden on the Sunday before Veterans Day in November and on Memorial Day in May. (Courtesy of Kelly Gauldin.)

Five

Profiles Past and Present

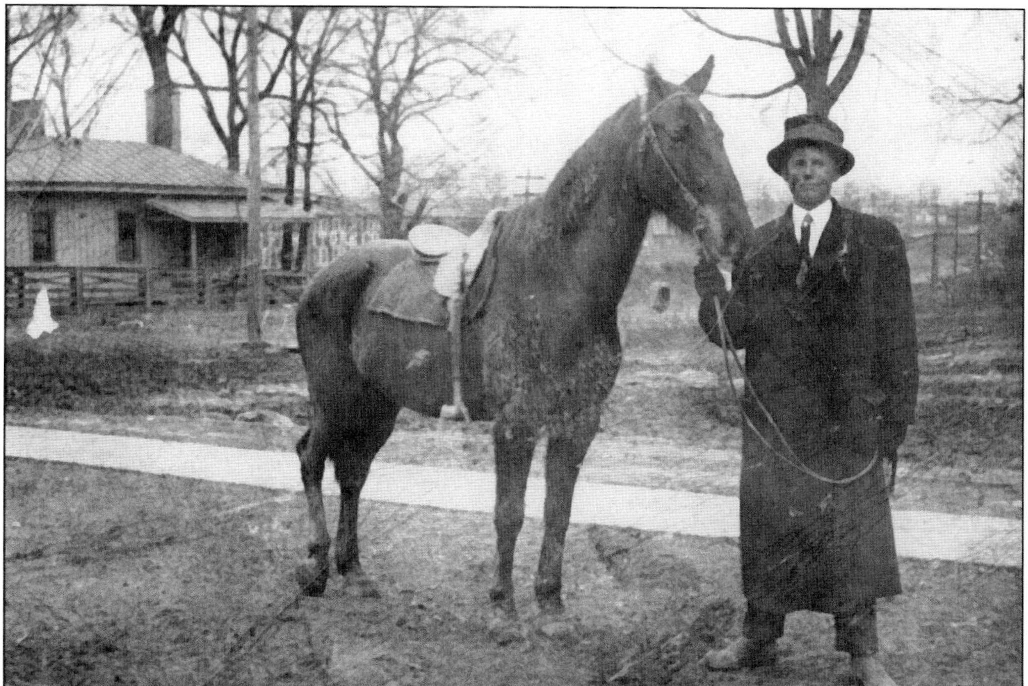

C.E. "Ed" Patterson was born in Kentucky but moved to Mebane with his family when he was a young boy. This undated photograph (probably around 1900) of Ed and his horse was taken next to the old Mebane railway station. White Furniture Company can be seen in the background. (MHM.)

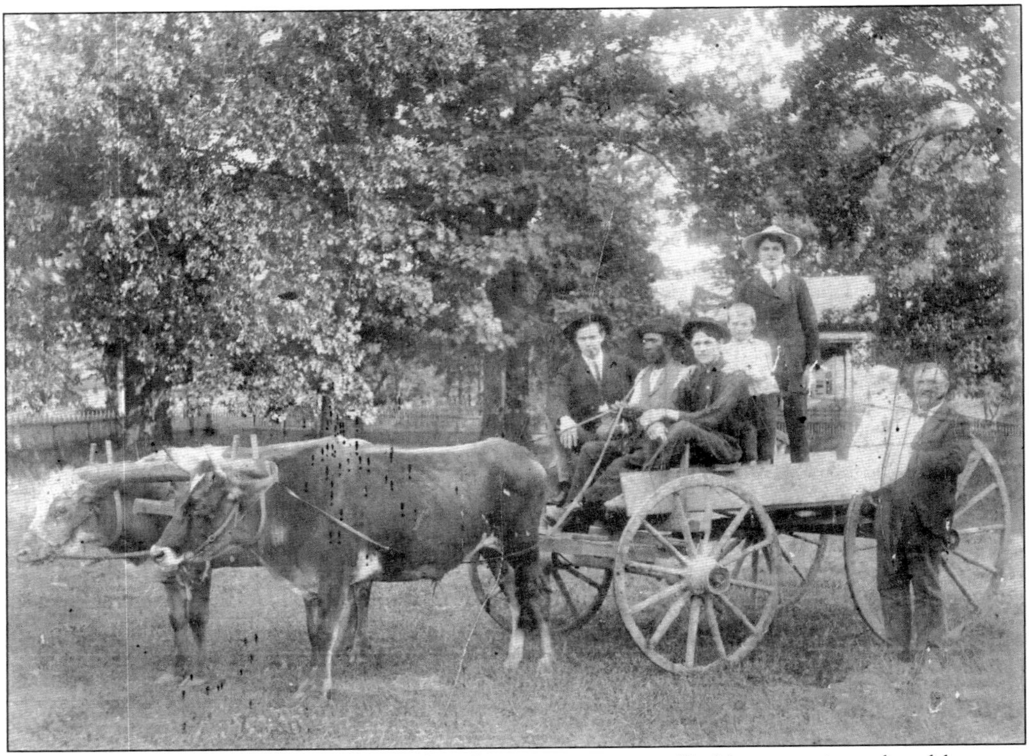

This unusual photograph of five people riding in a wagon pulled by oxen is undated but was probably taken in the late 19th century. (MHM.)

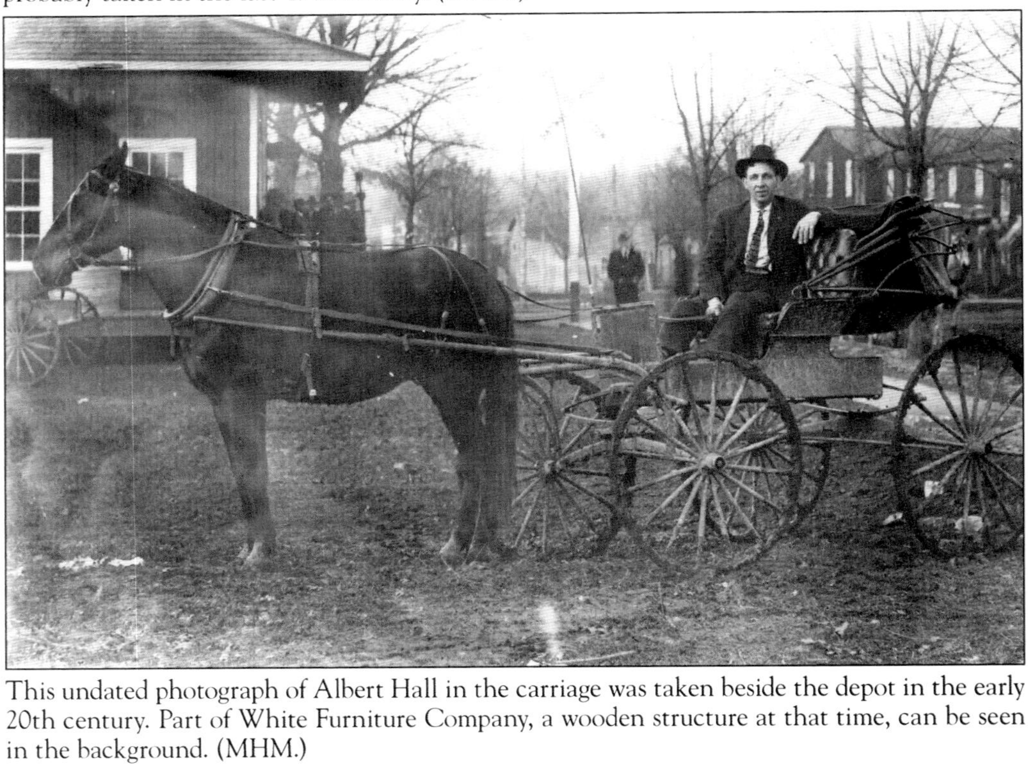

This undated photograph of Albert Hall in the carriage was taken beside the depot in the early 20th century. Part of White Furniture Company, a wooden structure at that time, can be seen in the background. (MHM.)

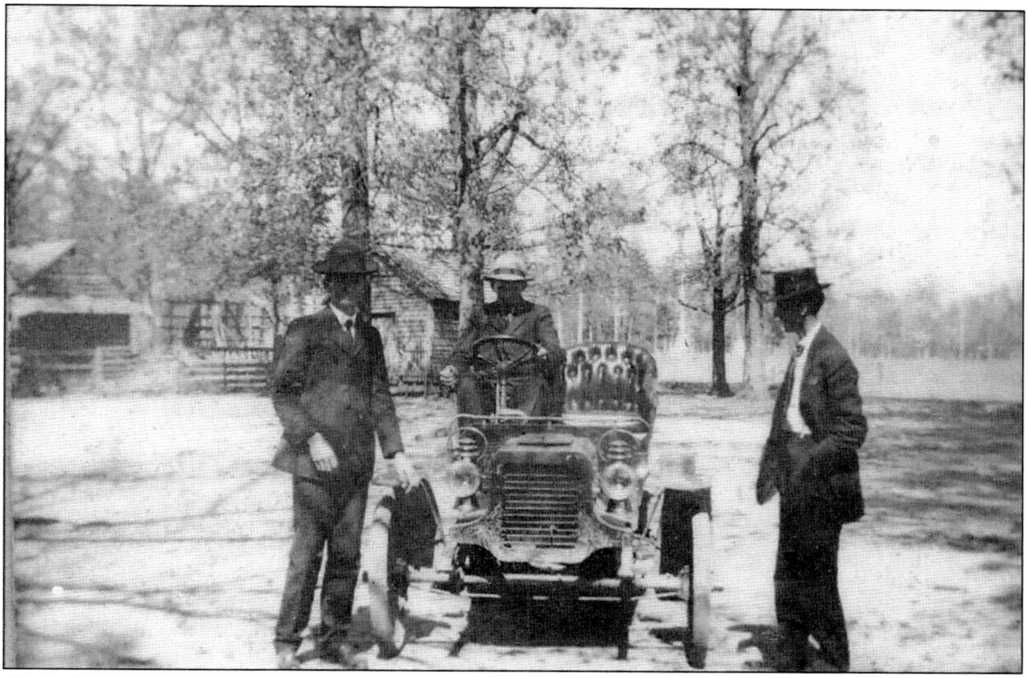

Clyde Compton is seated in his first automobile, a 1910 Ford, which has right-side steering. Standing at the right is Philip Cooper, owner of the first Ford garage in Mebane, who sold Compton the car. (MHM.)

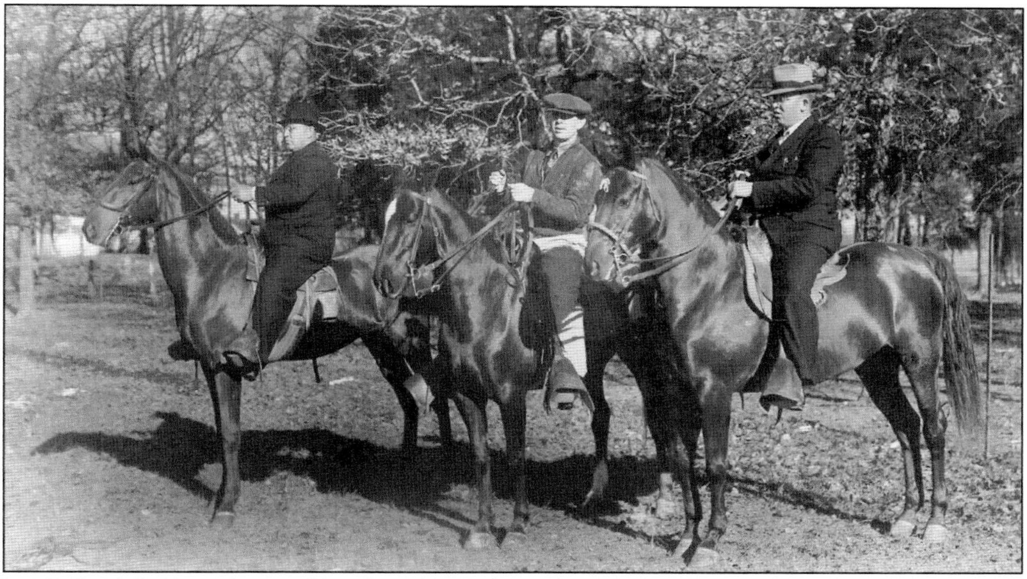

Joe Dillard (left) and two of his friends are dressed up to go for a horseback ride in the early 20th century. Dillard was a prominent businessman involved in the tobacco market and other ventures. (MHM.)

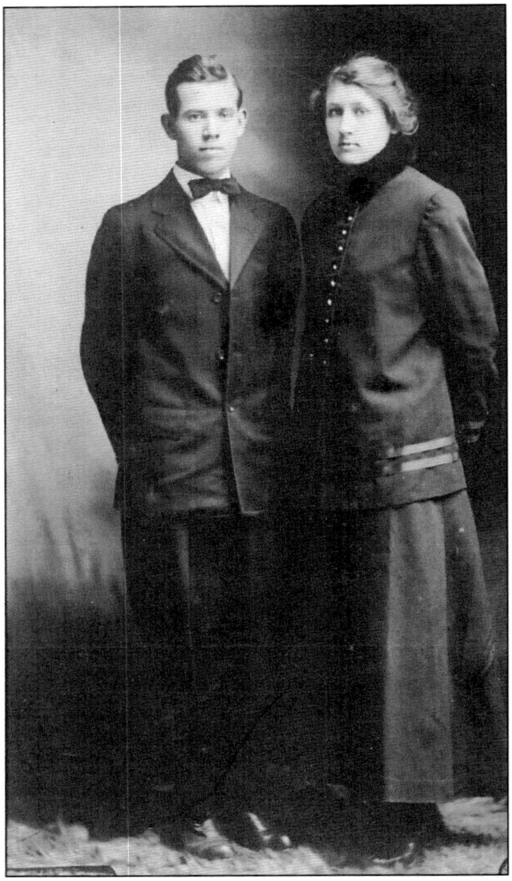

Bryant Carson Lankford and Callie Lavine Harris pose in their wedding attire in 1916. (Courtesy of Johnny Lankford.)

Nineteen years later, the expanded Lankford family gathers at the family home on Lebanon Church Road. Pictured are, from left to right, (first row) Marie and Ned; (second row) Callie, Carson (holding Johnny), Ruby, and Bryant. (Courtesy of Johnny Lankford.)

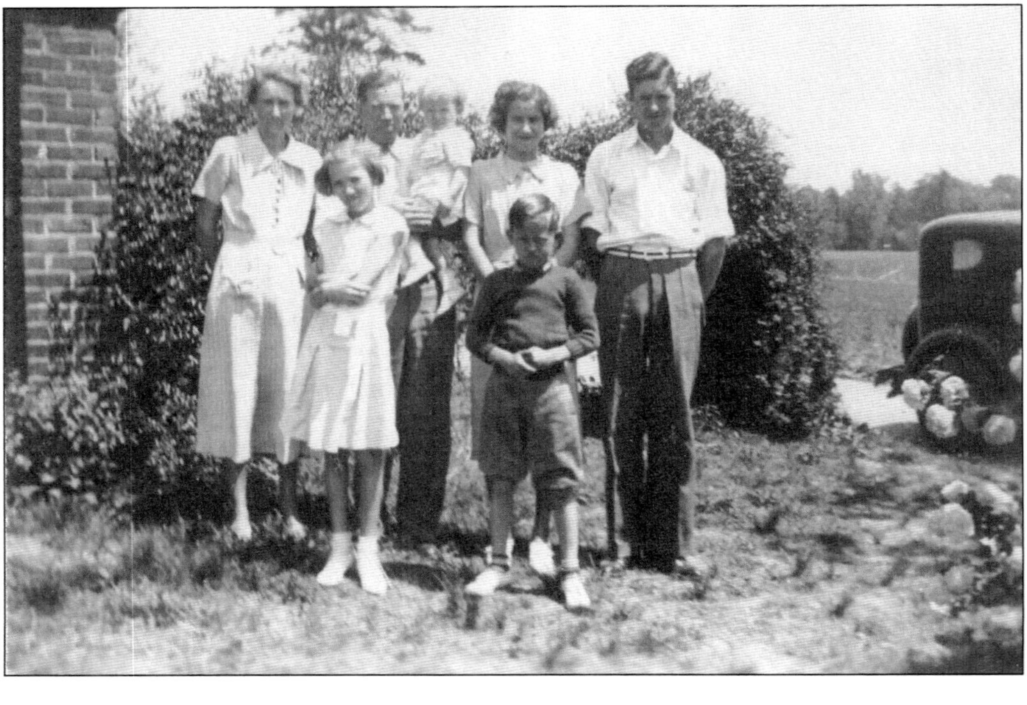

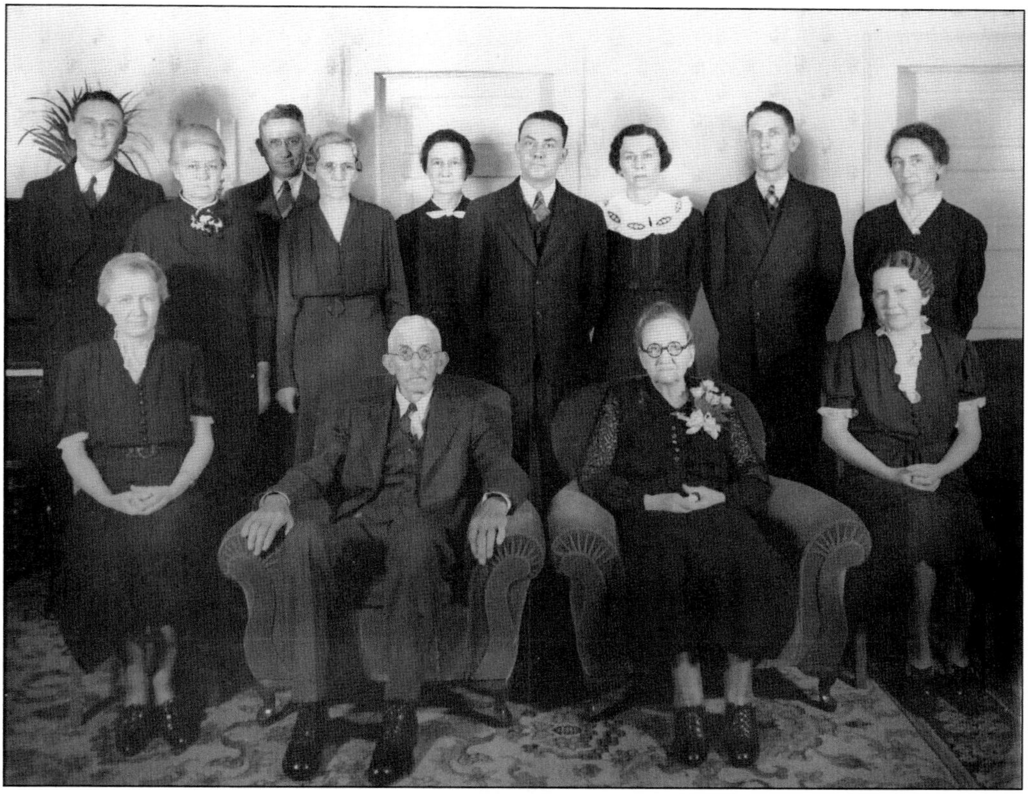

In the 1920s, members from several branches of the Jobe family sat down for a family portrait in their Sunday best. Pictured are, from left to right, (first row) Mary Jobe, Mr. Jobe, Mrs. Jobe, and Carrie Cheek; (second row) Talmadge Jobe, Bessie McAdams, Hifill Jobe, Lula ?, Patti Sykes, Albert Jobe, Corina Hightower, Neal Jobe, and Zella ?. (Courtesy of the Talmadge Jobe family.)

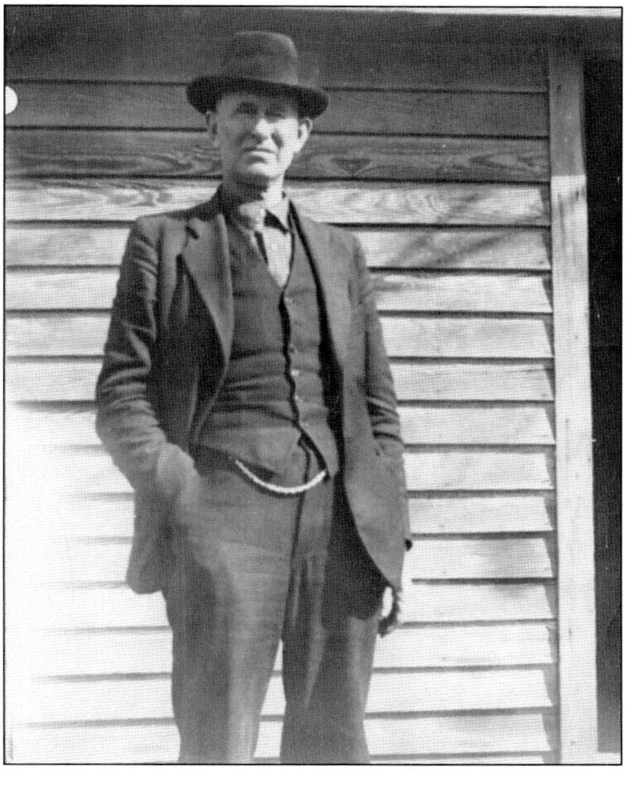

In the early 1920s, Dave Cheek stands on the front porch of his home on the corner of Holt and First Streets, directly across from Durham Hosiery Mill, where he worked as a night watchman. Like many of his coworkers, he had forsaken the hardscrabble life of a farmer for work in the hosiery mills that were springing up around Mebane. (Courtesy of Colleen Payne.)

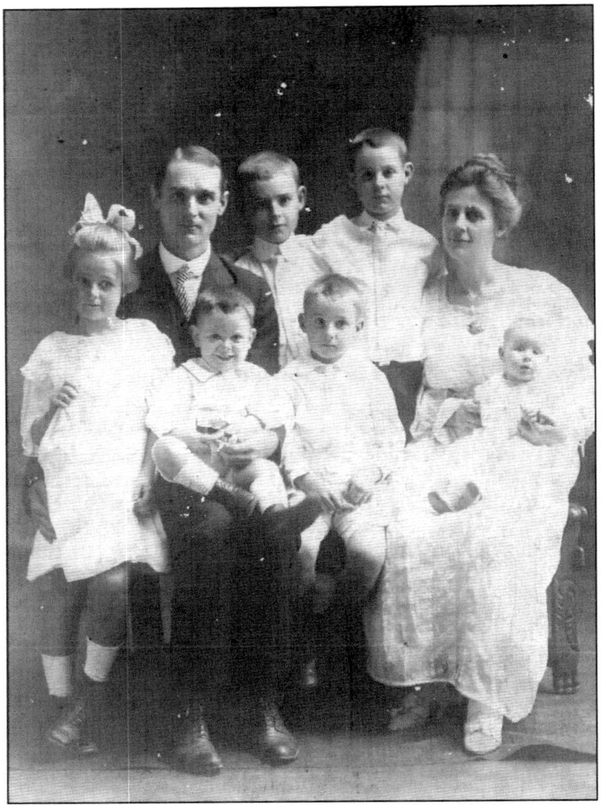

Jesse McRae Howard and Ellen Claire Harris Howard pose with their children in the 1920s. The children are, from left to right, (first row) Frances Baron Howard, Albert Howard, Bill Howard, and Nancy Alice Howard (baby on lap); (second row) Mac Howard and George Howard. (Courtesy of Ellen Turner Lawrence.)

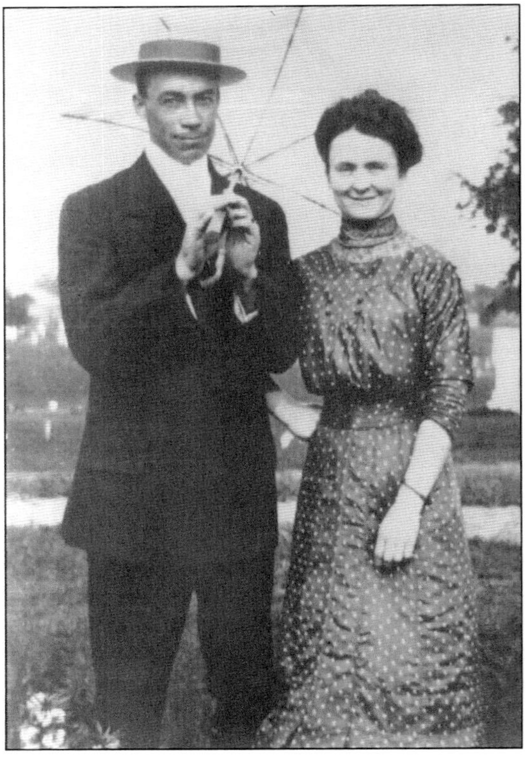

Mebane Home Telephone Company owner Sam Hupman Sr. and his wife, Mary, take a stroll on a sunny summer day in the 1920s. (Courtesy of Betty Tripp.)

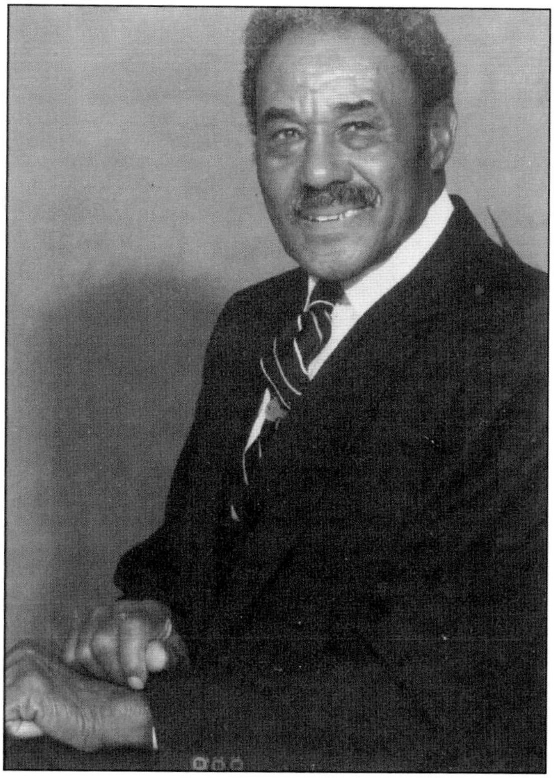

Octavious C. White, commonly called "Oc," was a highly respected automobile mechanic who worked out of a garage at his home on North Highway 119. Drawn by the common saying around town that "the car that Oc White can't fix hasn't been invented yet," his customers came from a wide area. The father of nine children, he worked 60 to 70 hours a week because, as he told the Burlington *Daily-Times News* in an interview in 1989, "I had all those mouths to feed." Below, White poses in his familiar work clothes in front of his shop. He always wore a tie, even under his overalls. (Both, courtesy of Linda Evans.)

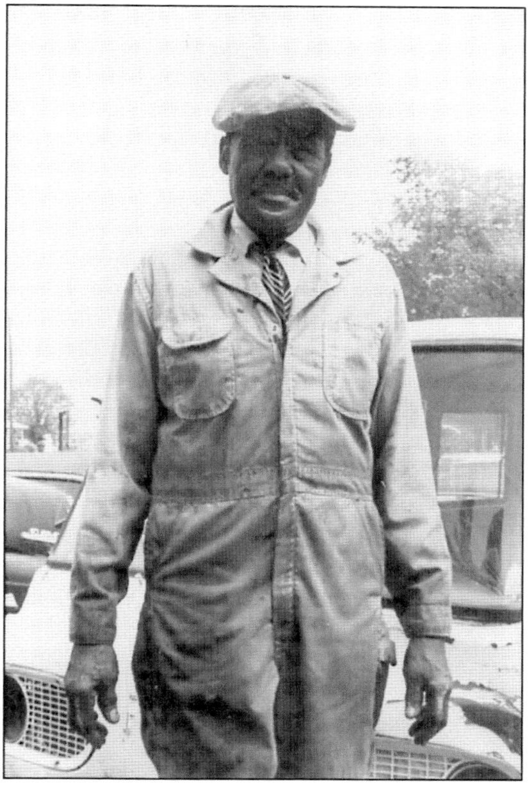

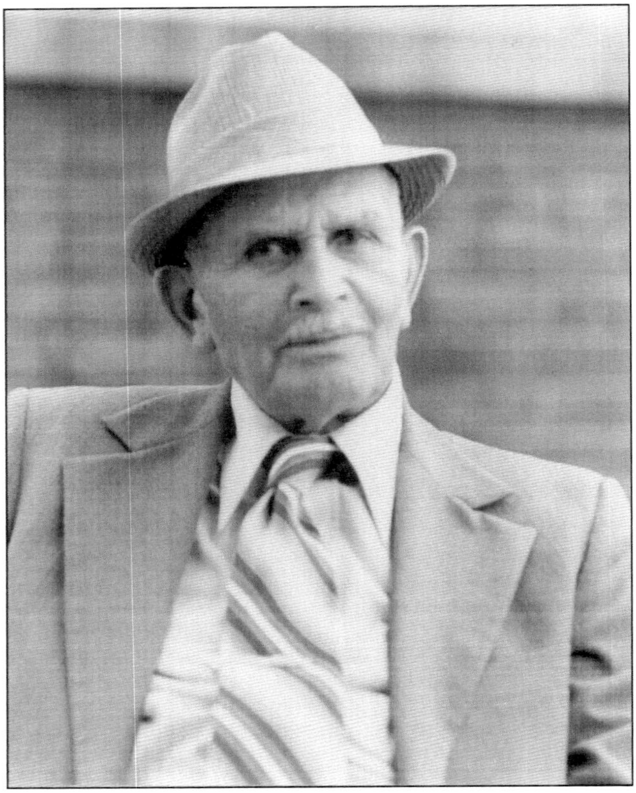

Born in 1902, Edward Compton was a highly respected African American contractor who lived north of Mebane in the White Level community. It was there that he built many homes, tobacco barns, and other structures. He died in 1902. His photograph still hangs today in the White Level Primitive Baptist Church. (Courtesy of Iris Chapman.)

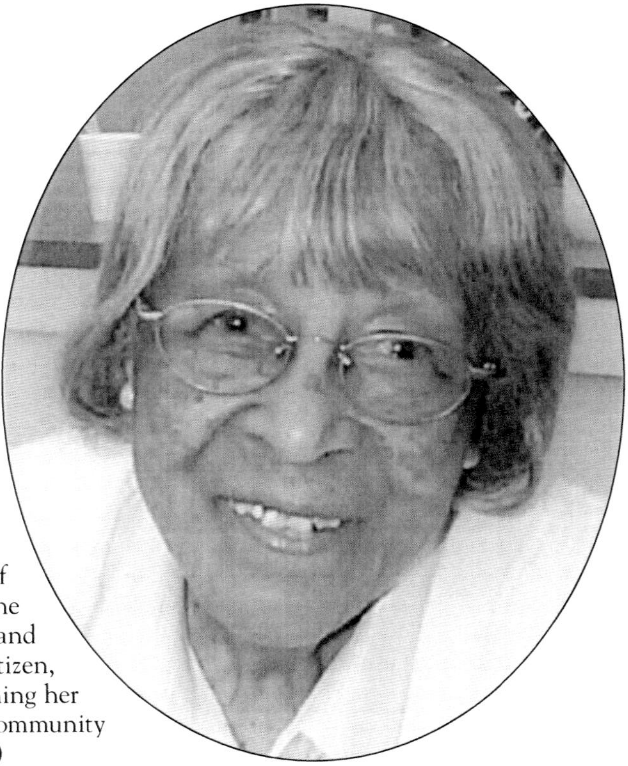

One of Mebane's oldest living citizens as of 2011, Mary Tate was born in 1909. She worked in New York for several years but has lived most of her life in the Mebane area, where she worked as a beautician, store clerk, and at several other jobs. As a senior citizen, she realized a lifetime dream by earning her high school diploma at Alamance Community College. (Courtesy of Iris Chapman.)

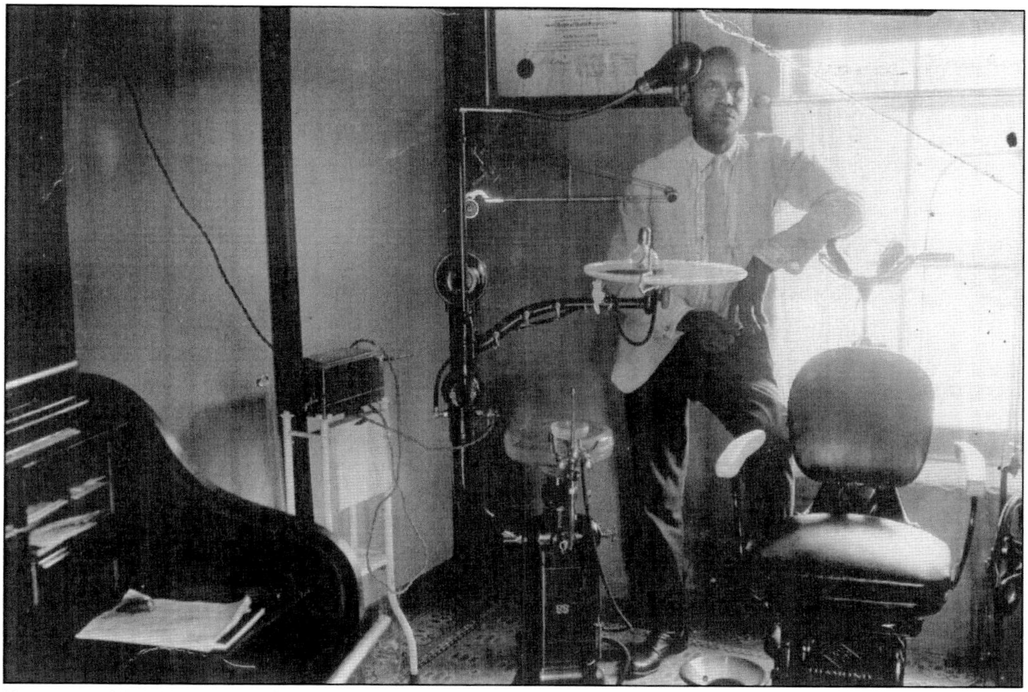

Born in 1886, Vance Walter Love grew up in Alamance County on Lynch Store Road. He was educated at the Palmer Institute in Guilford County and at the Meharry Medical College in Nashville, Tennessee. Unable to practice dentistry in Alamance County because of the segregation laws of the time, he worked for the State of North Carolina and then in his own private dental practice for many years. He died in 1971. (Courtesy of Iris Chapman.)

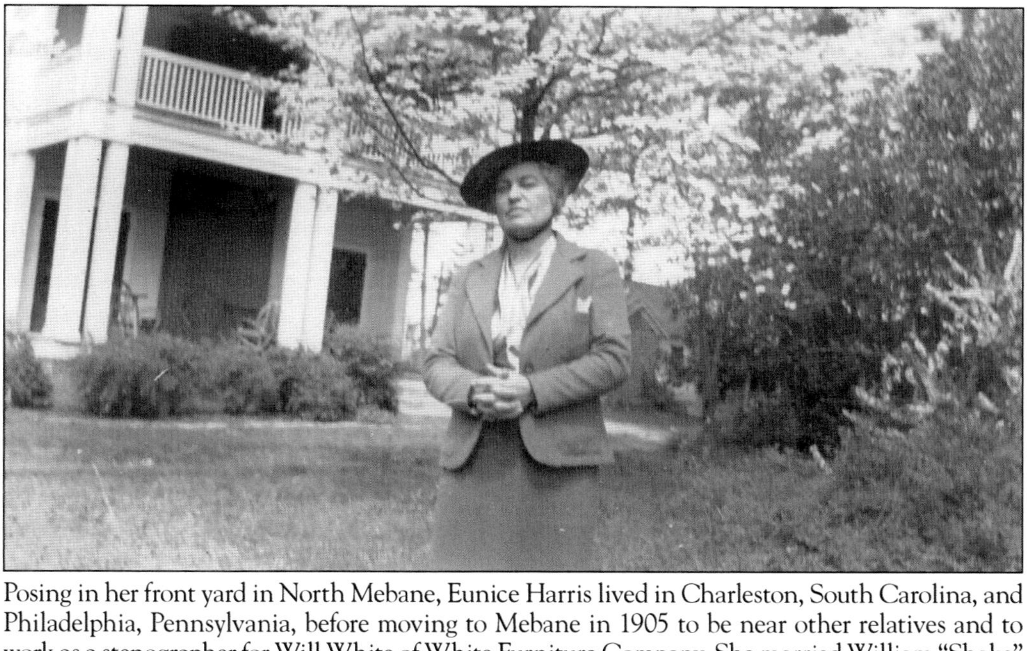

Posing in her front yard in North Mebane, Eunice Harris lived in Charleston, South Carolina, and Philadelphia, Pennsylvania, before moving to Mebane in 1905 to be near other relatives and to work as a stenographer for Will White of White Furniture Company. She married William "Shake" Shakespeare Harris in 1913. In 1930, she organized a literary book club, the Reviewers' Club, and led the effort to establish the Mebane Public Library. (Courtesy of Lennie Harris Stout.)

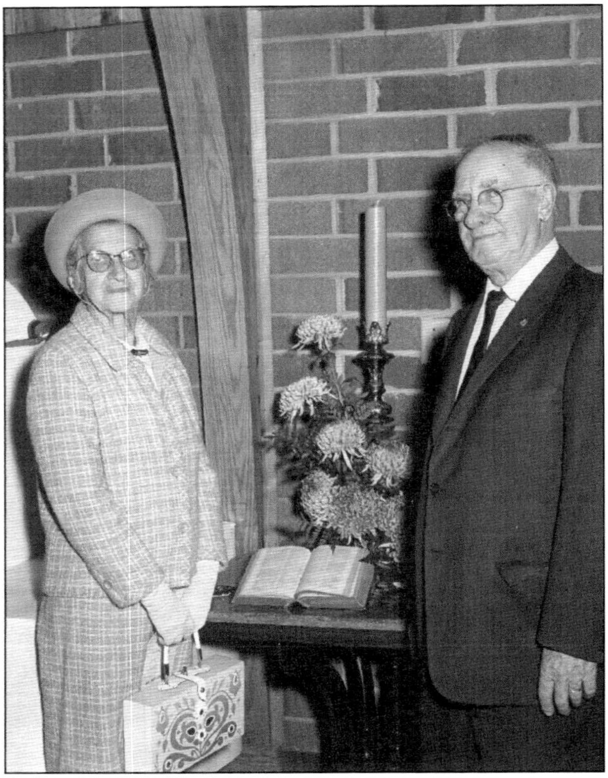

Leonarah Harris Corbett was the wife of William Warren Corbett, one of the founders of Kingsdown. She is shown here with her brother William Shakespeare Harris at a flower show held at the American Legion in 1970. Harris was Mebane's postmaster from the 1930s through the early 1950s. (Courtesy of Lennie Harris Stout.)

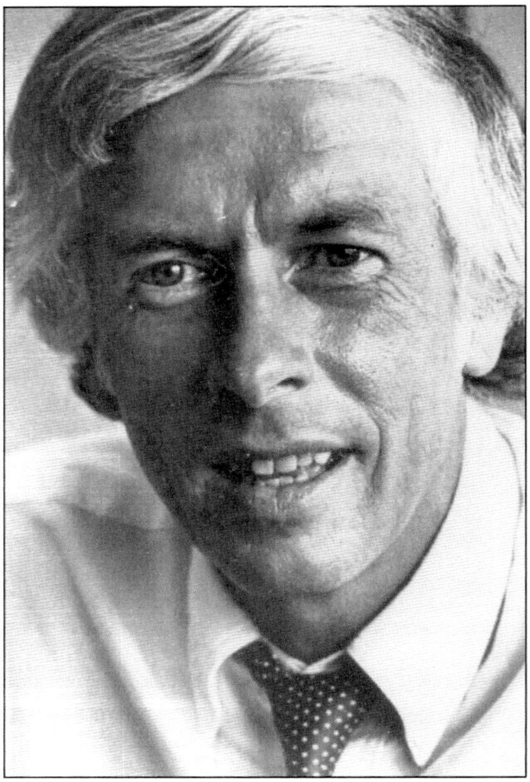

Ed Yoder Jr. was a 1950 graduate of Mebane High School. A Rhodes Scholar, he had a long and distinguished career as a journalist at the *Greensboro Daily News* and the *Washington Star*, where he won the Pulitzer Prize. He also has written several books, including *The Night of the Old South Ball*, a collection of essays that includes a fascinating reminiscence about growing up in Mebane in the 1930s and 1940s. (MHM.)

Lew Riggs poses in the Cincinnati Reds dugout in the late 1930s. A graduate of Mebane High School, he played professional baseball for several minor-league teams and for the St. Louis Cardinals, Cincinnati Reds, and Brooklyn Dodgers. He played in the World Series for the Reds and the Dodgers. After his retirement in 1950, he returned to his hometown and ran Riggs Shoe Store on Clay Street with his brother Hurley. In 1974, Bill Hunter of the Burlington *Times News* wrote, "Lewis Riggs was as nice a man as you'd ever want to meet." (MHM.)

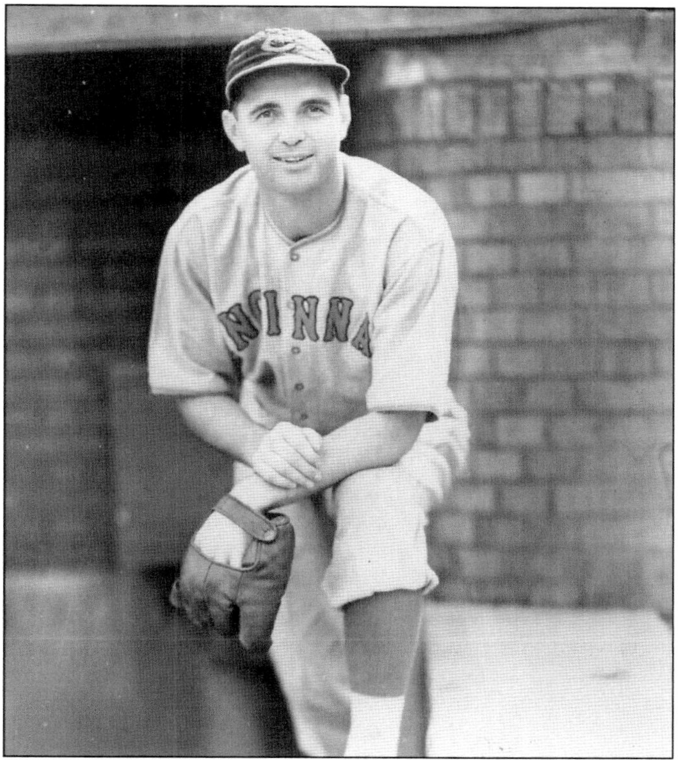

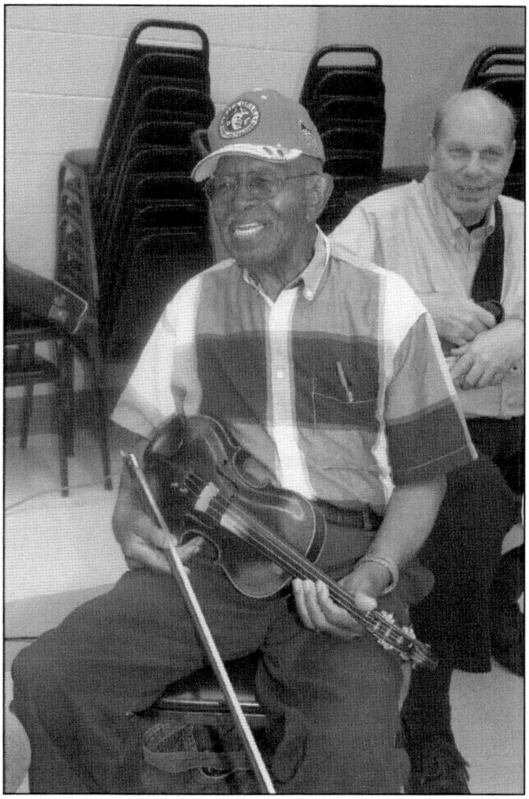

Born in Cedar Grove just outside of Mebane in 1918, Joe Thompson rose from humble beginnings to world fame as one of the last old-time African American fiddle players. For years, he and his cousin Odell Thompson performed across the United States and in foreign countries, playing in Carnegie Hall and other legendary venues. Odell died in 1994, but Joe has continued to perform on a very limited schedule. He received numerous awards, including the National Folk Heritage Award from the National Endowment for the Arts in 2007. (MHM.)

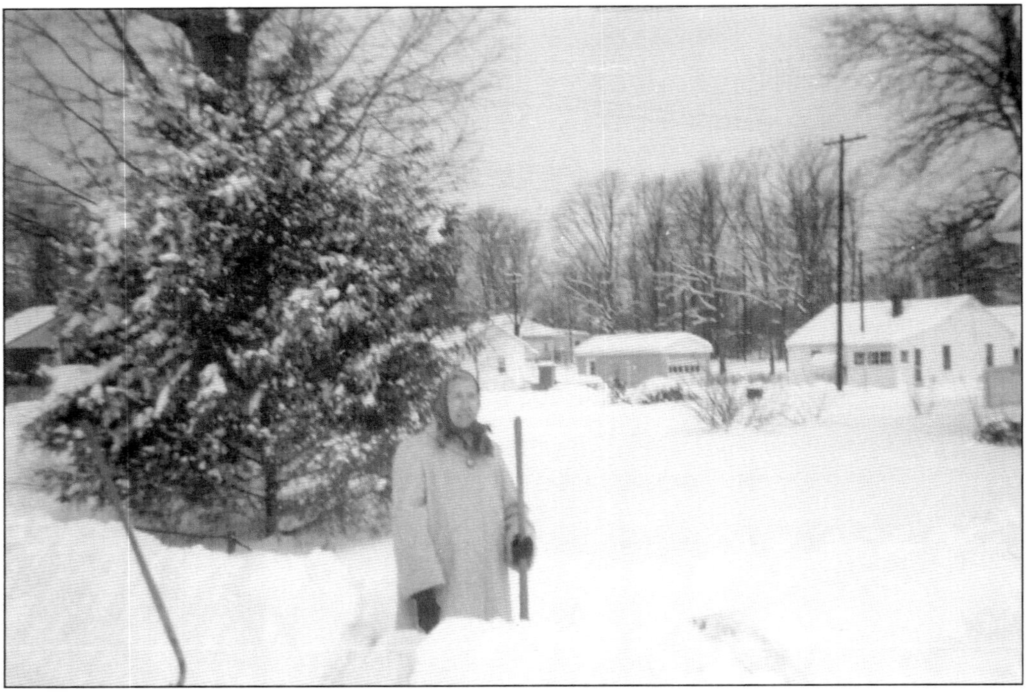

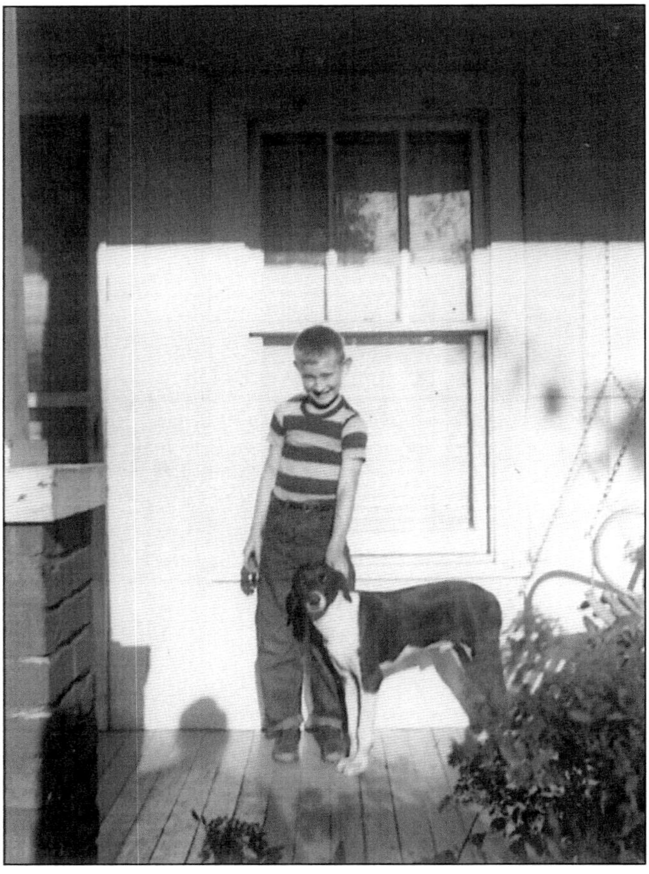

In 1960, Mebane received huge snowfalls on the first three Wednesdays in March. The total amount of snow on the ground at one time in Mebane and some other Alamance County areas was close to 18 inches. Carrie Oakley stands in her yard on Carr Street wondering how long it will be before she can see the ground again. (Courtesy of Colleen Payne.)

"Smokey" Lynch, son of John and Mabel Lynch, stands on the back porch of his home on North Highway 119 with his dog Skip, the most famous dog in town in the 1950s, when Mebane had no leash laws. Skip followed Smokey to school, regularly accompanied several young teenage boys as they delivered newspapers in the early morning or afternoon, and generally just went wherever he wanted to go. (Courtesy of Lennie Harris Stout.)

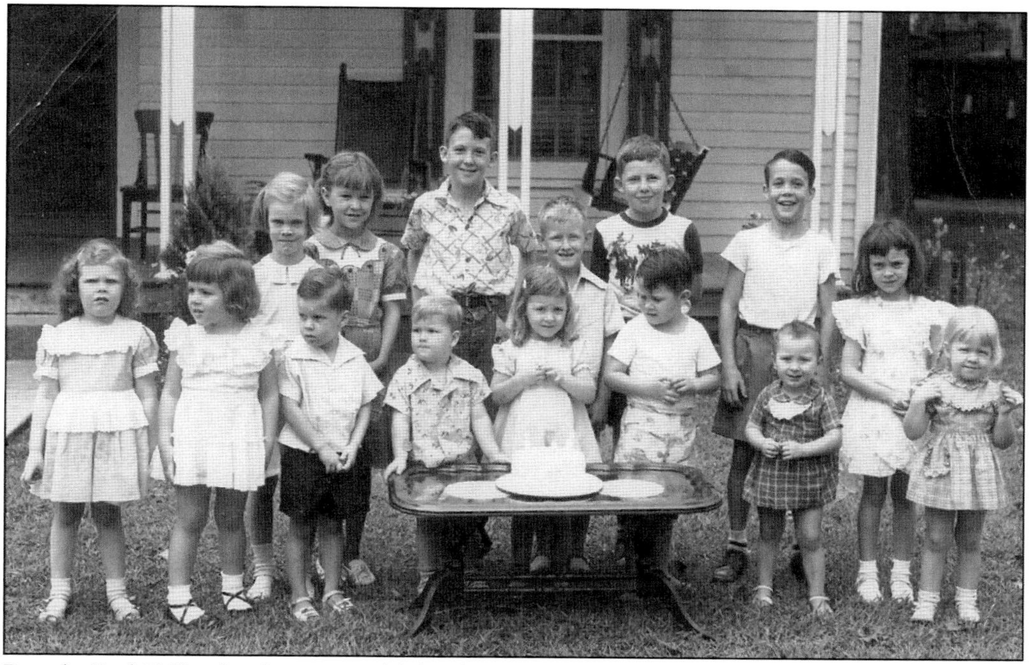

Brenda Gail Kelly, the three-year-old daughter of A.O. and Velma Kelly of Carr Street, stands behind her birthday cake at a party given in her honor by her grandmother Carrie Oakley and aunt Colleen Payne. The young guests included Linda Gettig, Pamela Sue Yates, Sandra Arnold, Jimmy Harris, Gary Yates, Mike Kelly, Jo Ann Kelly, Mary Ellen Phelps, Lennie Harris, May Ann Riley, Ronnie Oakley, Smokey Lynch, Garland McCauley, Jerry West, and Judy Harris. (Photograph by William Lynch, courtesy of Velma Kelly.)

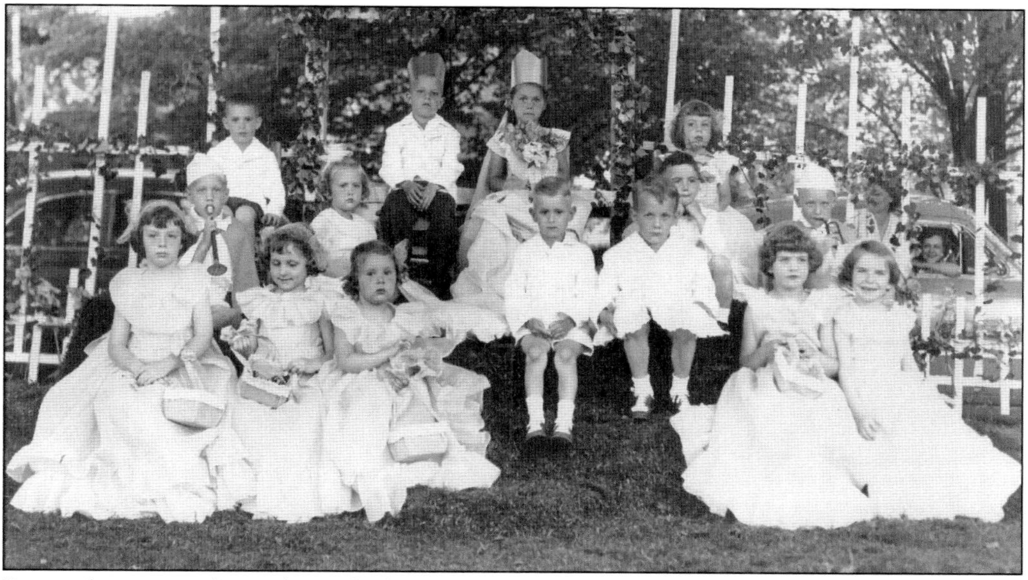

Pictured are several members of a local kindergarten class celebrating May Day in 1950 at a kindergarten operated by Louise Hawkins on South Fourth Street. Al Crumpler and Teena James were the king and queen. There were no public-school kindergartens in Mebane until the 1970s, so some parents sent their preschool children to private schools like this one. (Courtesy of Lennie Harris Stout.)

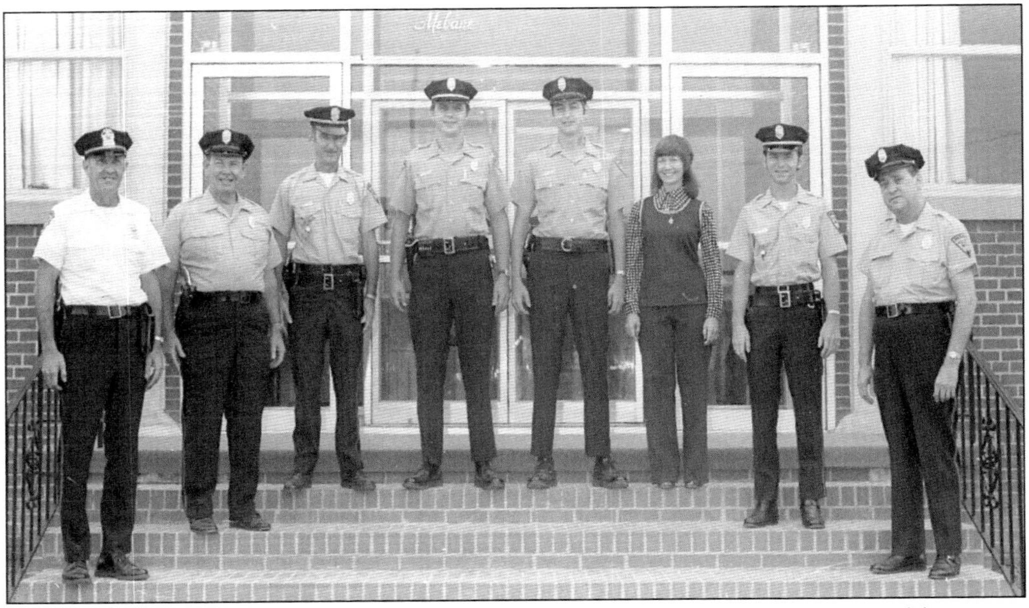

Over the years, the Mebane Police Department has been headquartered in several locations, including Fourth Street, the town hall, and the former post office on Center Street, its present location. This undated photograph shows the police officers in the 1970s or 1980s on the steps of the town hall. Pictured are, from left to right, Chief Dan Tate, Herley Dickey, Adrian Allen, Grant Kapp, John Byrd, Nina Anderson, Gary Bumgarner, and Cliff Wilkinson. (Courtesy of Gary Bumgarner.)

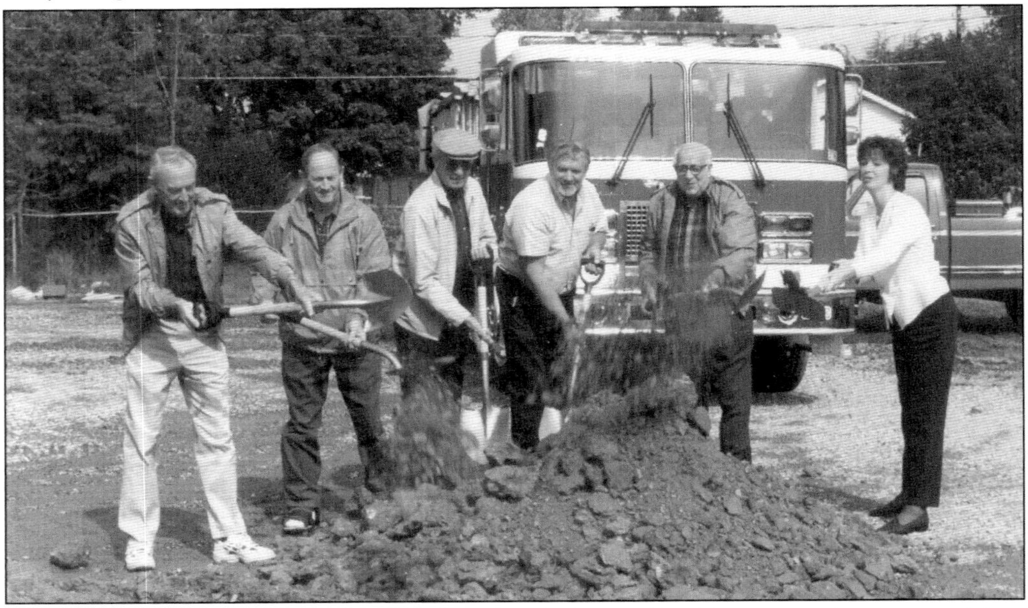

Several retired and active members of the Mebane Volunteer Fire Department break ground for a new fire station on North Highway 119 in 1996. For decades, the fire station was located on the south side of town, which was a major inconvenience and danger when trains passed through or stopped to unload freight, blocking the railroad crossings. All the men in photograph had been volunteer chiefs at one time. Pictured from left to right are Curtis Clark, Jack Lancaster, Irwin Copley, Jimmy Jobe, Zaner Sykes, and Lisa Hinson. (Courtesy of Curtis Clark.)

A.M. Michael served Mebane for 43 years in various capacities, including superintendent of public works. The town reservoir, built after a severe drought in the 1950s, was named Lake Michael in his honor. Today, the lake serves as a general recreation area popular with fishermen, boaters, hikers, and picnickers. (MHM.)

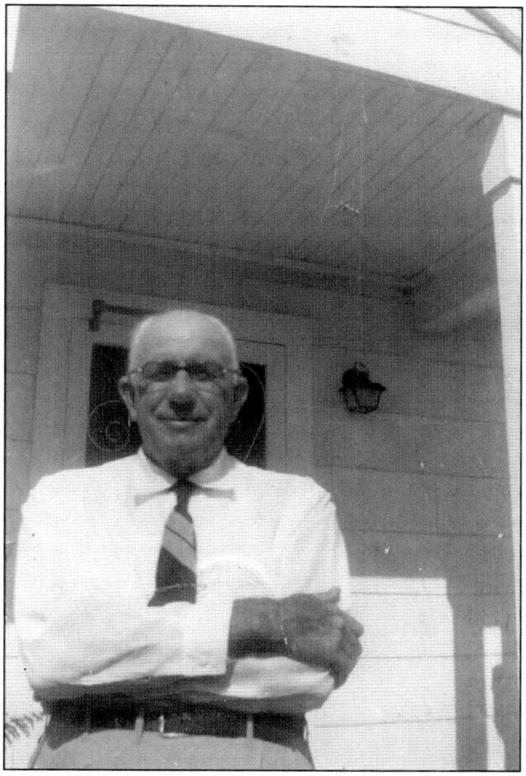

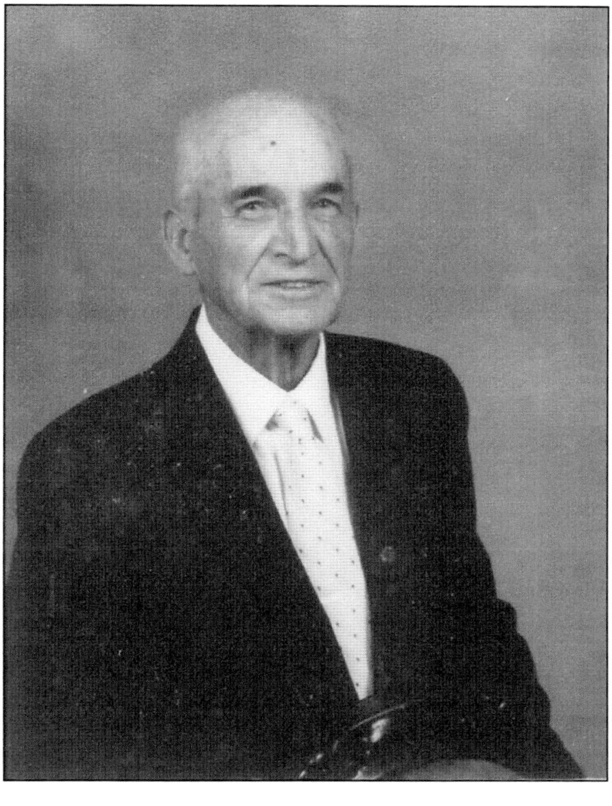

Gilbert Scarlett (1908–1999) was the water department supervisor for the town of Mebane for close to 40 years. His service was honored in 1974 in a special ceremony dedicating the Gilbert T. Scarlett Park on Washington Street across from today's city hall. (Courtesy of Jimmy Jobe and Marie Scarlett Perry.)

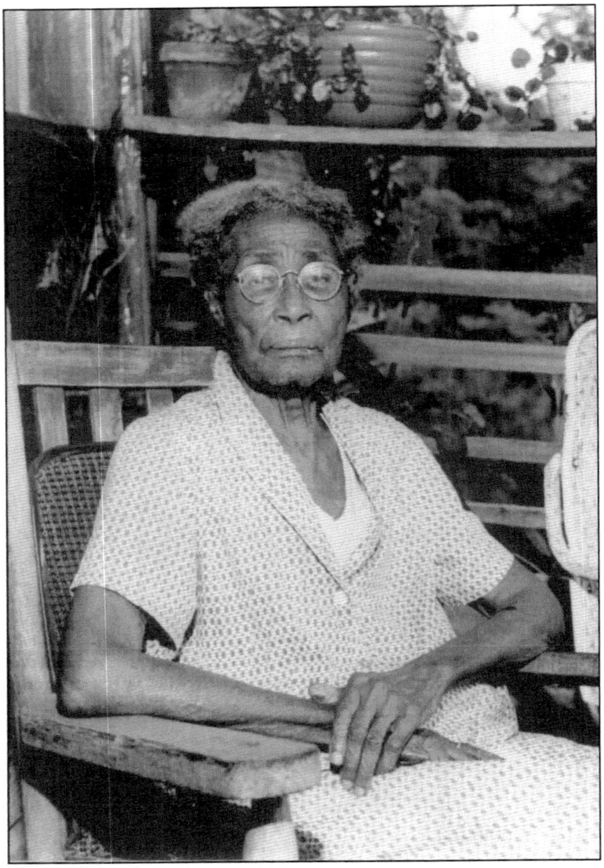

Effie Murray White (1884–1978) spent most of her life in a rural area north of Mebane near Cross Roads Presbyterian Church. The daughter of slaves on the Murray Plantation, she was the matriarch of a large family and a fountain of genealogical knowledge about her family and community. In 1974, near the end of his research for *Roots*, Alex Haley visited Effie, who was then 93, at her Cross Roads home to gather the final information he needed to complete his best-selling book that gave birth to the famous television series. Haley delivered the eulogy at her funeral in 1978. (Courtesy of Iris Chapman.)

In February 2011, the Mebane Historical Society presented a program on the connection between the Cross Roads community and *Roots*. Several members of the black and white branches of the Murray families attended the program and posed for this photograph at the end of the meeting. (Courtesy of the *Mebane Enterprise*.)

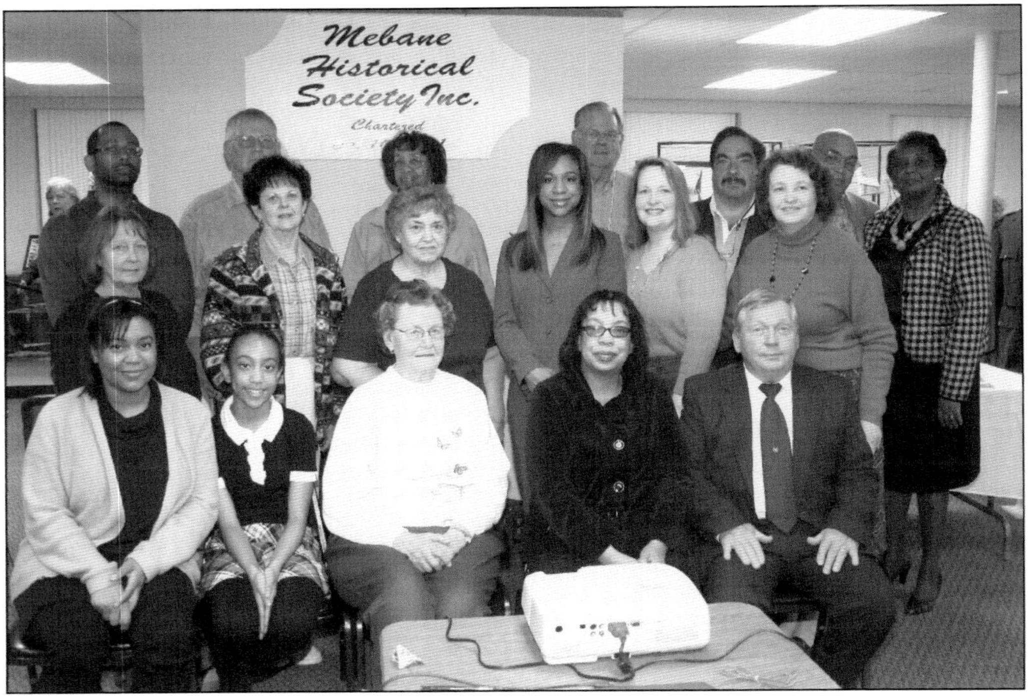

Six

Churches and Civic Clubs

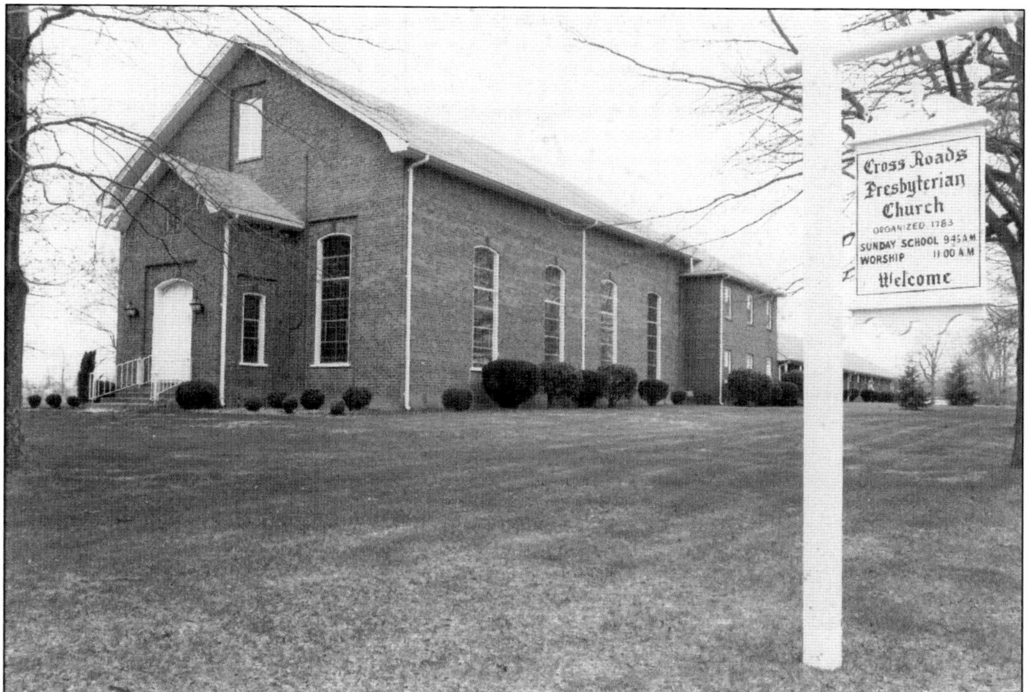

The settlers from the Northeastern colonies who migrated to the Alamance County in the 18th century wasted little time in constructing churches as places of worship and community gatherings. Cross Roads Presbyterian Church was organized in 1783, but the first structure, a small wooden building, was not constructed until 1790. A brick church was built in 1876. Both whites and slaves from the Murray Plantation and the surrounding areas worshipped at the church. Alex Haley's grandmother had been a slave on the plantation. (MHM.)

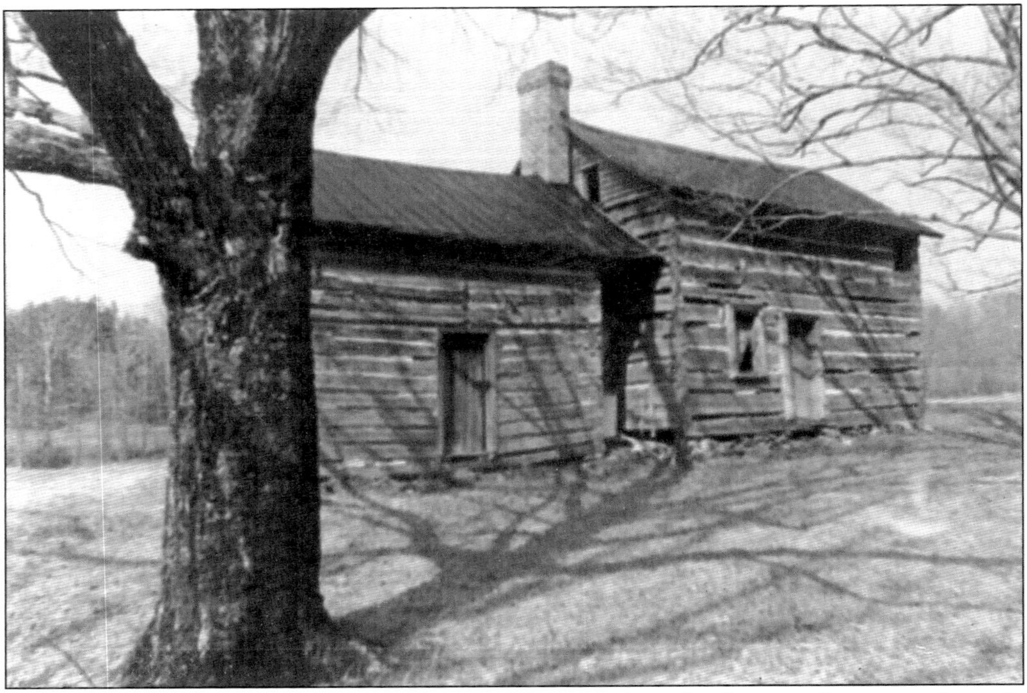

This image shows the humble home of Rev. William Paisley, who for several years in the early 19th century served as the pastor of the Cross Roads Presbyterian Church and of Hawfields Presbyterian Church on the south side of Mebane. (MHM.)

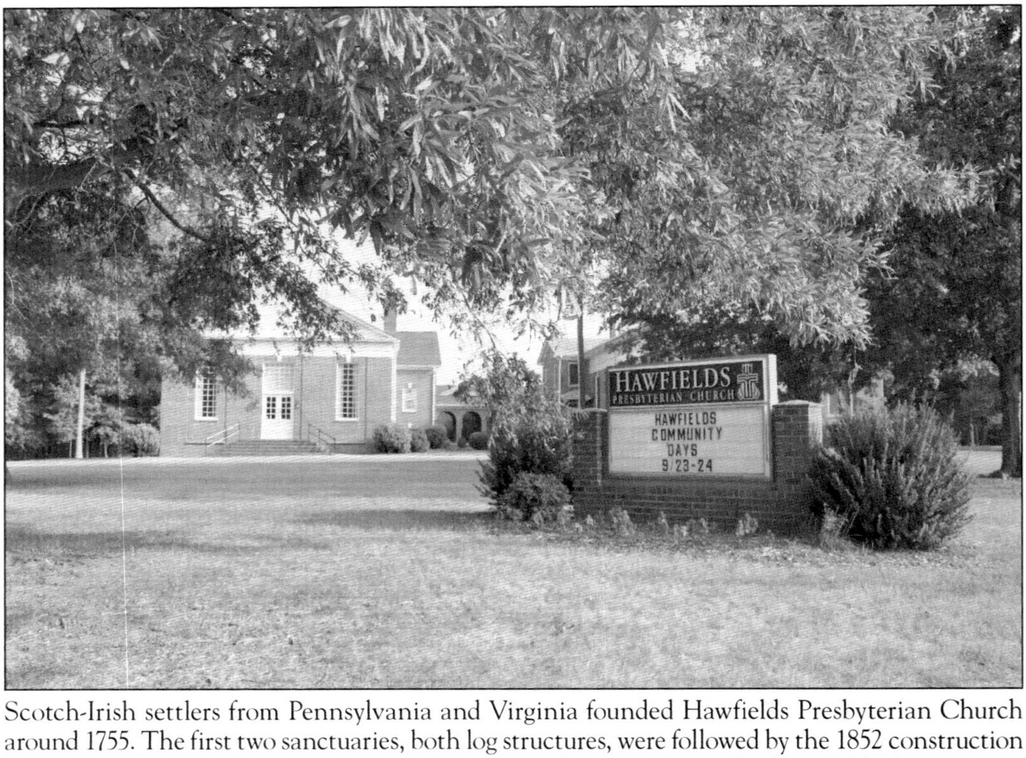

Scotch-Irish settlers from Pennsylvania and Virginia founded Hawfields Presbyterian Church around 1755. The first two sanctuaries, both log structures, were followed by the 1852 construction of the brick building that serves as the sanctuary today. (Courtesy of Kelly Gauldin.)

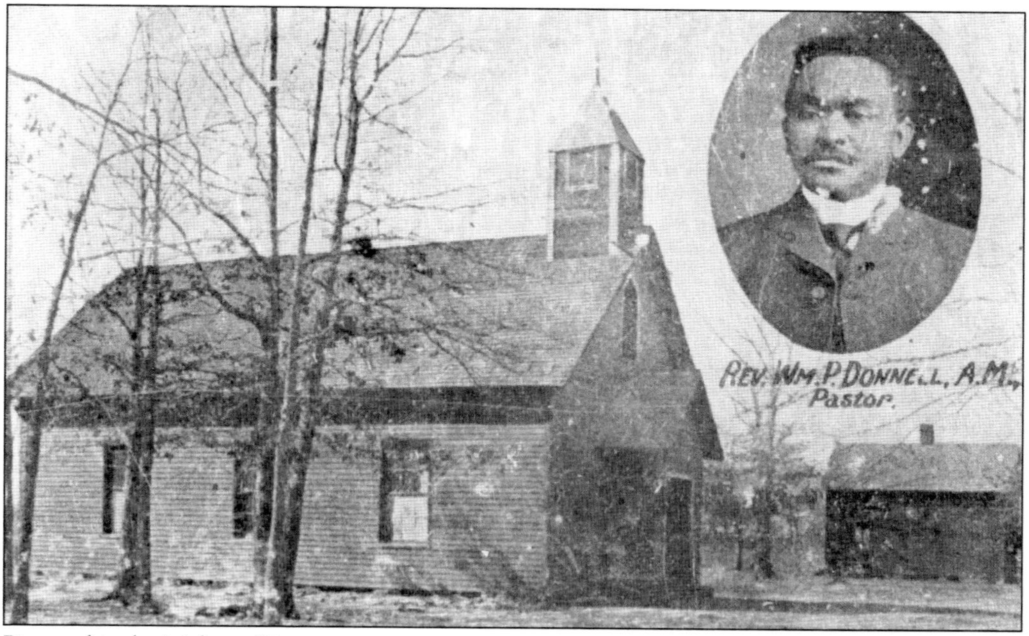

Pictured is the Mebane First Presbyterian Church, built on Holt Street in 1864. The inset on the right of the photograph is Rev. William P. Donnell, one of its later pastors. This building served the congregation until a new church was built near West End School in 1938. In 1971, the present church was built on the corner of Moore Road and West Holt Street. Rev. James W. Brown is the minister. (Courtesy of Thomas Vinson.)

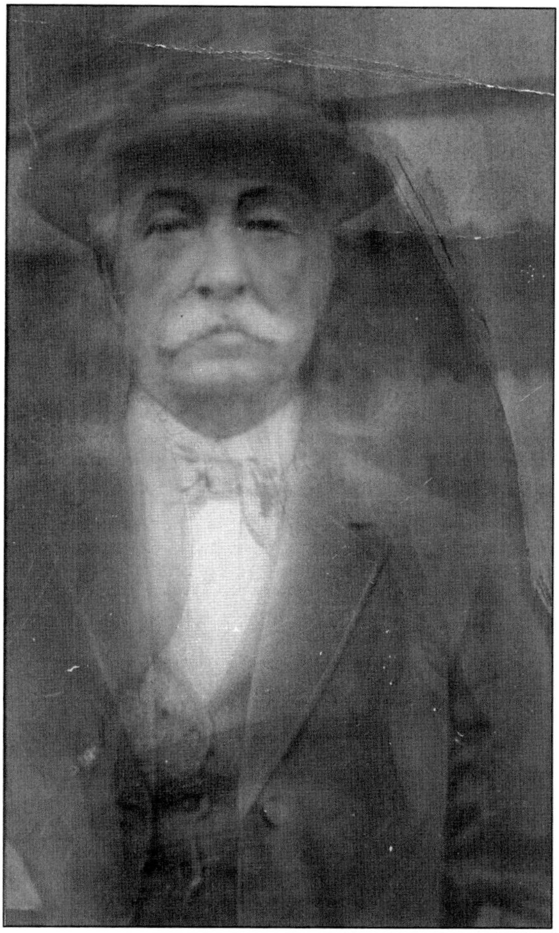

The organizer and first pastor of the Mebane First Presbyterian Church was Rev. W.A. Scott. (Courtesy of Thomas Vinson.)

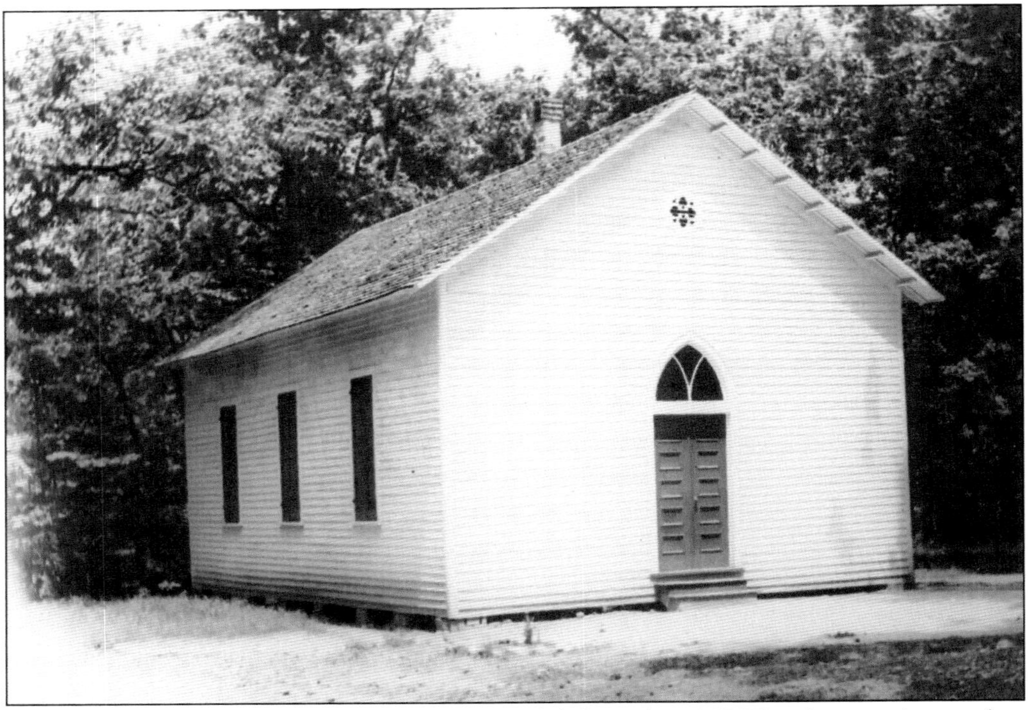

Lebanon Methodist Episcopal Church was built and dedicated in 1887. This photograph was taken years before the 1936 tornado that destroyed the Mebane Theater and Mebane Motor Company, travelled several miles, and touched down again on Lebanon Church Road. (MHM.)

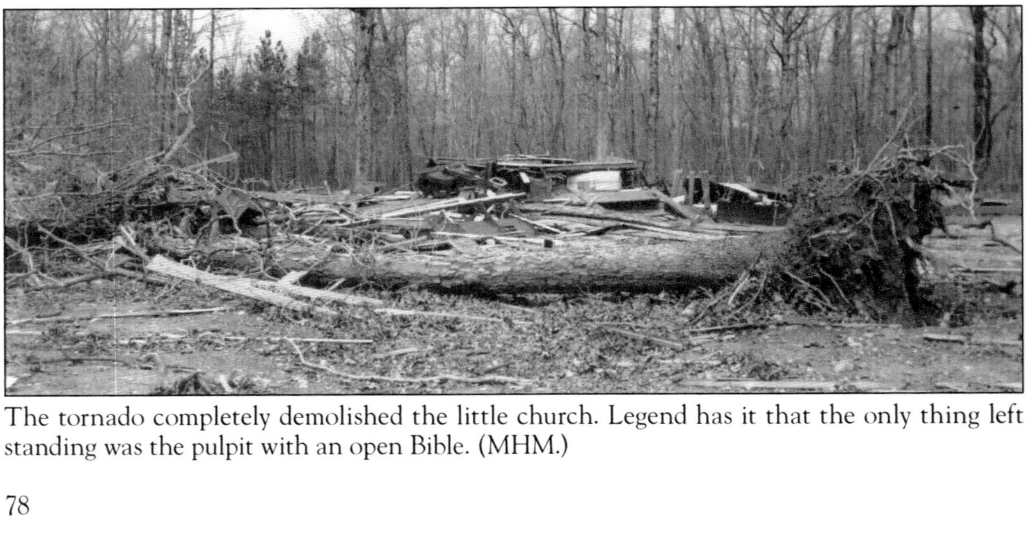

The tornado completely demolished the little church. Legend has it that the only thing left standing was the pulpit with an open Bible. (MHM.)

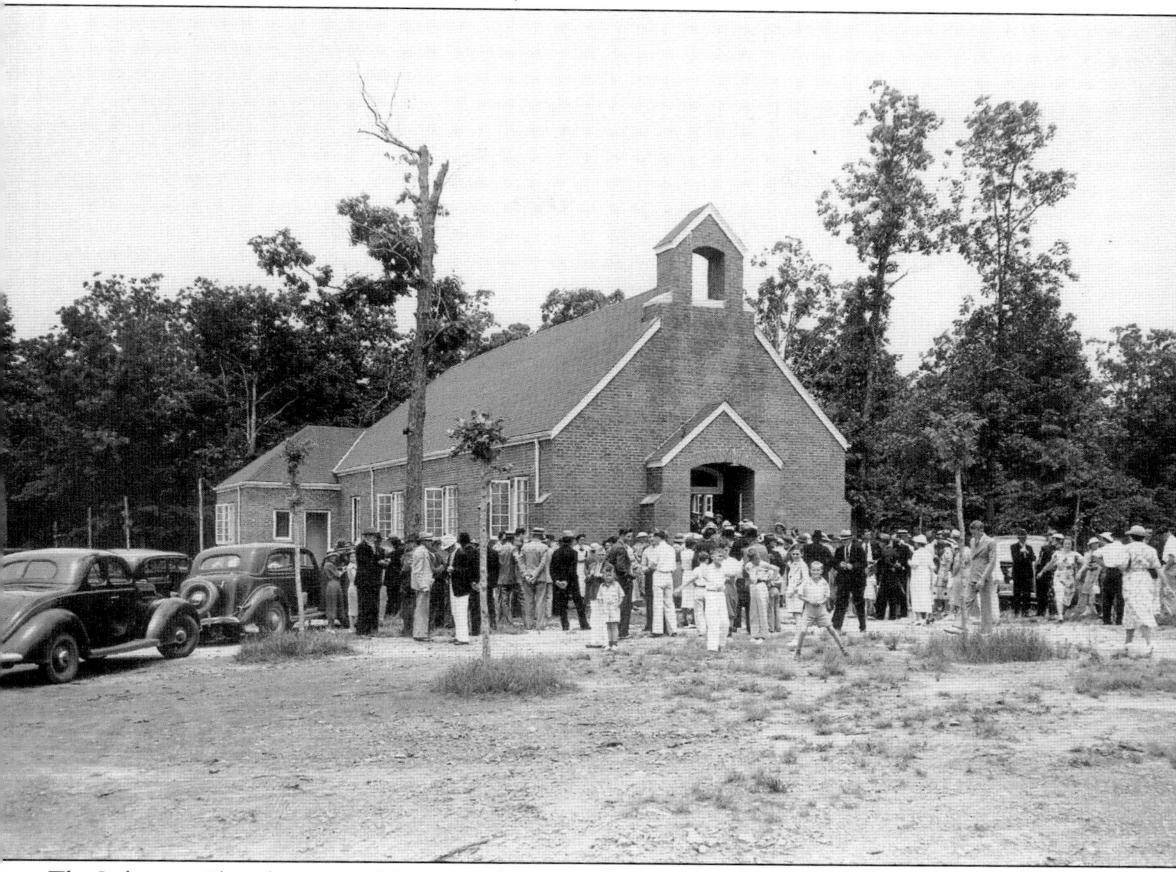

The Lebanon Church was quickly rebuilt, bigger and stronger. Most of the congregation showed up for the dedication of the new structure on June 26, 1938. (MHM.)

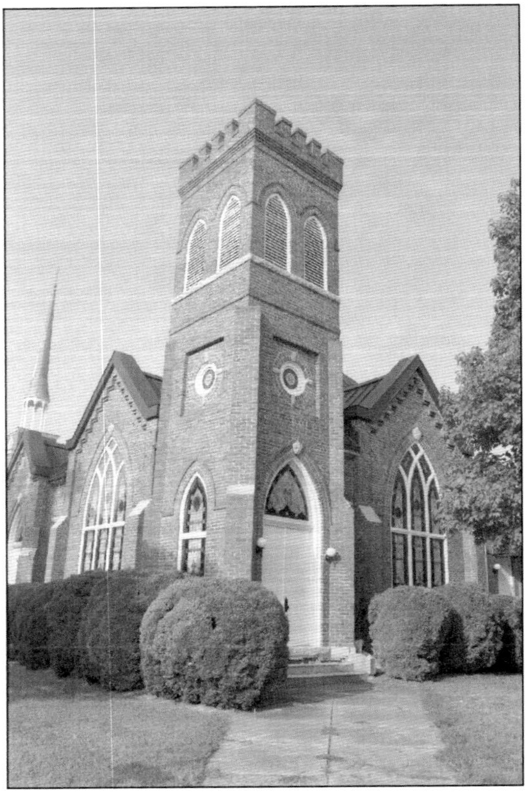

The Mebane Presbyterian Church on Fifth Street was founded in 1868 with 12 members and Rev. Calvin M. Morrow as the first pastor. This image, taken in 2011, shows the original building. (Courtesy of Kelly Gauldin.)

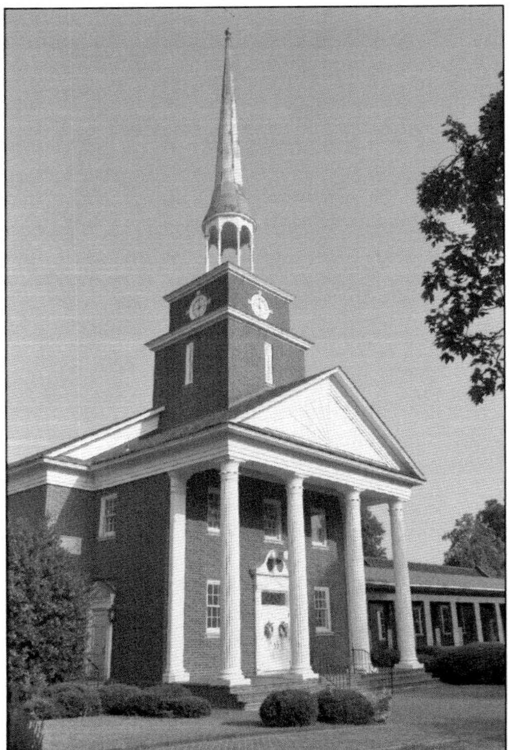

This image shows the Mebane Presbyterian Church built beside the old one in the late 1950s. (Courtesy of Kelly Gauldin.)

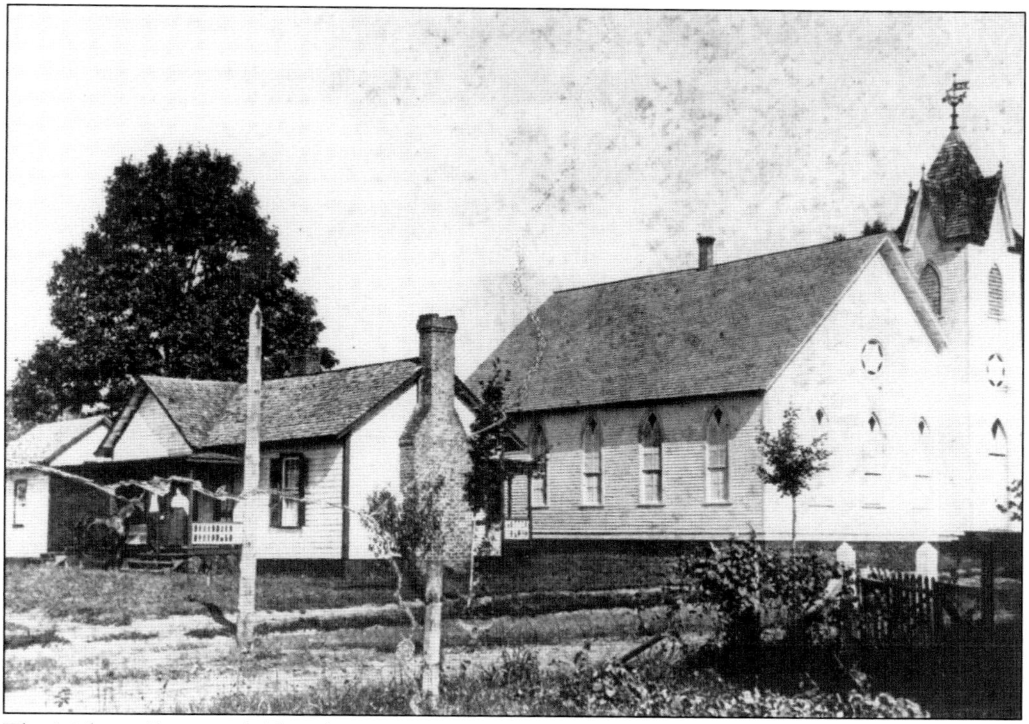

The Mebane Episcopal Church South was a wooden structure built on the corner of South Fourth Street and Holt Street in 1902. (MHM.)

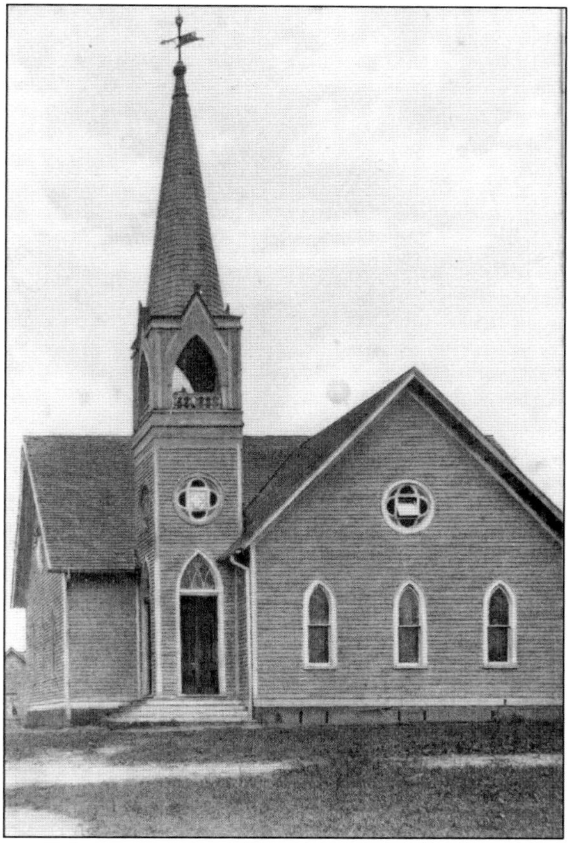

The Mebane Protestant Church was constructed on the corner of North Third Street and Ruffin Street in 1911. It was in the downtown area, close to three tobacco warehouses. The building was later remodeled and transformed into an apartment building. (MHM.)

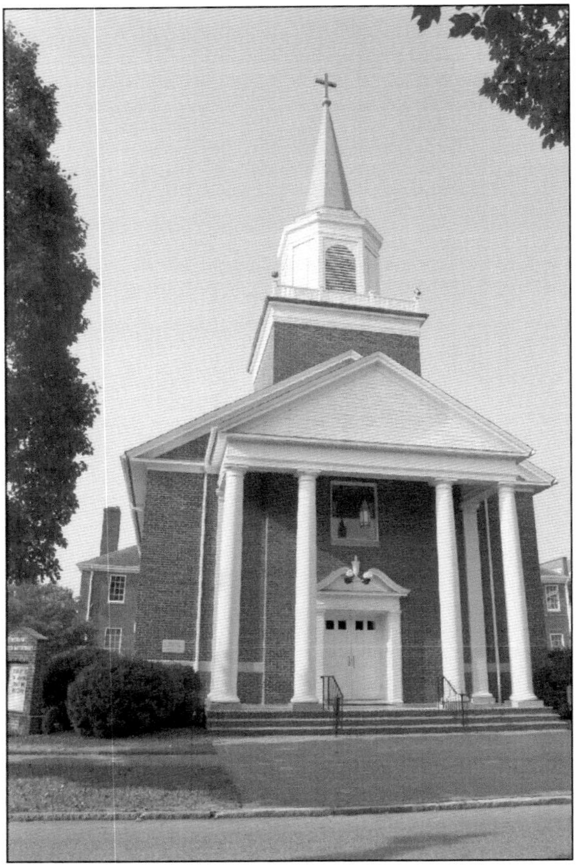

In 1947, the Mebane Episcopal Church South and the Mebane Protestant Church merged into the Mebane United Methodist Church, located on the corner of Holt Street and Fourth Street. This photograph shows the church in 2011. (Courtesy of Kelly Gauldin.)

Twenty-one local citizens founded the Mebane Baptist Church in 1901. The small congregation met in space generously provided by the Mebane Presbyterian Church until it was able to raise $700 to build a church of its own, a wooden structure on the corner of Third Street and Jackson Street, in 1907. After a fire destroyed the sanctuary in 1928, worshippers met in its educational building until the construction of the present brick church in 1948, two years after the church officially changed its name to the First Baptist Church. (Courtesy of Kelly Gauldin.)

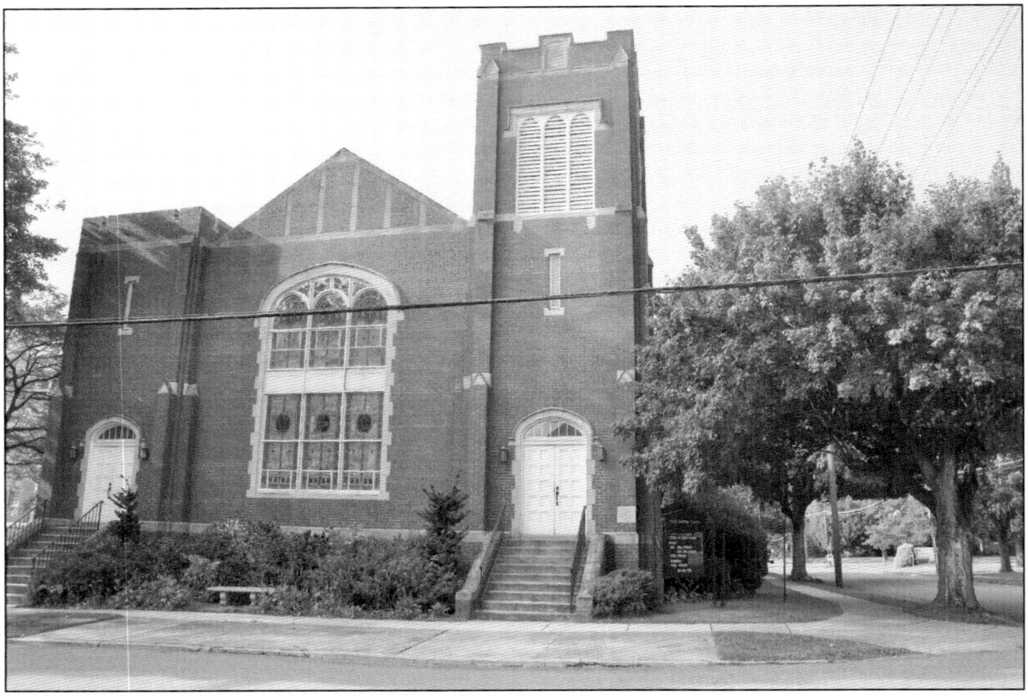

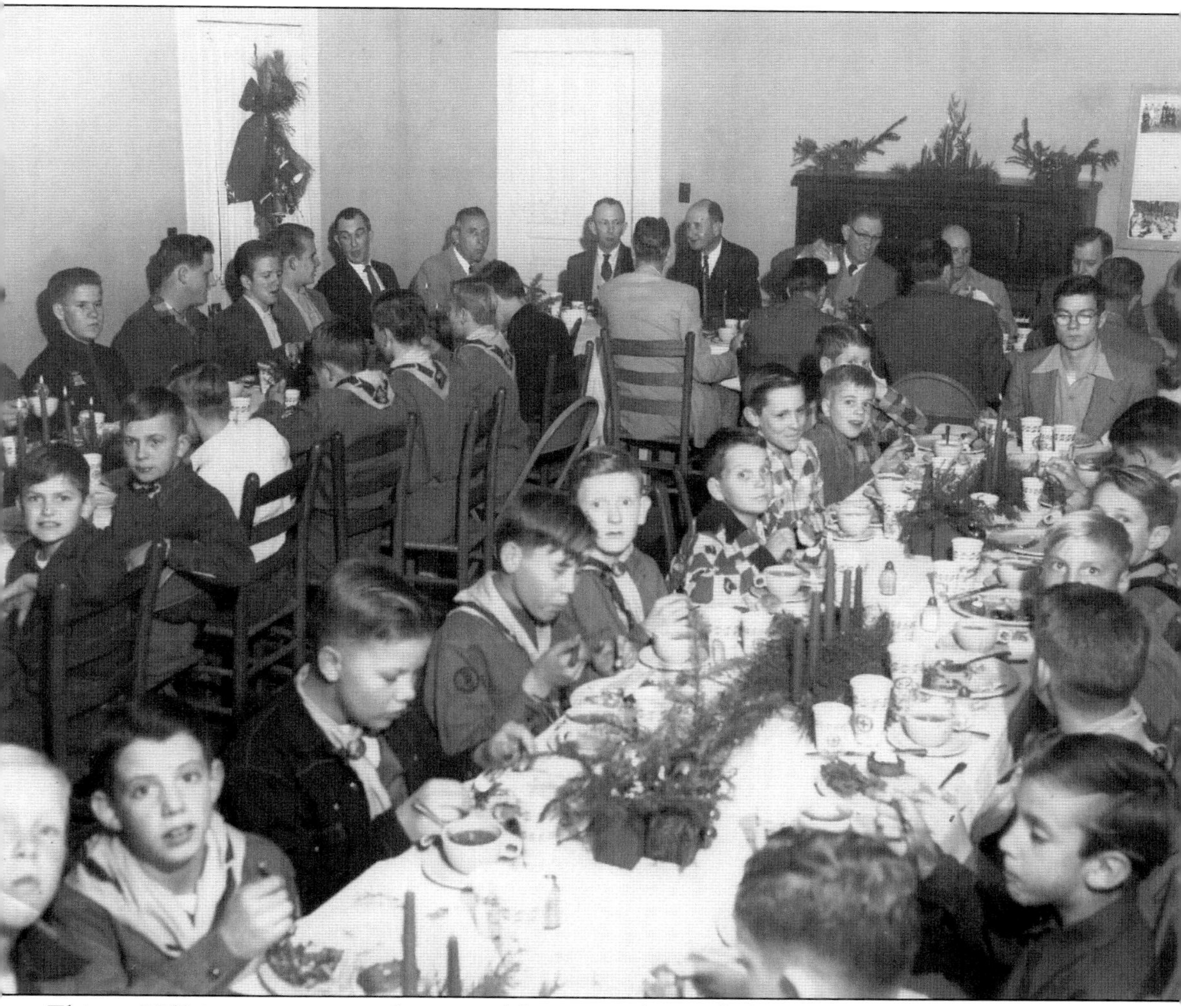

This c. 1950 image captures the annual honorary dinner held in a local church for the Boy Scouts. The Scouts were sponsored by the churches and local civic clubs. (Courtesy of Kenneth Wilkinson.)

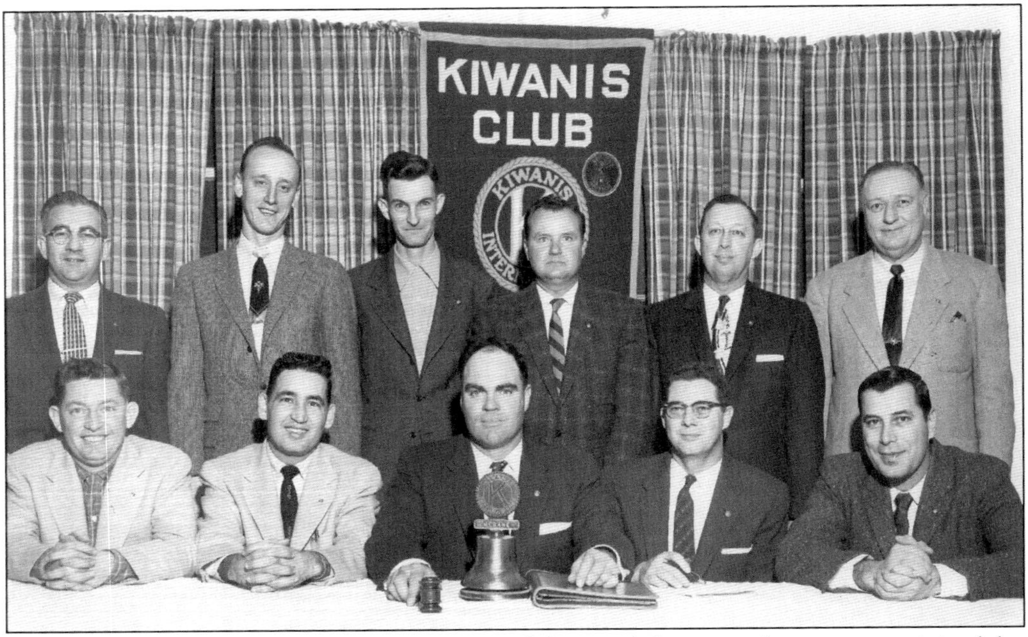

The Mebane Kiwanis Club has long been one of the town's largest and most active civic clubs. This photograph shows the president and other officers of the club in 1955. Pictured are, from left to right, (first row) Bill Sutton, Bill Warren, Charles Jay Harris (president), Jim Bell, and Ray Payne; (second row) Pete Bradley, unidentified, Tom Townsend, Jack Nash, Conrad Sutton, and Guy Rawls (a visitor from Raleigh). (Courtesy of Lennie Harris Stout.)

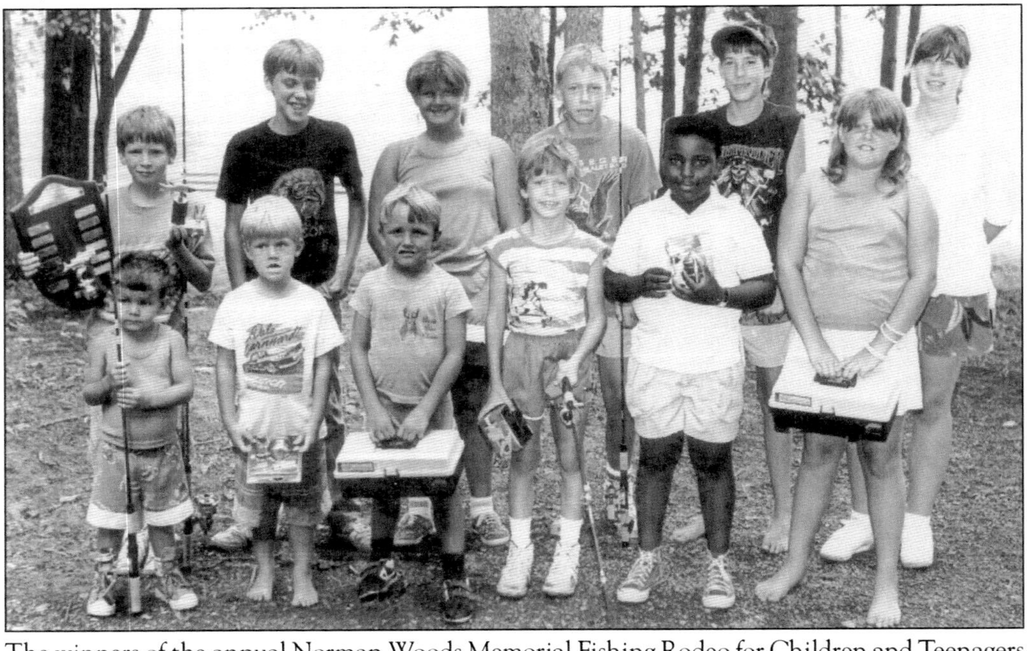

The winners of the annual Norman Woods Memorial Fishing Rodeo for Children and Teenagers are seen posing at Lake Michael in 1988. From left to right are (first row) Jeremy Shaw, Patrick Dodson, Kevin Carmichael, David Chambers, Tiant Fearrington, and Cheryl Dodson; (second row) Ben Florece, John McAdams, Emily Dodson, Scott Atkins, Scott Douglas, and Sandra Hughes. (MHM.)

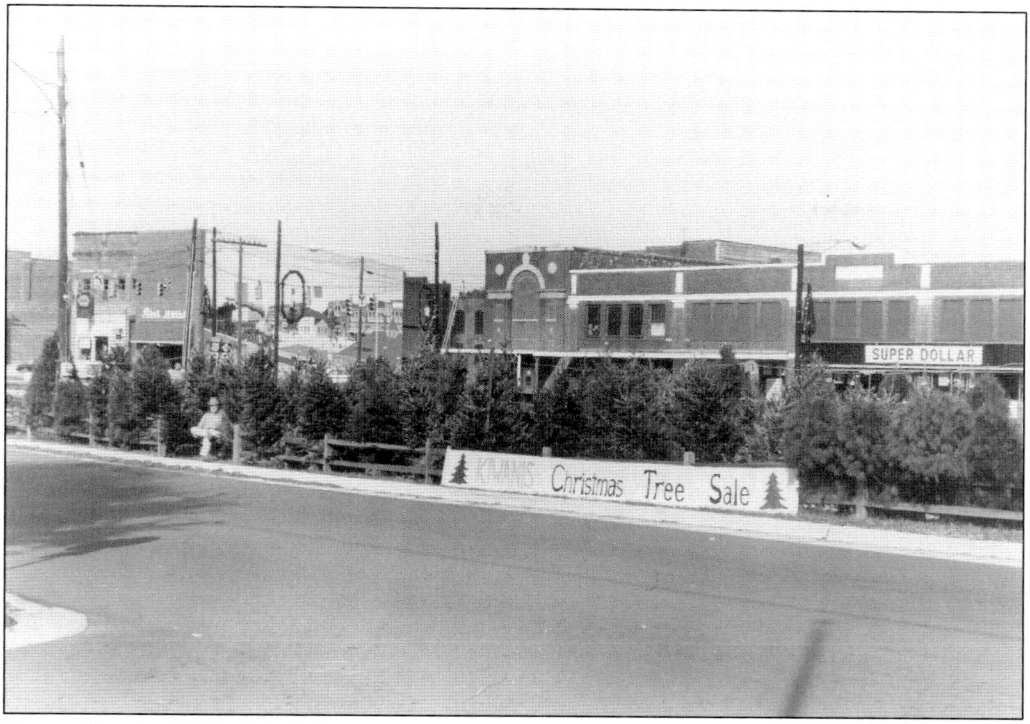

Pictured in the 1980s, Hugh Bass waits patiently for customers at the Kiwanis Club's annual Christmas tree fundraising sale. In the background is Center Street from Rice's Jewelry to Super Dollar. (MHM.)

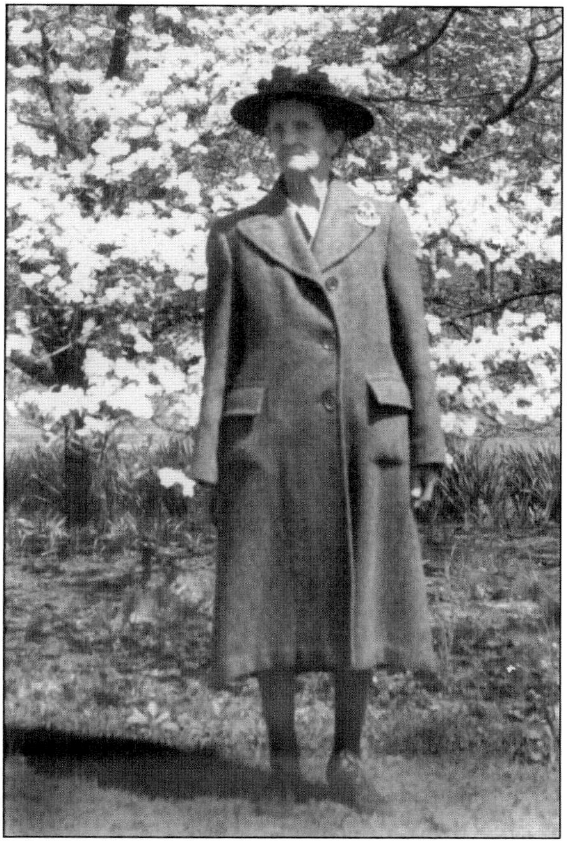

This undated photograph shows Emma Harris (1867–1965), affectionately called "Miss Emma" by everyone who knew her, standing in the garden of her home on the corner of Carr Street and Wilba Road. She moved into the two-story brick home around 1920 and lived there for most of the rest of her long life with her housekeeper and friend, Georgia Bradley. Miss Emma was a member of several organizations and was instrumental in establishing the first garden club in Mebane in 1928, when she was 60 years old. It was called the Mebane Garden Club, and she was the first president, a post she held for 28 years. The club was later renamed the Emma Harris Garden Club. (Courtesy of Lennie Harris Stout.)

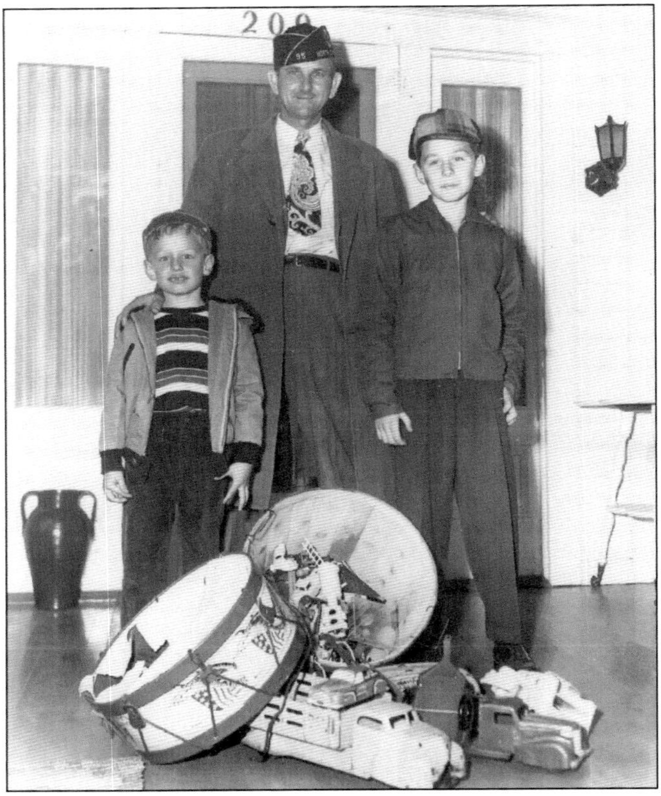

From left to right, Milton McDade, Tal Jobe, and W.Y. Jobe stand behind the toys they helped the American Legion collect for underprivileged children for Christmas around 1950. American Legion Post No. 95 was organized in Mebane in 1921 by veterans of World War I. Legionnaires first met at the Masonic Lodge but later constructed their own lodge on West Clay Street. (Courtesy of the Talmadge Jobe family.)

The American Legion was also the site of a Christmas party held for children in the 1950s. (Courtesy of the Talmadge Jobe family.)

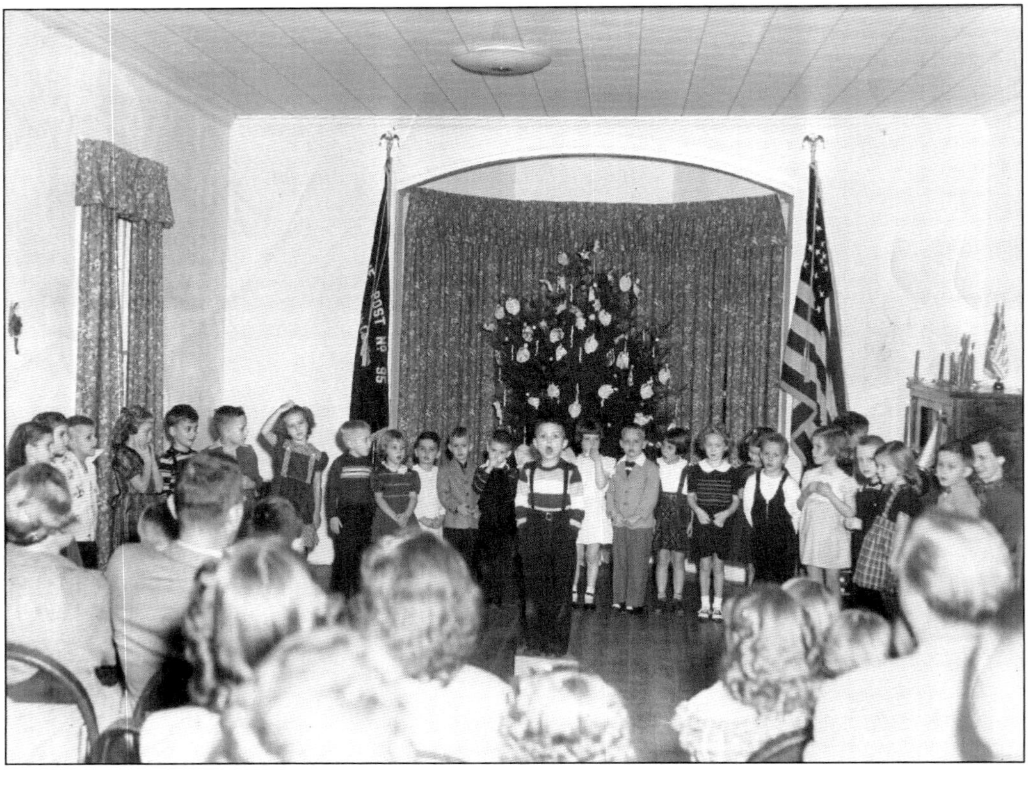

Seven

Recreation and Sports

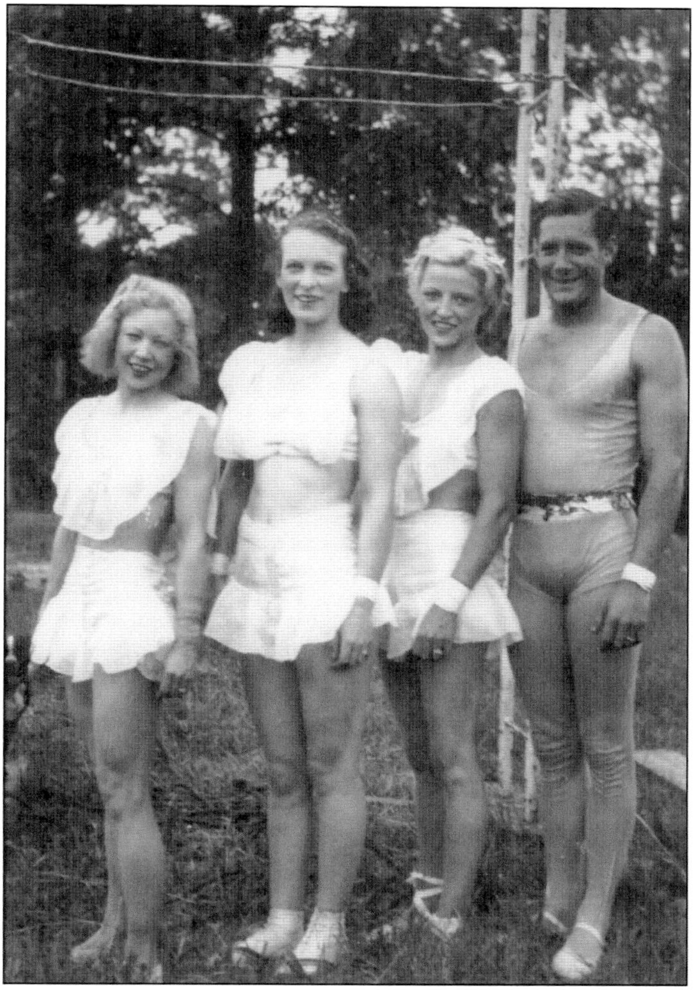

The Mebane Fair was an annual fall event for Mebane residents from 1919 until the late 1950s or early 1960s. The early fairs were staged in the downtown area but were later held on vacant lots on West Highway 70 on the outskirts of town. With the arrival of television and other amusements, the fair soon became a thing of the past. Lawrence and Peaches and the Queens, the performing group pictured here in 1936, was a popular act for several years. (MHM.)

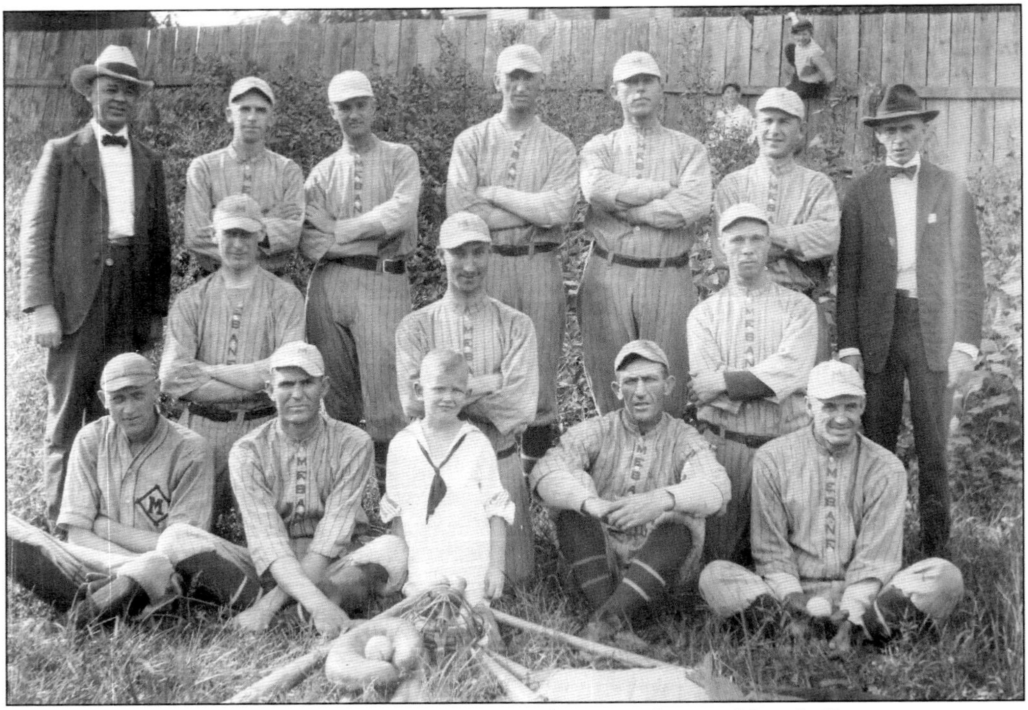

In the first half of the 20th century, amateur and semiprofessional baseball teams were very popular all across the nation. This 1915 photograph shows a Mebane team that was a member of the Bi-State League. From left to right are (first row) Guy Britton, Dr. Thompson, Melvin Thompson, Lucian Barnett, and Bob Howard; (second row) Herbert Craig, Hugh Smith, and Lee Hooks; (third row) Crockett Fitch, Clyde Allred, Shields Cheek, C.L. Malone, Dock High, Shorty Gaston, and unidentified. The photograph may have been taken in the school ballpark that is today Walker Field. (Courtesy of Nancy Wells.)

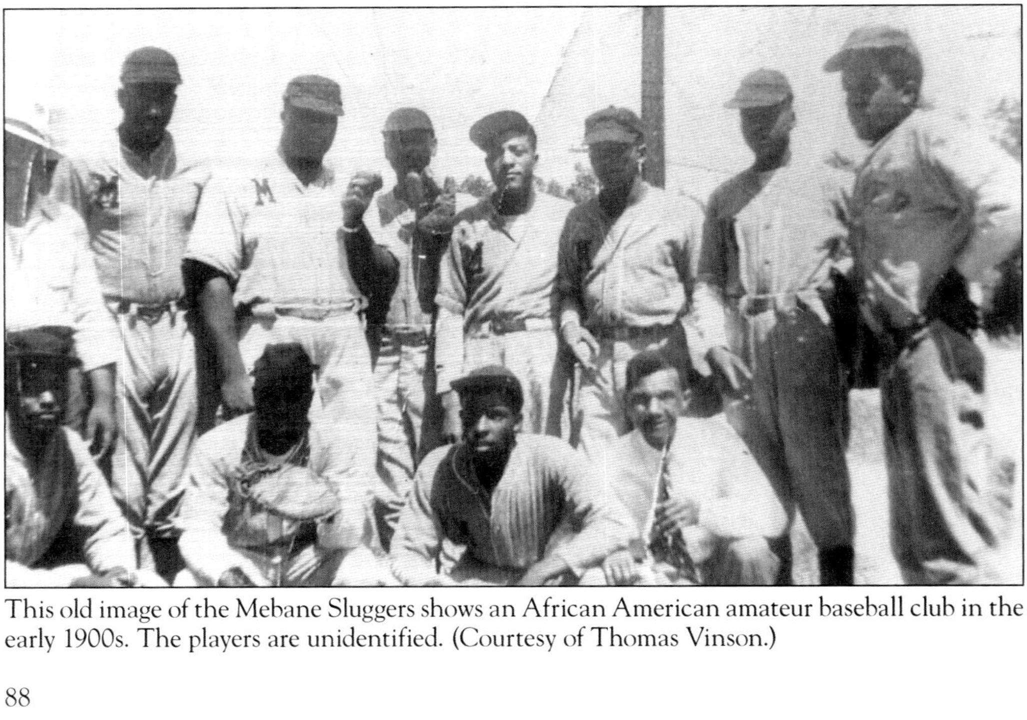

This old image of the Mebane Sluggers shows an African American amateur baseball club in the early 1900s. The players are unidentified. (Courtesy of Thomas Vinson.)

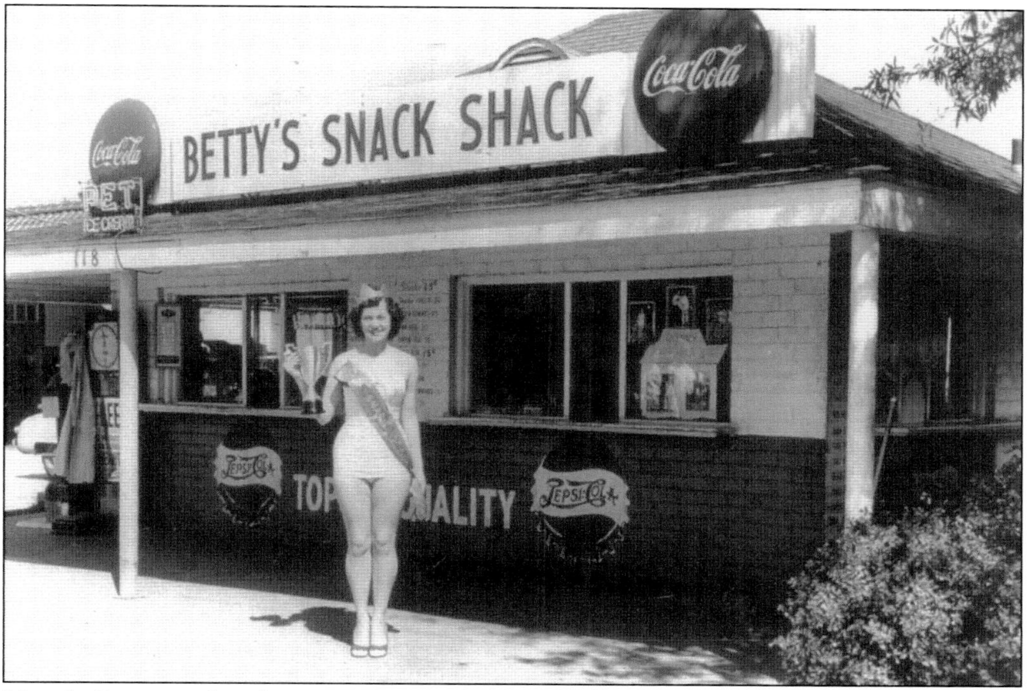

Mary Jo Foxx posed as the 1949 Miss Betty's Snack Shack in front of the town's most popular walk-up restaurant. (MHM.)

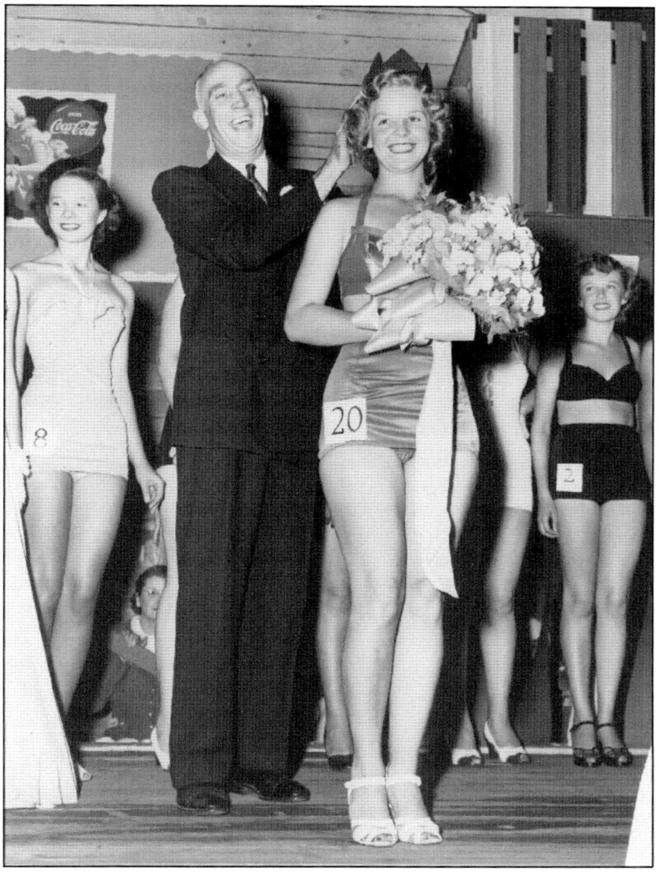

Mary Ann Wilson is crowned Miss Tobacco Festival Queen 1950. She later married George Sykes, who operated Sykes Electric Company on Clay Street and served for many years as a volunteer fireman. (Courtesy of Ann Sykes.)

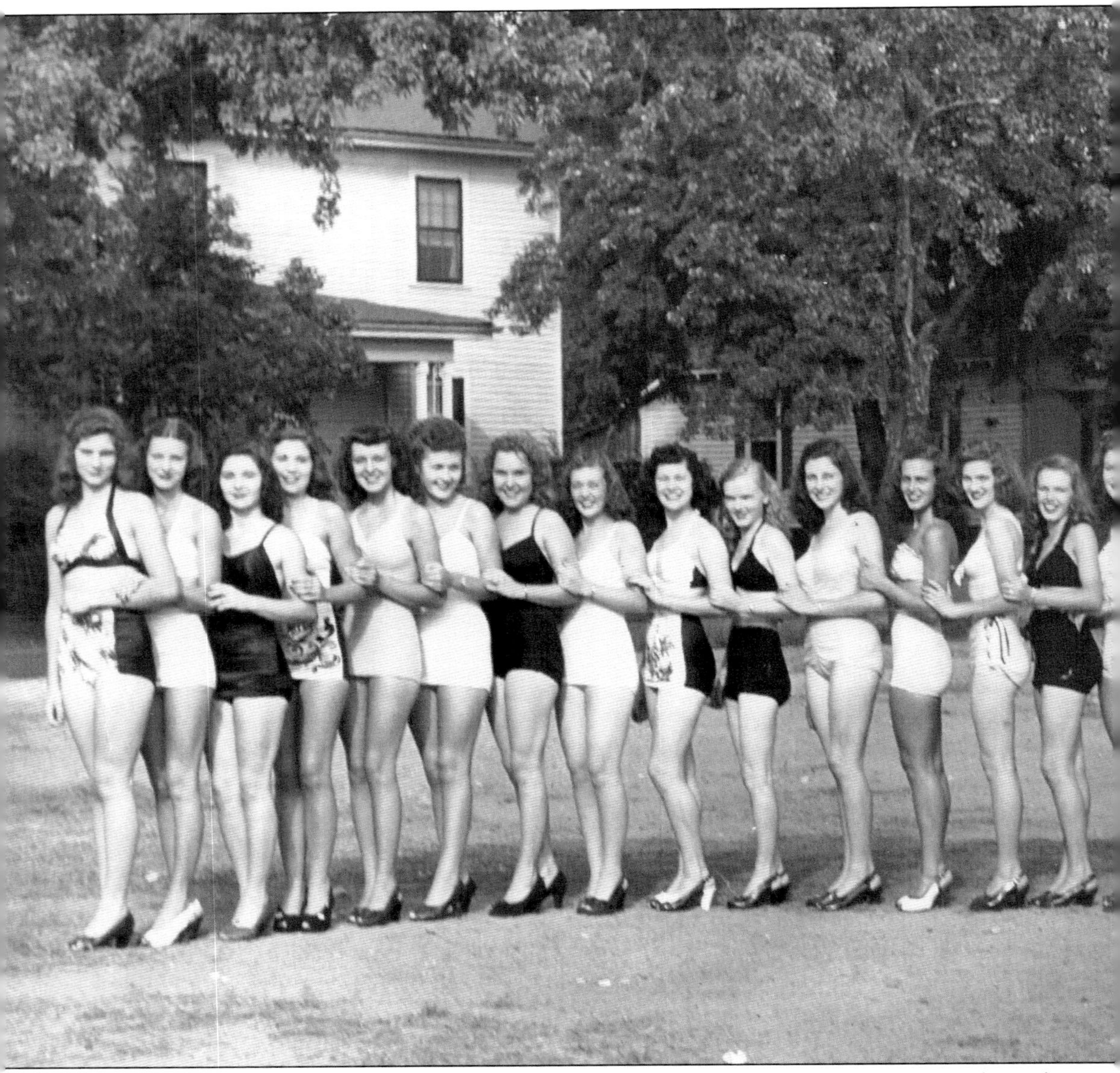

The contestants for the 1947 Miss Tobacco Festival Queen pose for a group photograph on the school playground across from the teacherage. The contestants were chosen to represent the town's civic clubs and businesses, which also sponsored the pageant. On the day of the parade, the contestants took their seats in vehicles and were joined by bands and majorettes to travel down

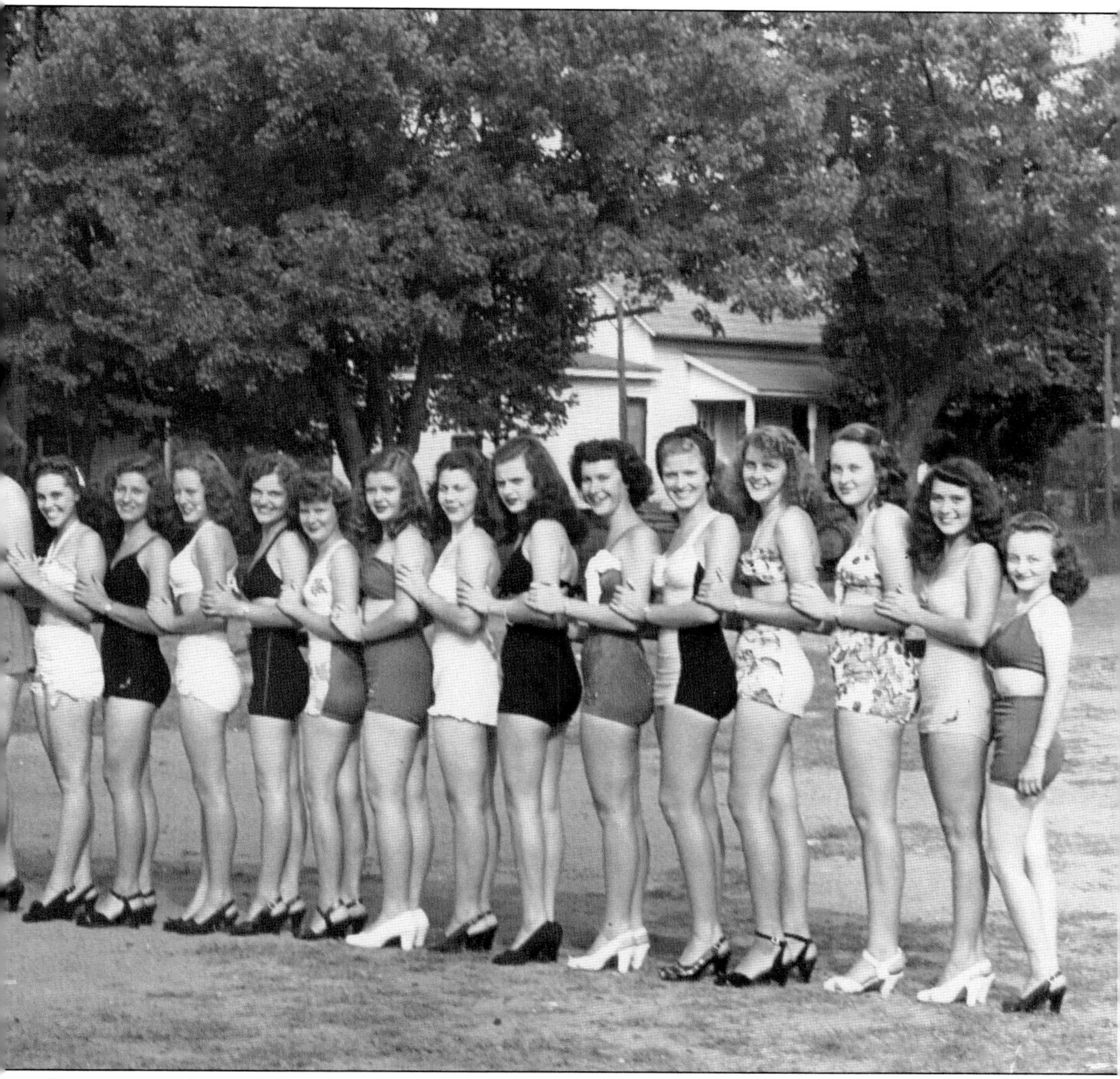

Center and Clay Streets as large crowds looked on. At the end of the parade, the contestants mounted a large stage set up on Third Street between Center and Clay Streets for the selection and crowning of the new queen. A dance that was held in the streets and warehouses followed the ceremony and often went late into the night. (Courtesy of Betty Tripp.)

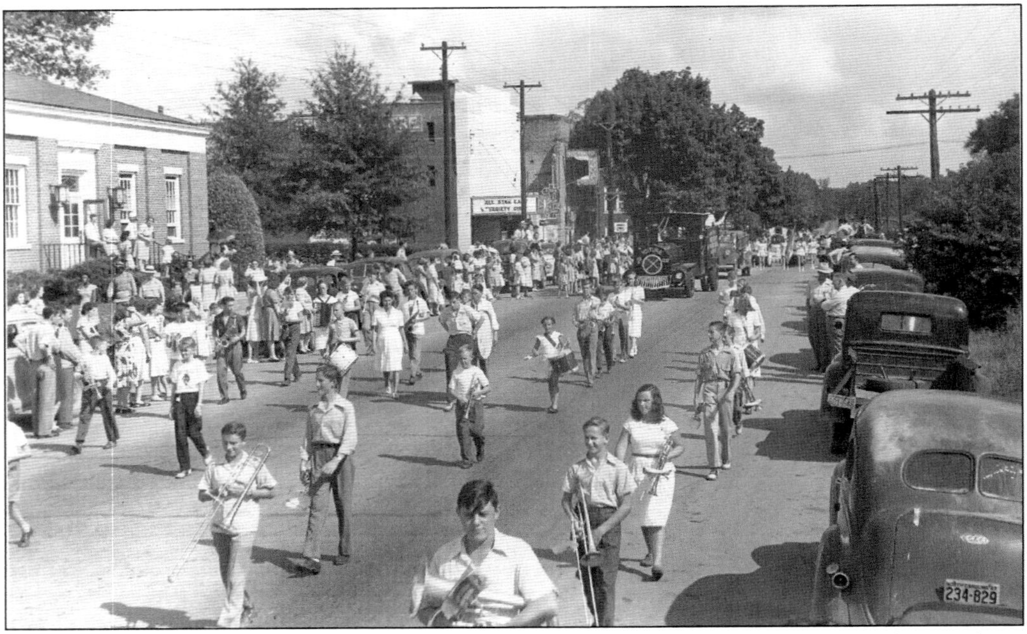

The annual Tobacco Festival Parade was always a popular event. This 1947 parade is making its way down Center Street by the Mebane Theater, the vacant lot beside the theater, the post office, and on past Betty's Snack Shack. (MHM.)

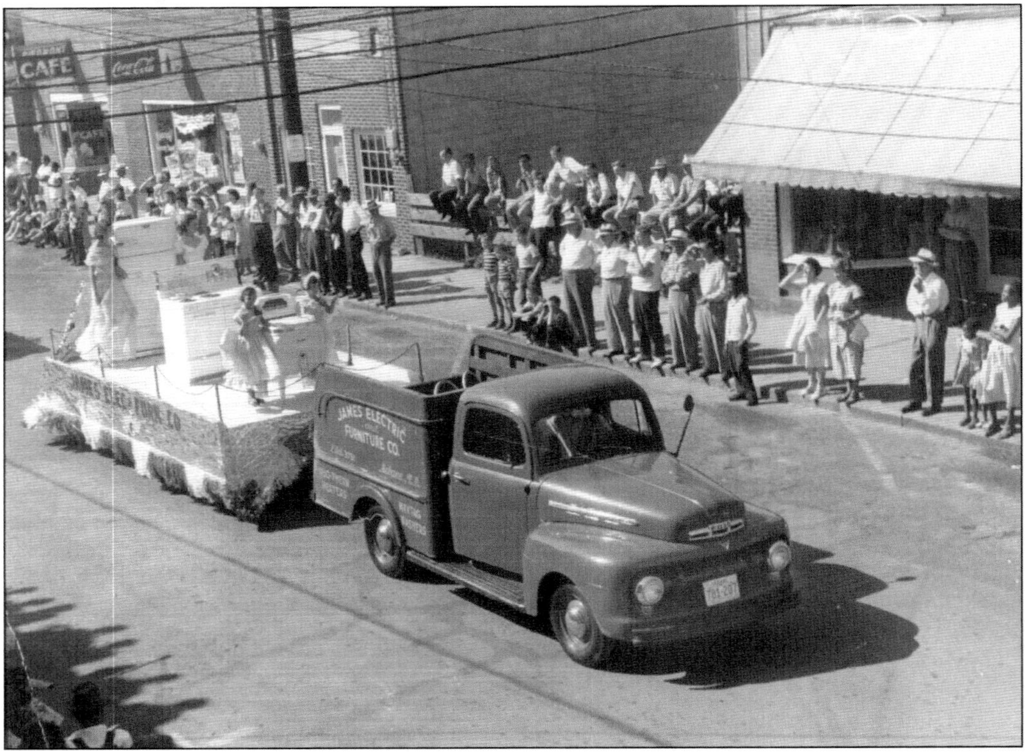

In a 1947 parade, these contestants are sitting on floats advertising the appliances of their business sponsors as they pass by the Piedmont Café, Rascoe's Grocery, and other businesses on Clay Street. (MHM.)

Additional entertainment came to town during the Tobacco Festival in the form of popular country music performers like "Little" Jimmy Dickens and other members of the Grand Ole Opry Touring Company, who performed on a stage at one of the local warehouses before huge crowds. This photograph of Dickens appeared in an advertisement for the Tobacco Festival in the late 1940s. (MHM.)

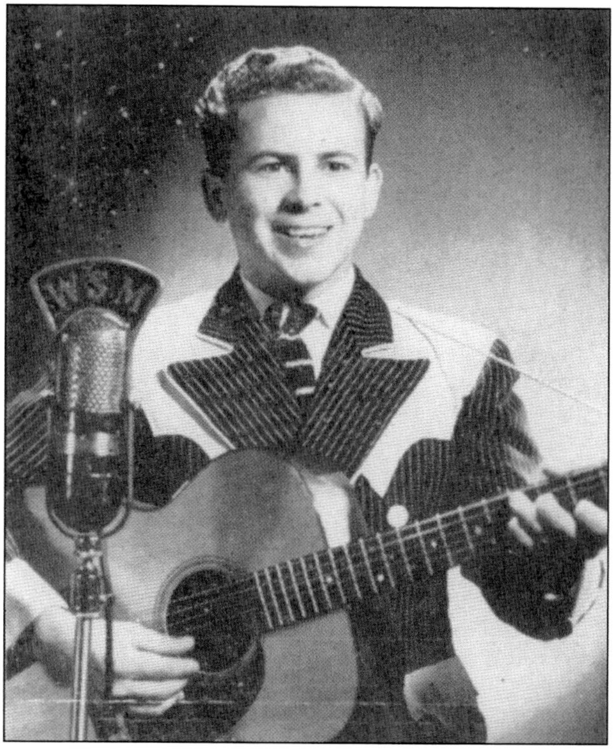

One of the most popular hangouts for young people was the Dollar Soda Shop, a combination bus station, restaurant, and poolroom adjoining the movie theater. It was operated by Harry and Annie Dollar from 1941 to 1955. The poolroom in the back of Dollar Soda Shop was popular with local men. The "No Gambling" and "No Cursing" signs were undoubtedly frequently ignored. (MHM.)

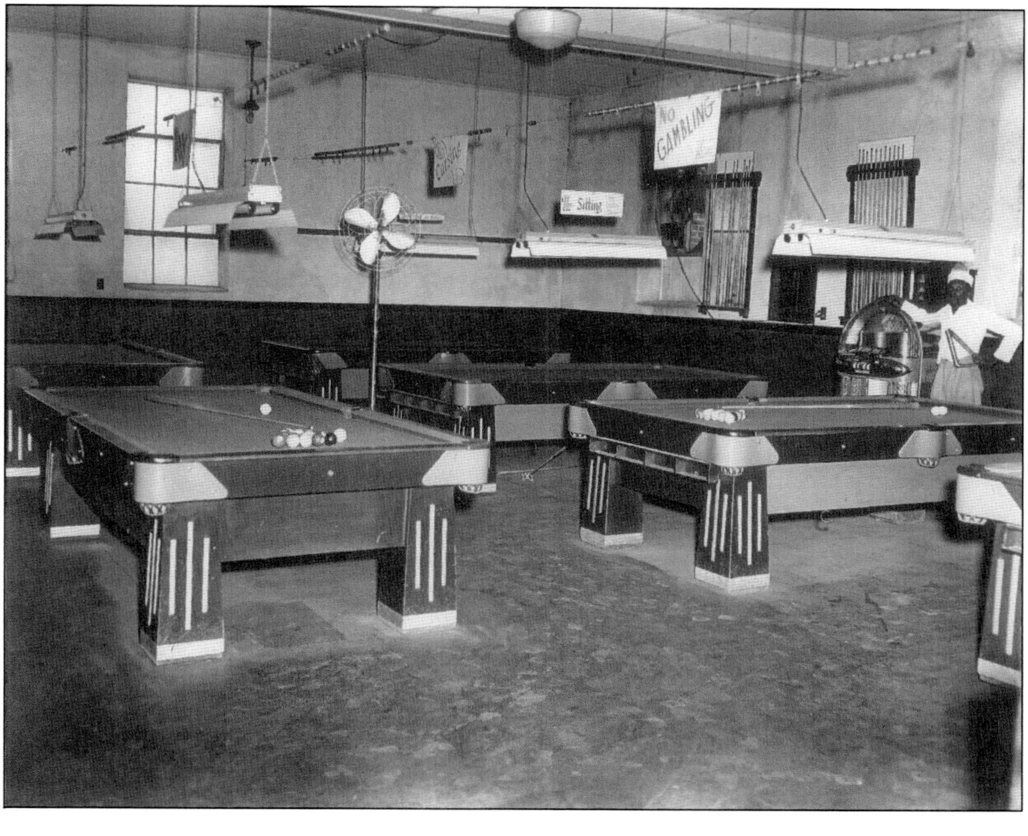

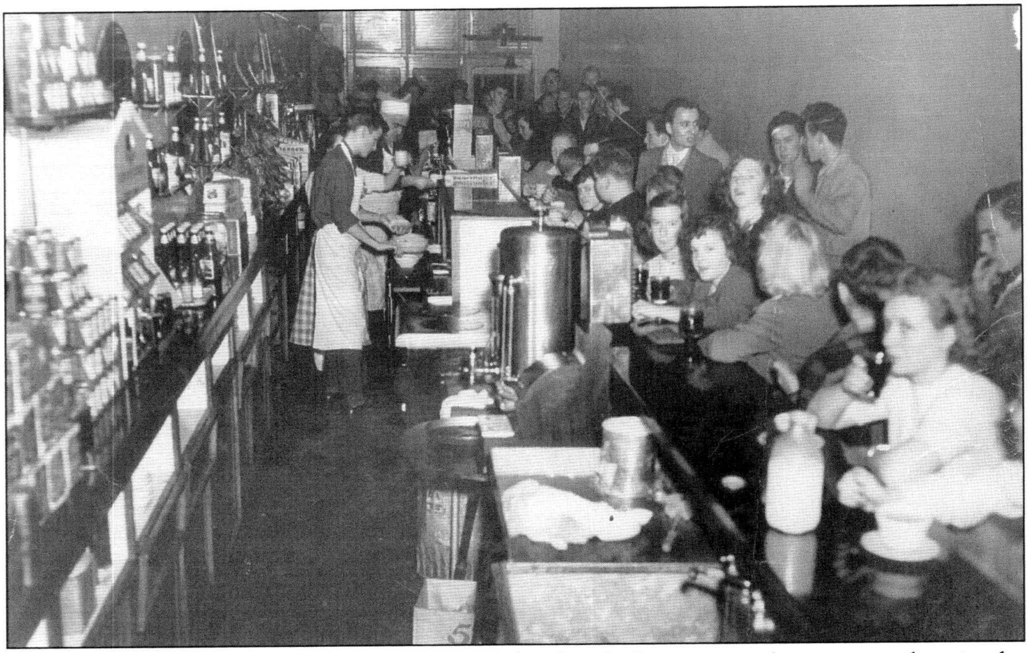

The Dollar Soda Shop was always busy after school and after a movie let out next door in the Mebane Theater. (MHM.)

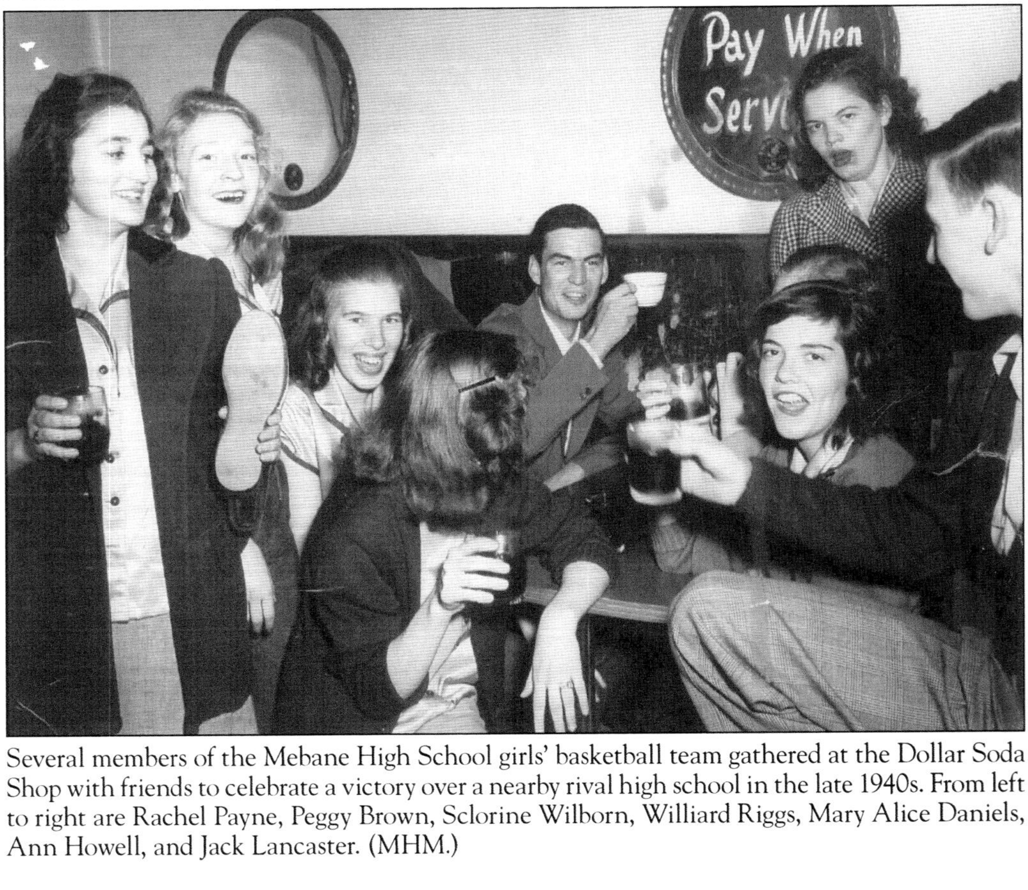

Several members of the Mebane High School girls' basketball team gathered at the Dollar Soda Shop with friends to celebrate a victory over a nearby rival high school in the late 1940s. From left to right are Rachel Payne, Peggy Brown, Sclorine Wilborn, Williard Riggs, Mary Alice Daniels, Ann Howell, and Jack Lancaster. (MHM.)

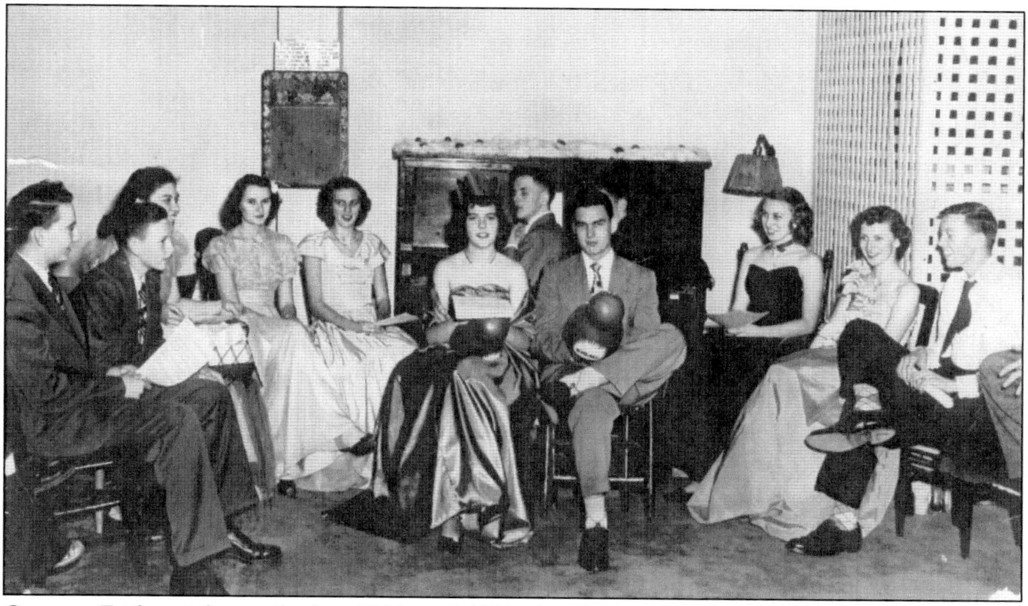

On most Friday nights in the late 1940s and 1950s, local teenagers climbed the steps to the a large empty storage room over Rose's Dime Store to enjoy dancing, ping-pong, and other activities at the Teenage Club, sponsored by the Junior Woman's Club. In the photograph above, taken at a 1949 Valentine's Dance, Leo Wilkinson sits at the piano surrounded by, from left to right, Henry Dixon, Edwin Yoder Jr., Iris Abernathy, Sarah Cook, Betty Jean McLeod, Ann Howell, Williard Riggs, Martha Jeffries, Mary Ann Lancaster, and Benny Sutton. (MHM.)

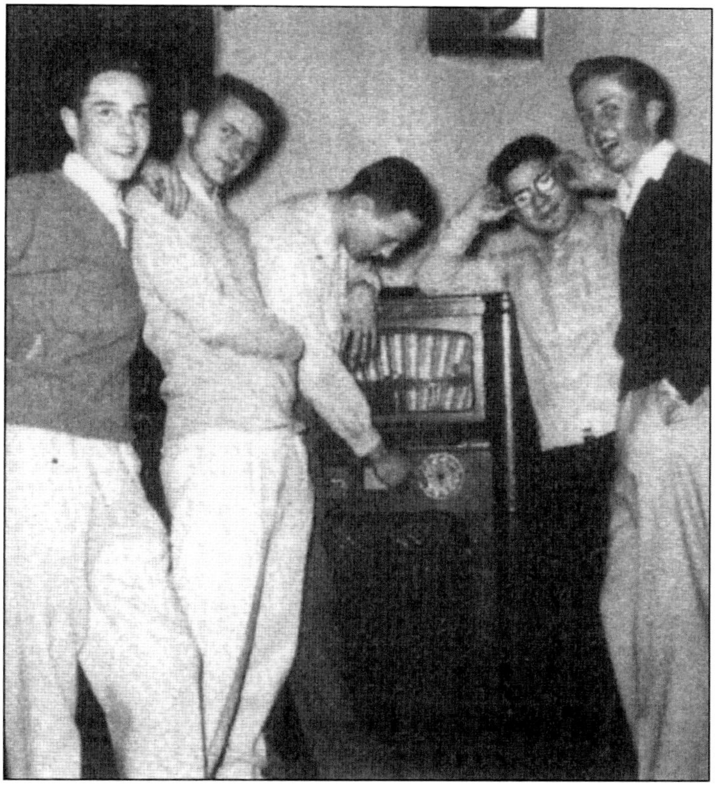

Teenagers often gathered around the club's Wurlitzer jukebox as it played the latest rock 'n' roll songs for the dancers on the floor. From left to right are Edwin Robinson, Bobby Wynn, Marshall Southern, Fred Carter, and Billy Lineberry. (MHM.)

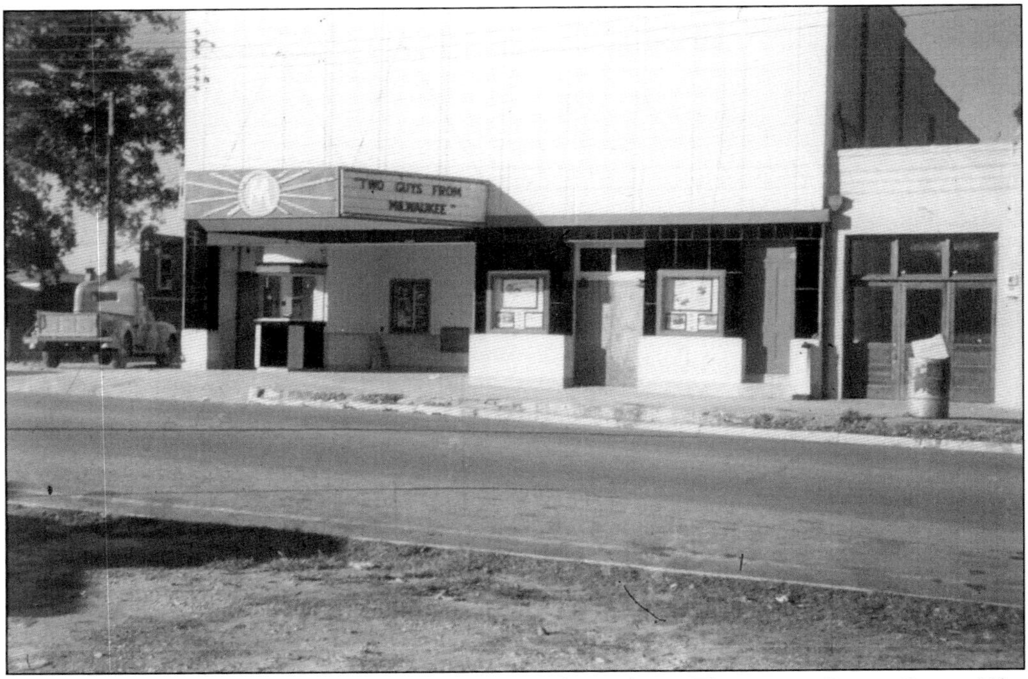

Two Guys From Milwaukee was playing in 1947 at the Mebane Theater on Center Street. The theater was a popular downtown attraction for over half of the 20th century. Lightning struck and burned the theater during same 1936 tornado that destroyed Lebanon Church. It was soon rebuilt, burned again in 1944, and was rebuilt in 1945. After World War II, television came along and cut into its profits and eventually caused it to close in the late 1960s. Today, the old remodeled theater is the site of Welcome Finance Company. (MHM.)

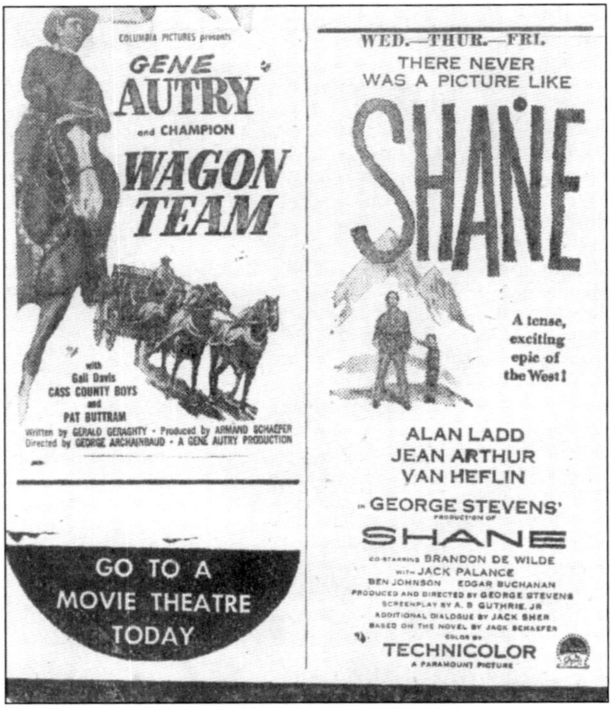

This 1953 theater advertisement in the *Mebane Enterprise* shows the popularity of Westerns and musicals during that decade. The theater was open in the afternoons and evenings from Monday through Saturday and was closed on Sundays for most of its existence. (MHM.)

On April 2, 1936, a tornado and fire destroyed the Mebane Theater in spite of the prompt response of the Mebane Fire Department. (MHM.)

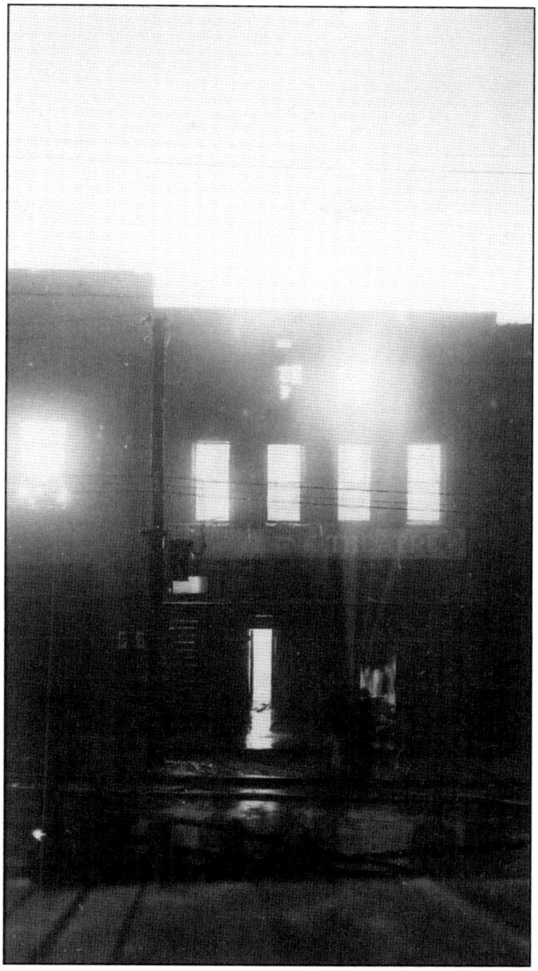

The Mebane Motor Company, located next door to the theater, burned along with it in 1936. It was also a total loss. (MHM.)

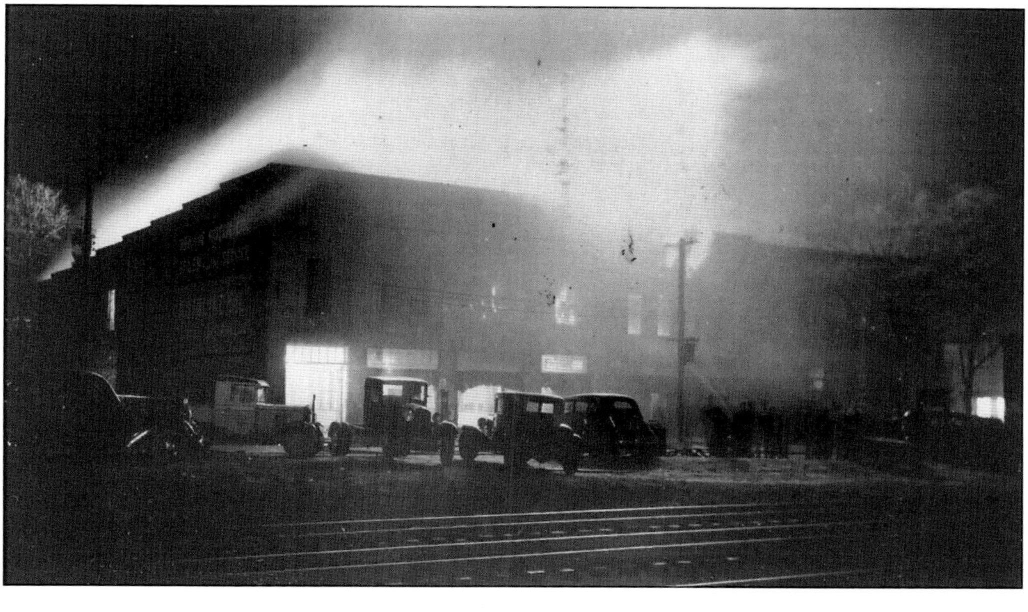

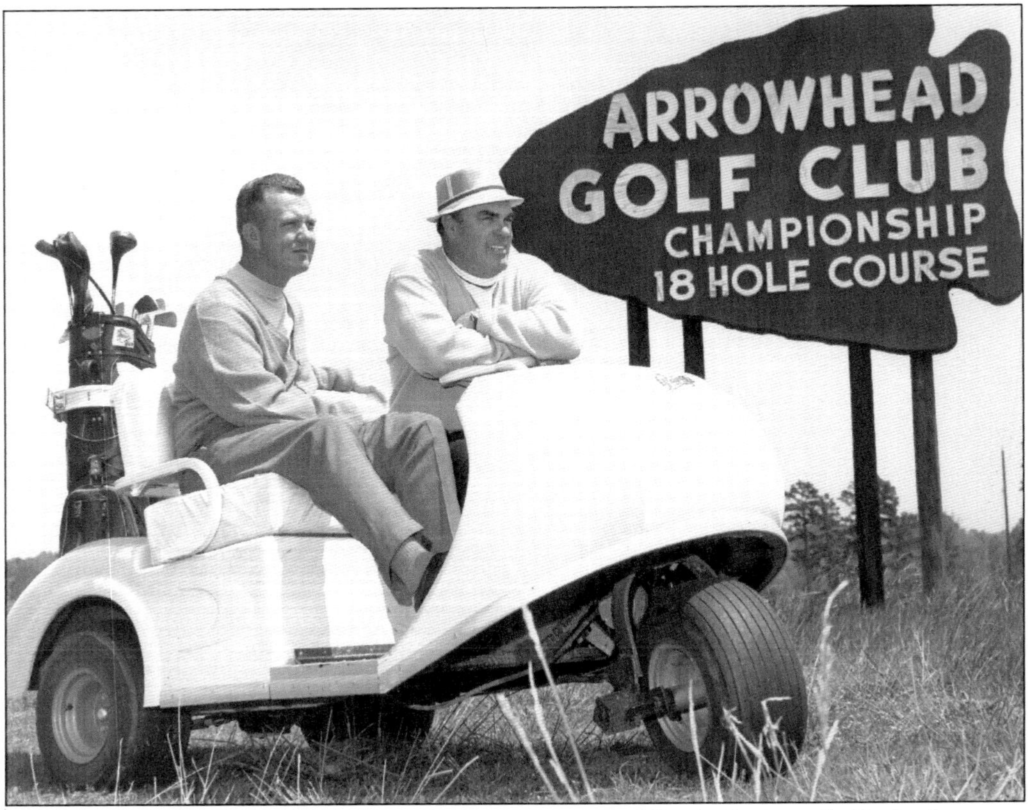

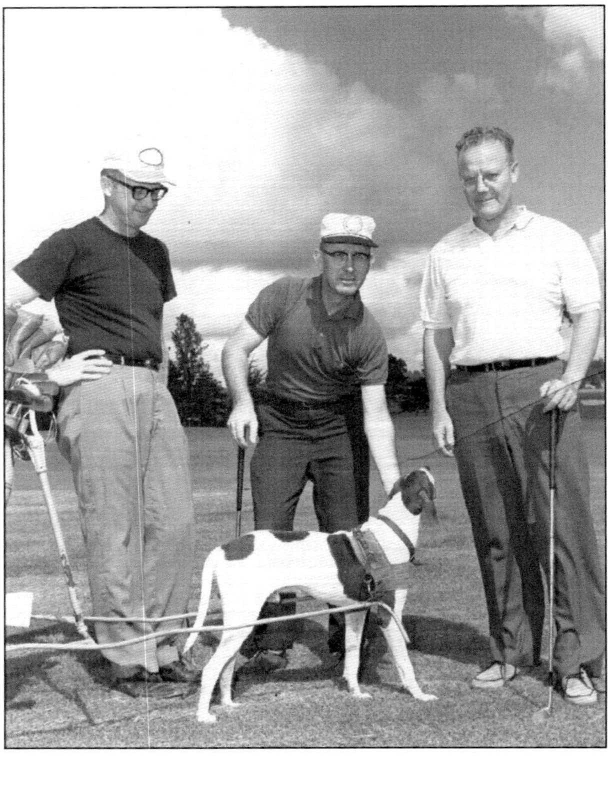

Woody Durham (left), the future "Voice of the Tarheels," and Shake Harris enjoy a round of golf on the new Arrowhead Golf Course on Mebane Oaks Road in 1964. Harris had earlier owned the Dogwood Golf Course on Fifth Street Extension. (Courtesy of Lennie Harris Stout.)

White Furniture Company president Steve White (right) and two friends were frequent golfers at the course. White trained the dog to pull his golf bag on the course. (Courtesy of Lennie Harris Stout.)

Eight

School Days

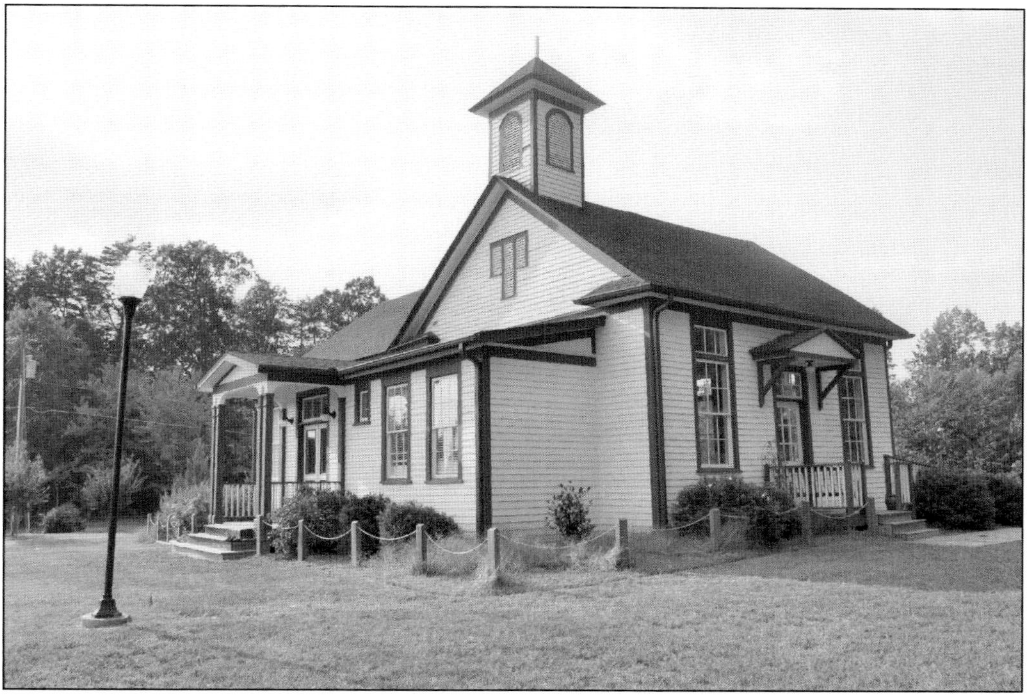

Beginning as a one-room log school near Cooks Mill in 1901, Woodlawn School later moved to its current location on Mebane Rogers Road. The elementary grades were taught there until the school closed in 1934; the students were then moved to other elementary schools in the county. Later remodeled and updated, it became a popular site for meetings, class reunions, weddings, plays, and other activities. (Courtesy of Kelly Gauldin.)

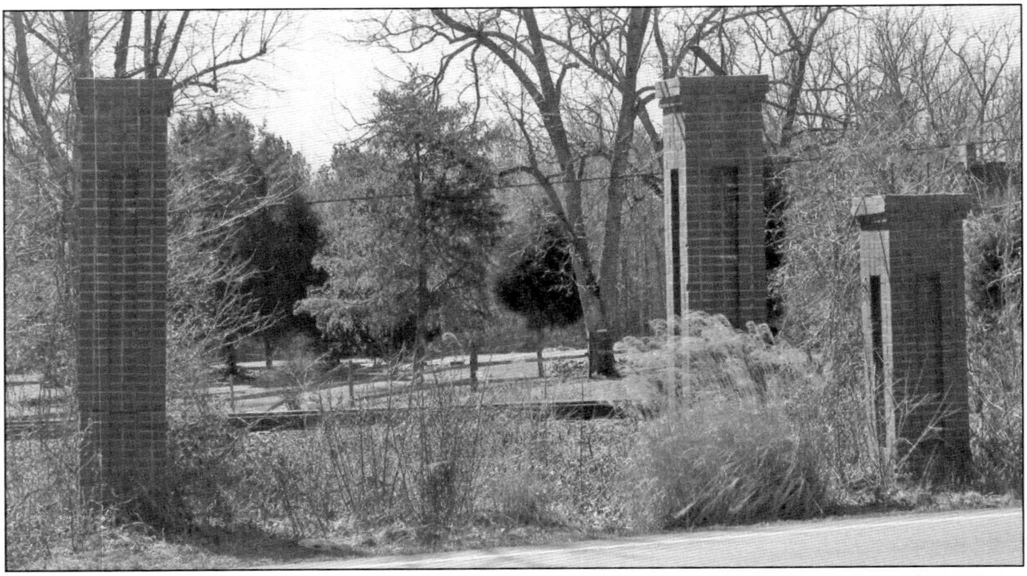

These old brick columns along the railroad track mark the former entrance to the old Bingham School on East Highway 70 near King Tire. The school was originally established as a private academy in Wilmington, North Carolina, by William Bingham in 1793, but over the next century, it moved to several other cities in the state, including four different sites in Alamance County, the only county in the state with four historical markers for the same historic site. In Mebane, it operated as a boys' military academy and attracted students from 33 states and several foreign countries before moving to Asheville in 1891. (Courtesy of Fred and Mary Archer.)

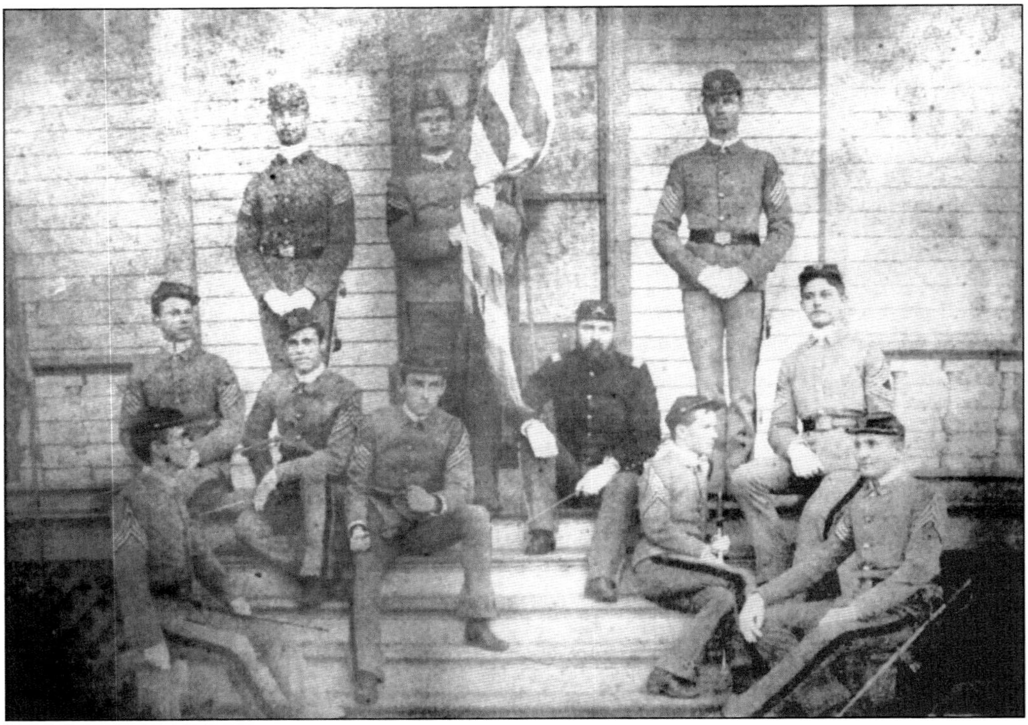

This undated photograph shows several unidentified Bingham School students during the Civil War era. (Courtesy of Giles Mebane.)

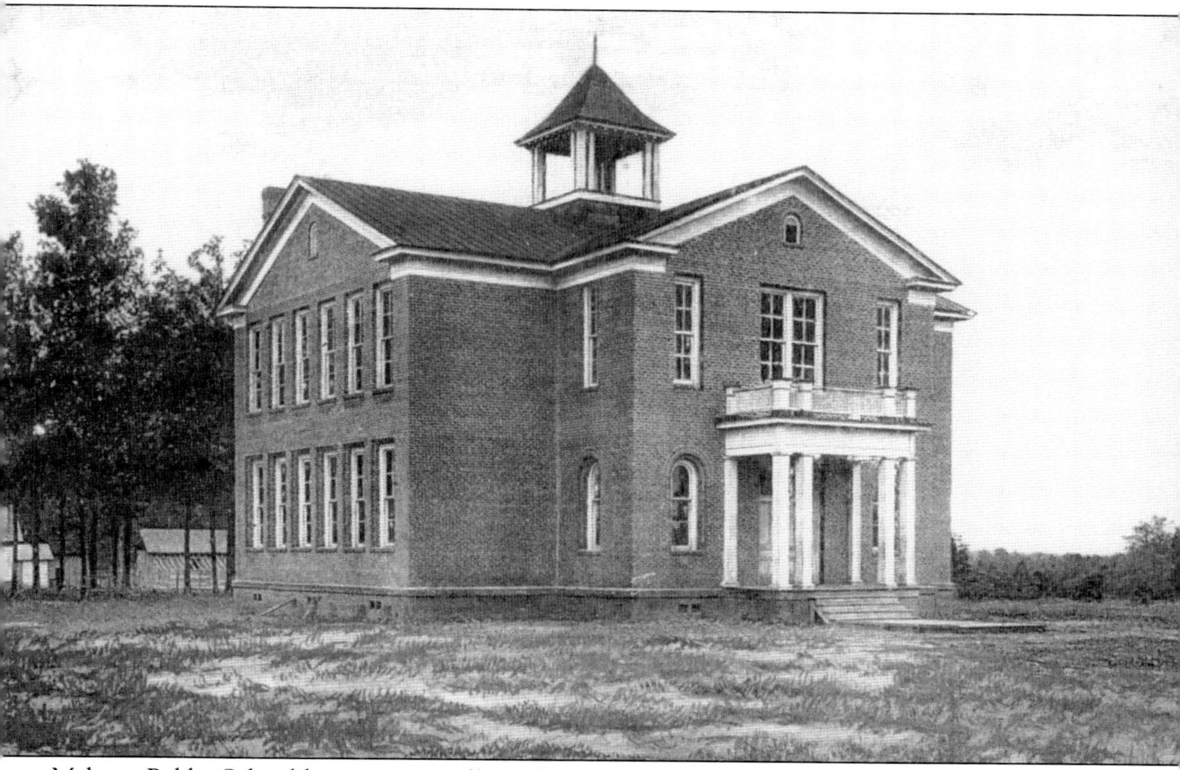

Mebane Public School began as a small wooden structure in 1903 but was replaced by a brick building around 1910 and renovated and expanded several times over the years. It was a small, intimate school in a small, intimate town. During this era of school segregation, the school was the center of the white community and received strong support from white citizens. As Mebane's population increased, E.M. Yoder Elementary School was built across town in 1952 and South Mebane Elementary School was constructed in 1957. (MHM.)

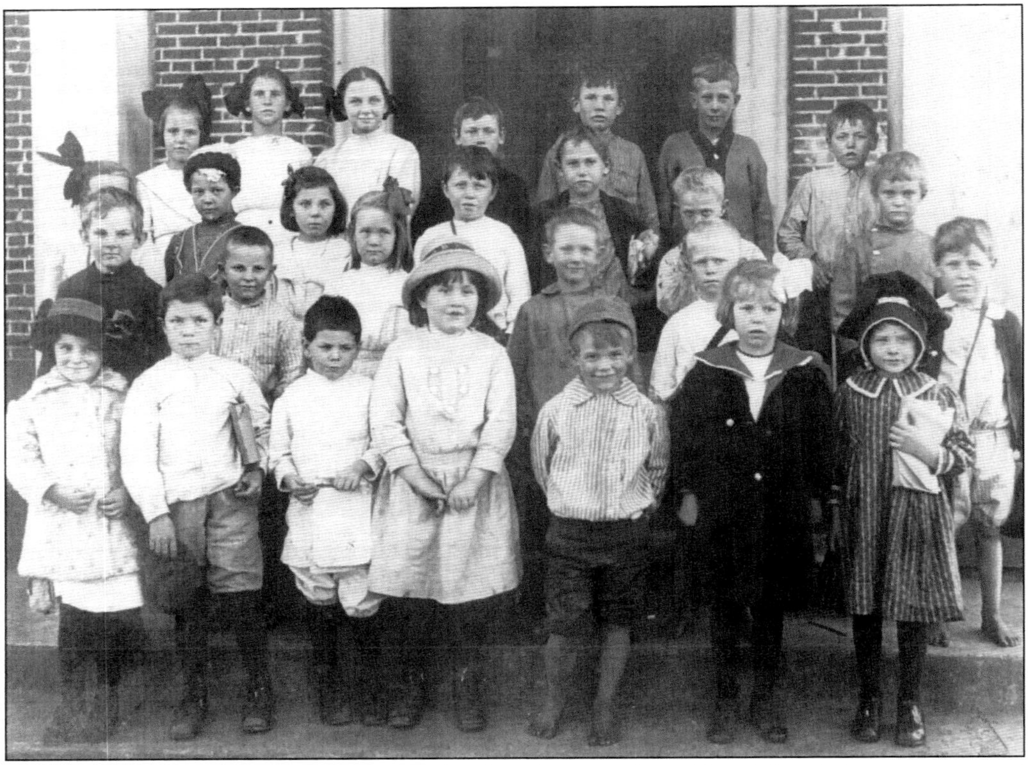

The students at Mebane School posed for this photograph in 1910. The clothing on most of these young people reveals that they came from low-income families working in factories and farming. (MHM.)

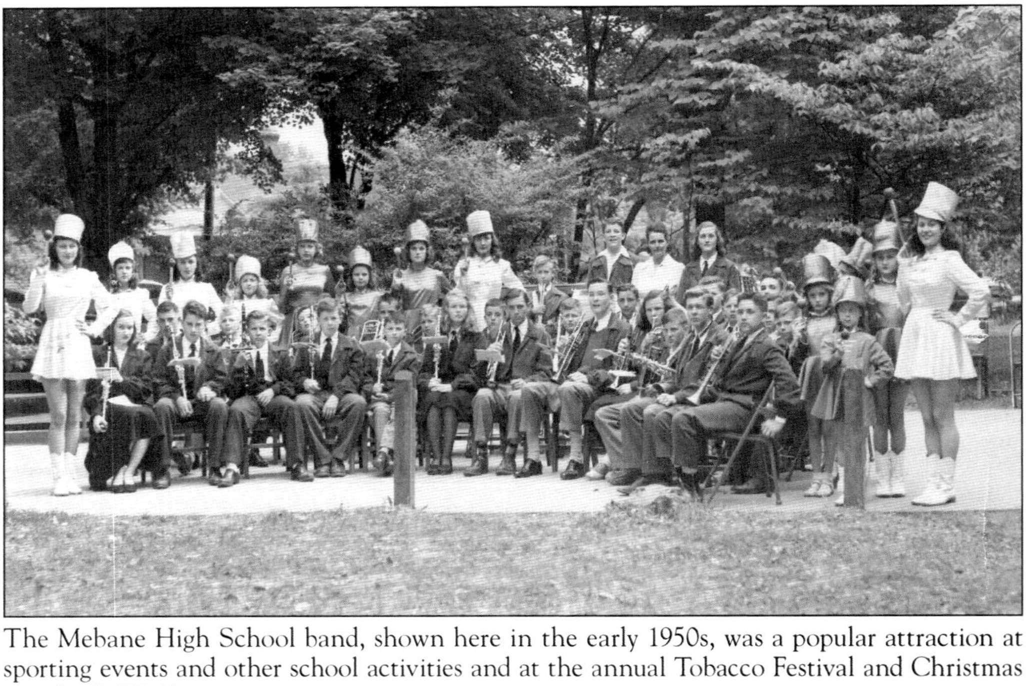

The Mebane High School band, shown here in the early 1950s, was a popular attraction at sporting events and other school activities and at the annual Tobacco Festival and Christmas parade. (MHM.)

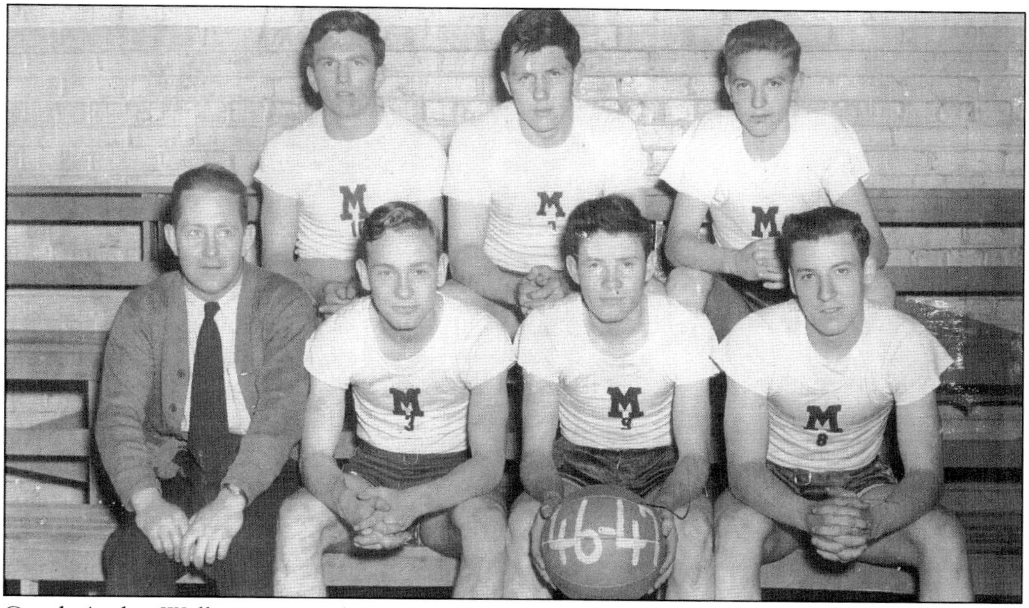

Coach Archie Walker poses with the 1946–1947 high scool boys' basketball team. Pictured from left to right are (first row) Archie Walker, Baxter Bowen, Walter Cook, and Harry Dollar Jr.; (second row) Nick Bartis, Kenneth Lynch, and Bernice Staley. (MHM.)

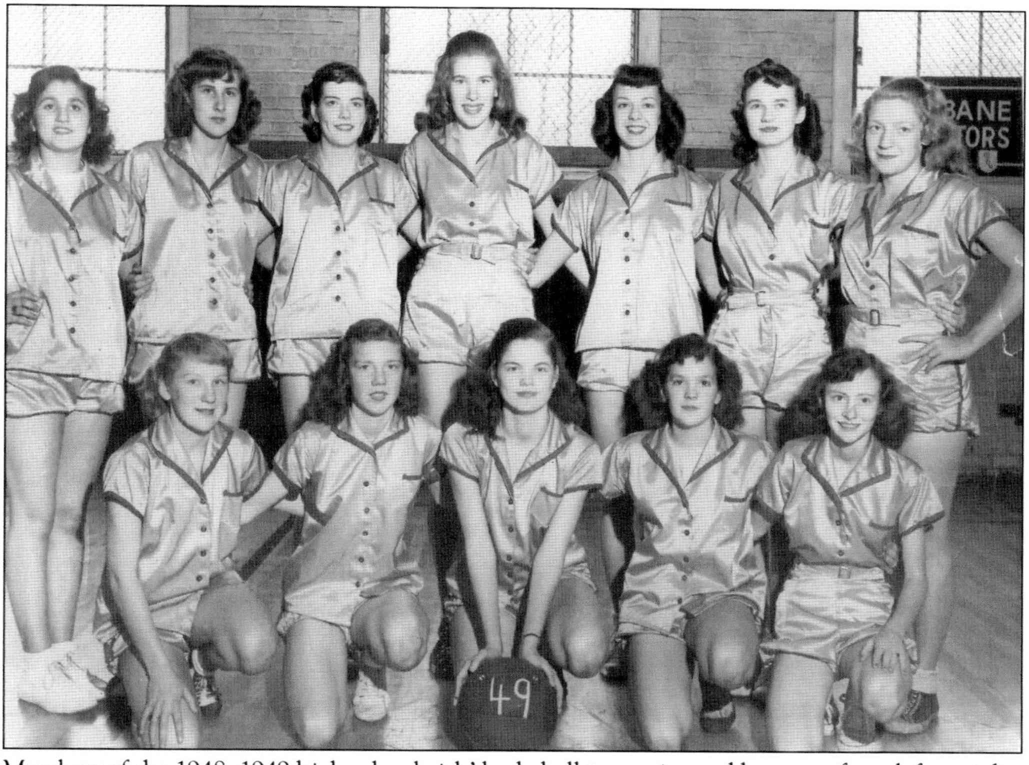

Members of the 1948–1949 high school girls' basketball team pictured here are, from left to right, (first row) Joyce Workman, Elizabeth Andrews, Mary Alice Daniels, Clara Jean West, and Elizabeth Stephenson; (second row) Rachel Payne, Frances Keasler, Anne Howell, Sclorine Wilborn, Minnie Lee Hooks, Sarah Ann Cook, and Peggy Brown. (MHM.)

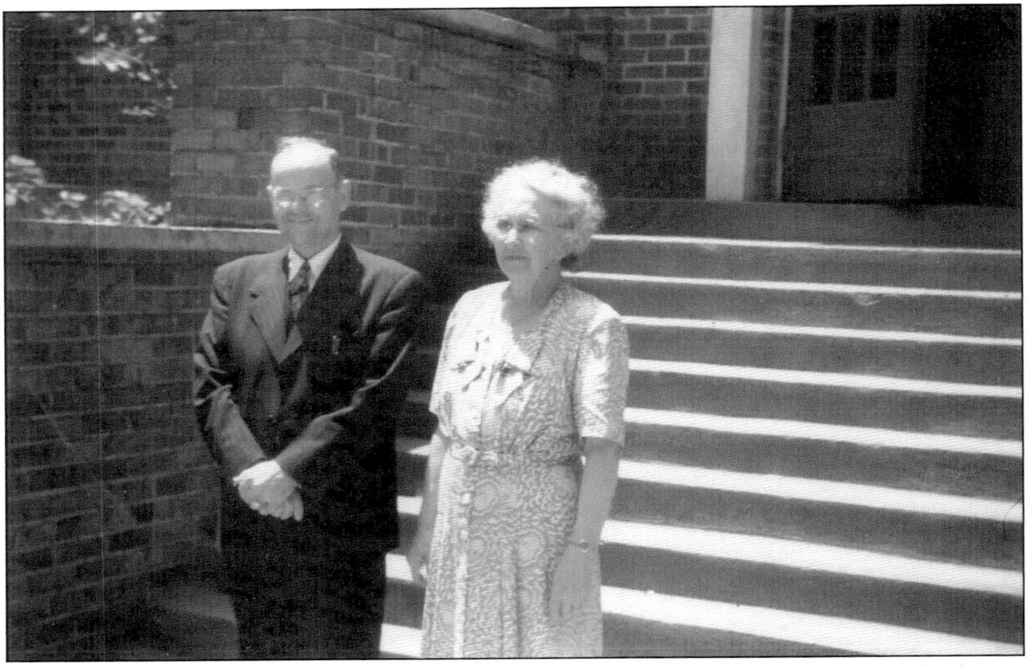

Principal E.M. Yoder and legendary teacher Annie Young Crawford stand on the school steps in this undated photograph. Yoder was the principal of Mebane High School from 1935 to 1962. After Eastern opened, he remained the principal of the middle school in the former high school until he retired in 1966 after a long and illustrious career in public education. (MHM.)

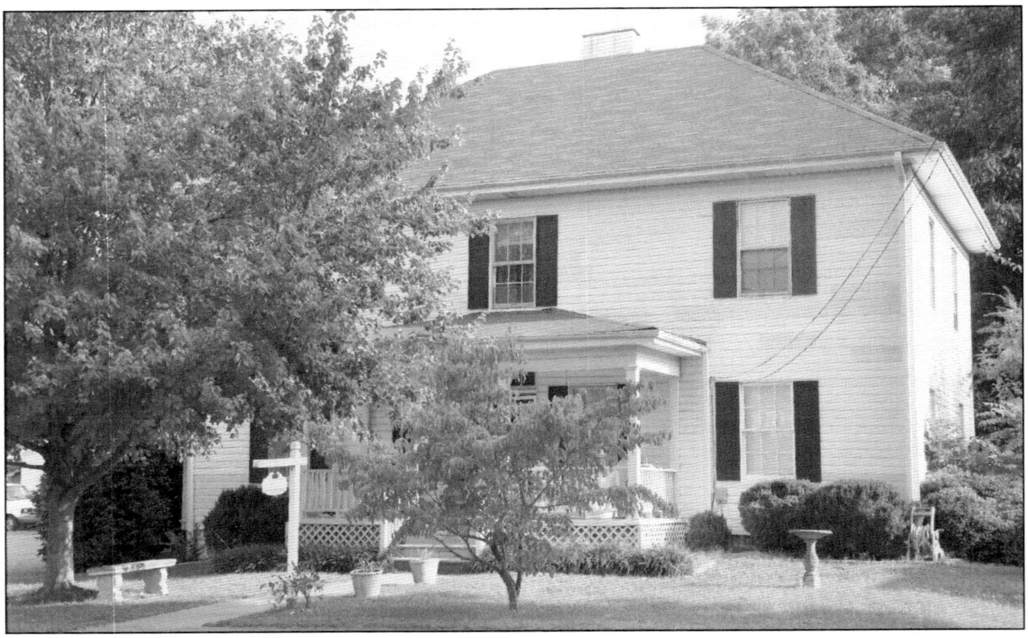

Across the street from the Jackson Street entrance to the school was the teacherage, a two-story house built in 1910. It was carved up into small apartments in the early 1940s for single young female teachers who often had trouble finding convenient living quarters in the small town in the 1940s and 1950s. Approximately 20 of them married Mebane men in 1940s. The teacherage eventually became a private residence once again. (Courtesy of Kelly Gauldin.)

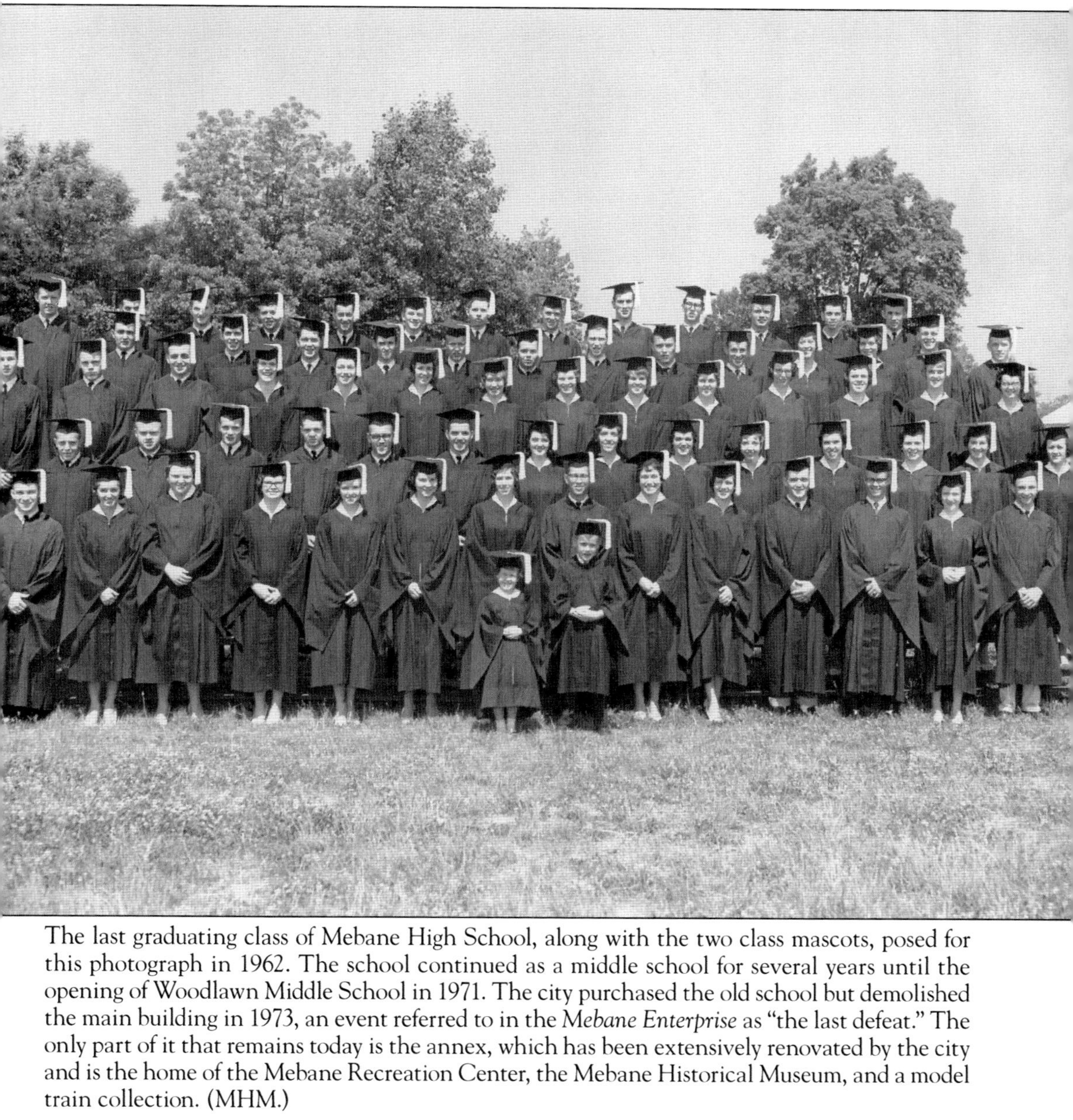

The last graduating class of Mebane High School, along with the two class mascots, posed for this photograph in 1962. The school continued as a middle school for several years until the opening of Woodlawn Middle School in 1971. The city purchased the old school but demolished the main building in 1973, an event referred to in the *Mebane Enterprise* as "the last defeat." The only part of it that remains today is the annex, which has been extensively renovated by the city and is the home of the Mebane Recreation Center, the Mebane Historical Museum, and a model train collection. (MHM.)

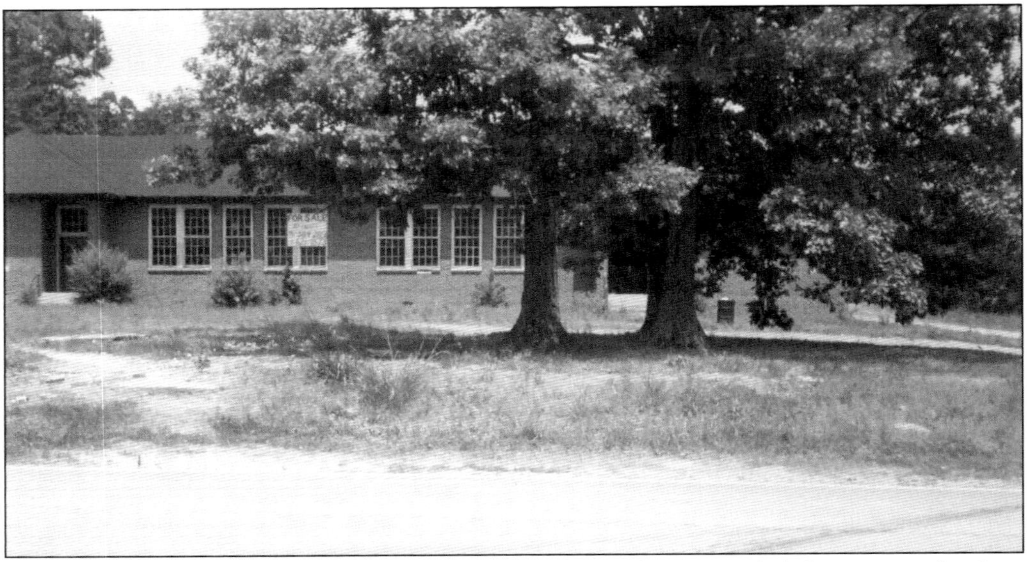

During the era of school segregation, African American students attended elementary schools in the county and high schools in Graham or Burlington. A new elementary school built in the mid-1930s went through several name changes before becoming West End Elementary. This undated photograph of the school was taken long after it closed. (Courtesy of Linda Evans.)

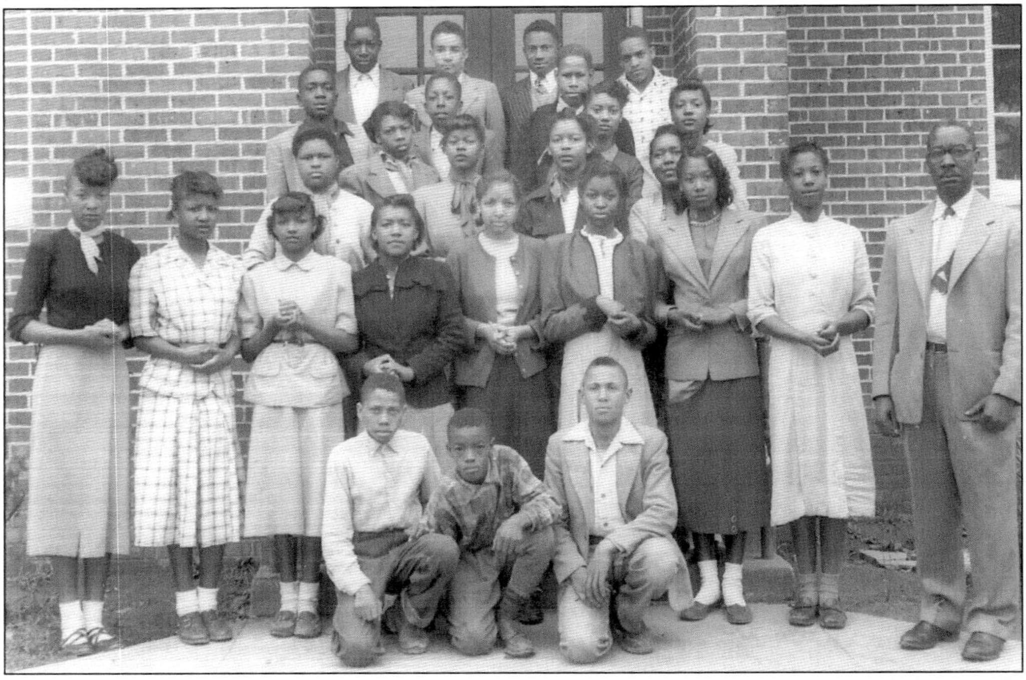

The seventh-grade class at West End Elementary poses with its principal in this undated photograph. From left to right are (first row) Claude Haith, Edward Mebane, and Ernest White; (second row) Sarah Morrow, Nettie Curry, Remonia Pettiford, Odessa Mebane, Armedella Graves, unidentified, Peggy Foust, Annie Davis, and Principal Dempsey Pettway; (third row) Carrie Crawford, Helen Packingham, Margie Degraffreindt, Loretta Day, and Annie Holt; (fourth row) Bobbie Tate, Douglas Hester, Donald Tinnin, Dorothy Smith, and Mary Foust; (fifth row) Billy Murphy, Leory Wilson, James Minor, and Archie Lea. (Courtesy of Linda Evans.)

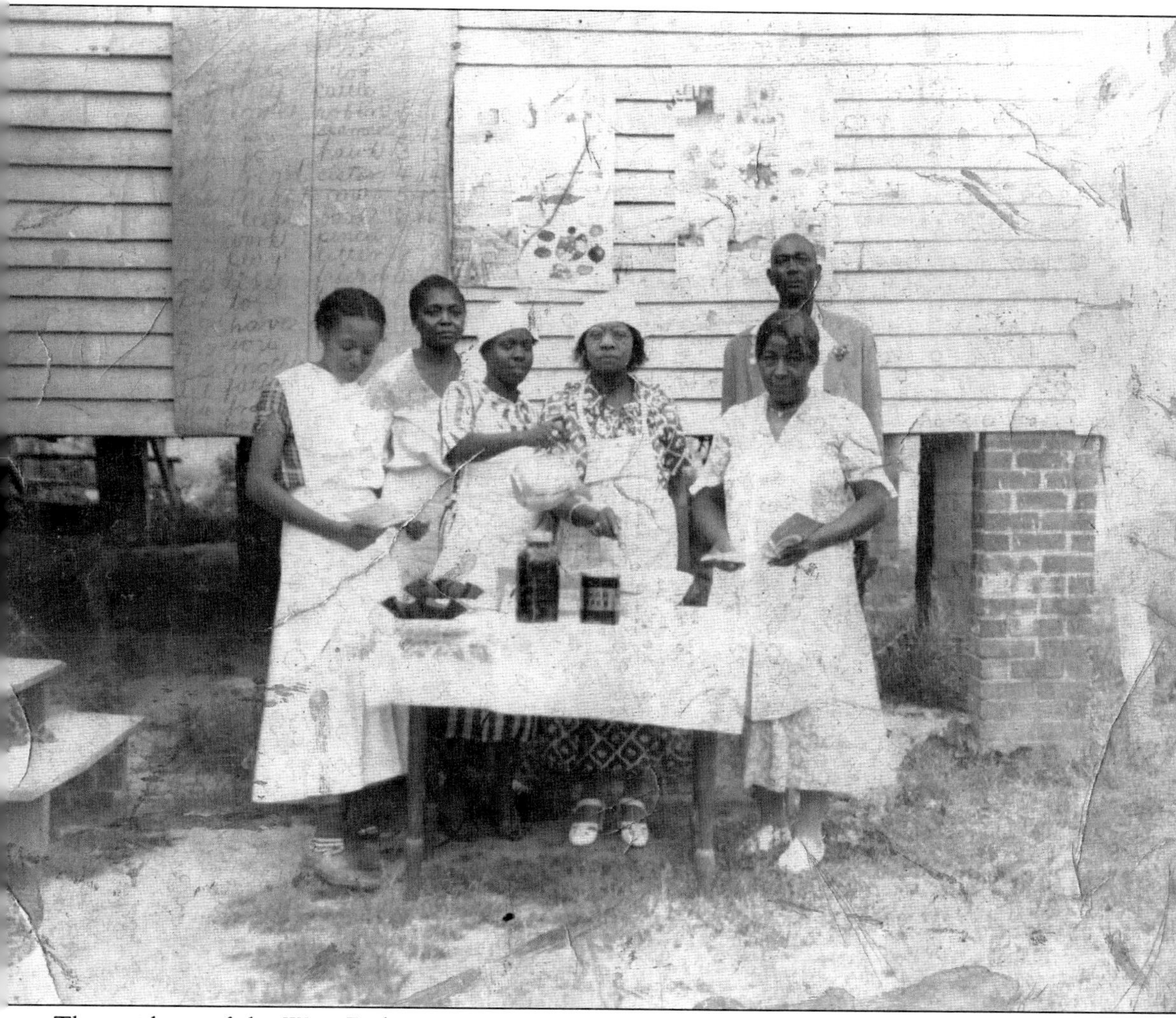

The residents of the West End community were strong supporters of their local school. This undated photograph shows community volunteers preparing for a food sale to benefit their school. The women are, from left to right, unidentified, Badie Conyard, Ollie Mae Holt, Alice Glenn, and unidentified. The man on the right in the back is John Thompson. (Courtesy of Linda Evans.)

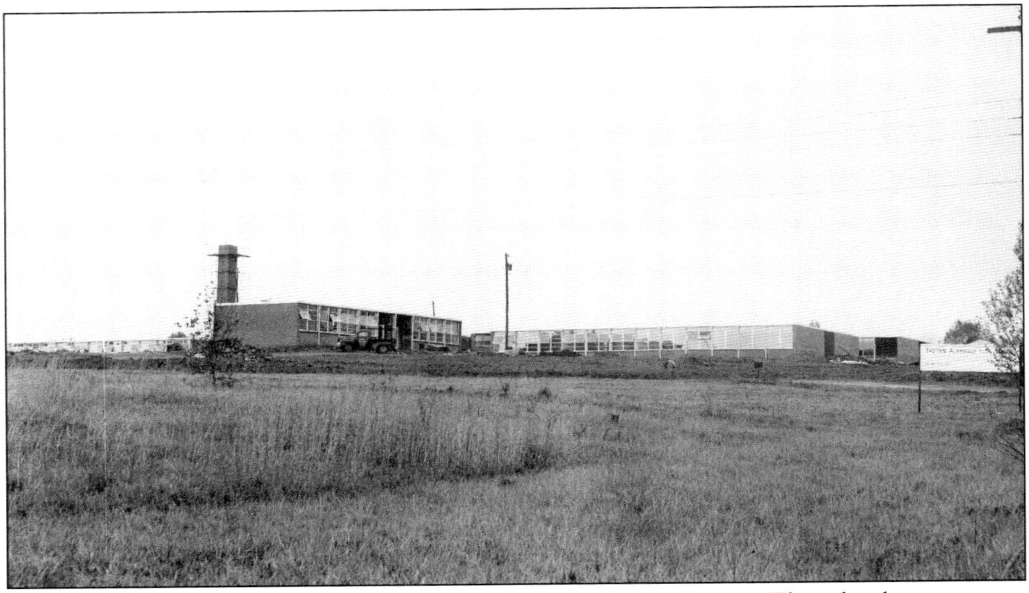

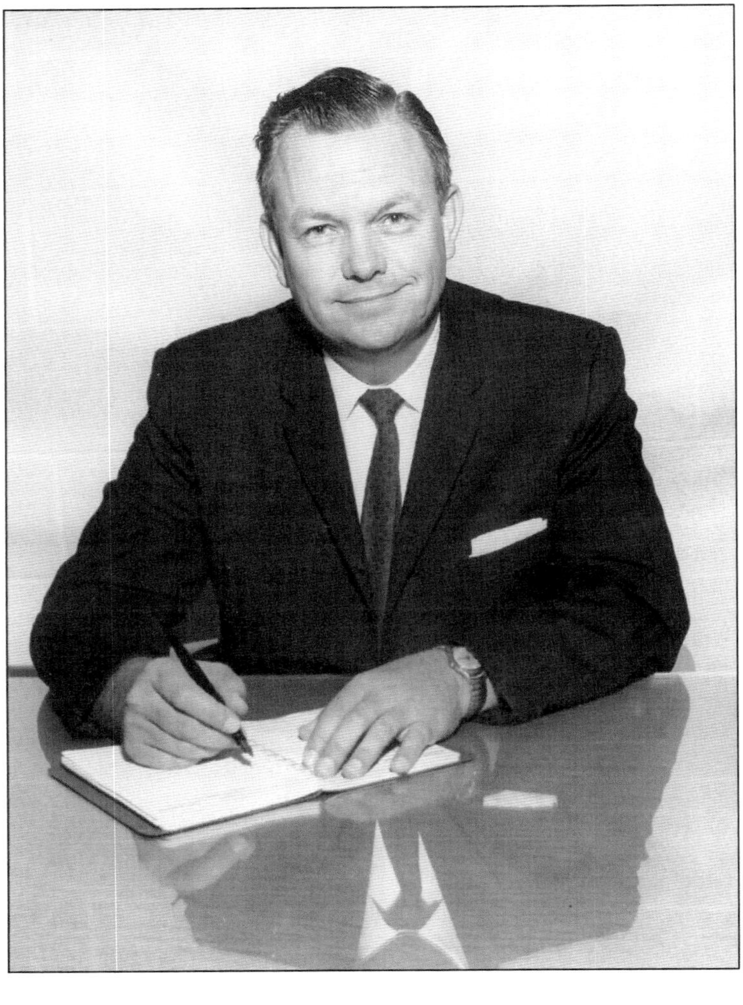

The school consolidation and integration movements eventually brought the merger of the high schools in Mebane, Haw River, and Pleasant Grove to form the new Eastern High School, which opened on Mebane Rogers Road in 1962. (MHM.)

Principal Elmo Allgood was the first principal of Eastern High. He had the difficult job of merging the faculty, students, and curriculums of the three high schools, which had been strong and sometimes bitter rivals in athletics and other areas. (Courtesy of Tal Jobe.)

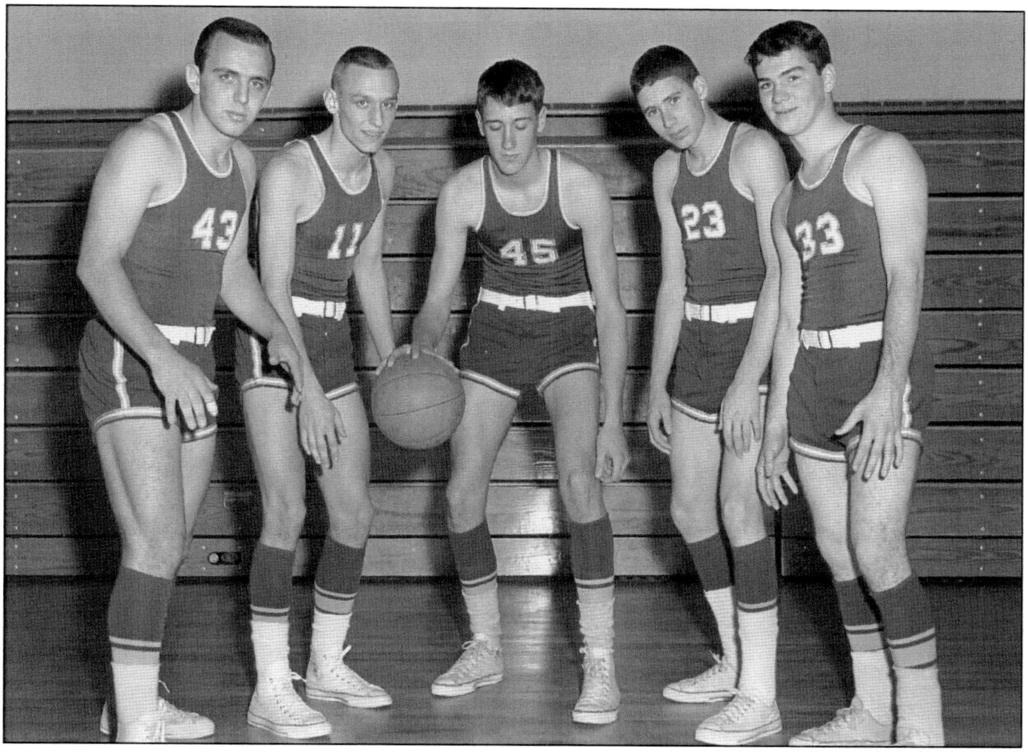

The starting team of Eastern High School's boys' basketball team poses in the gym in the early 1960s. From left to right are Ronnie Poteat, Tal Jobe, Gerald Smith, Tommy McLamb, and Dwayne Ray. Jobe would later return to the school as a teacher and coach and would lead the Eagles to their first state championship in 1991. (Courtesy of Tal Jobe.)

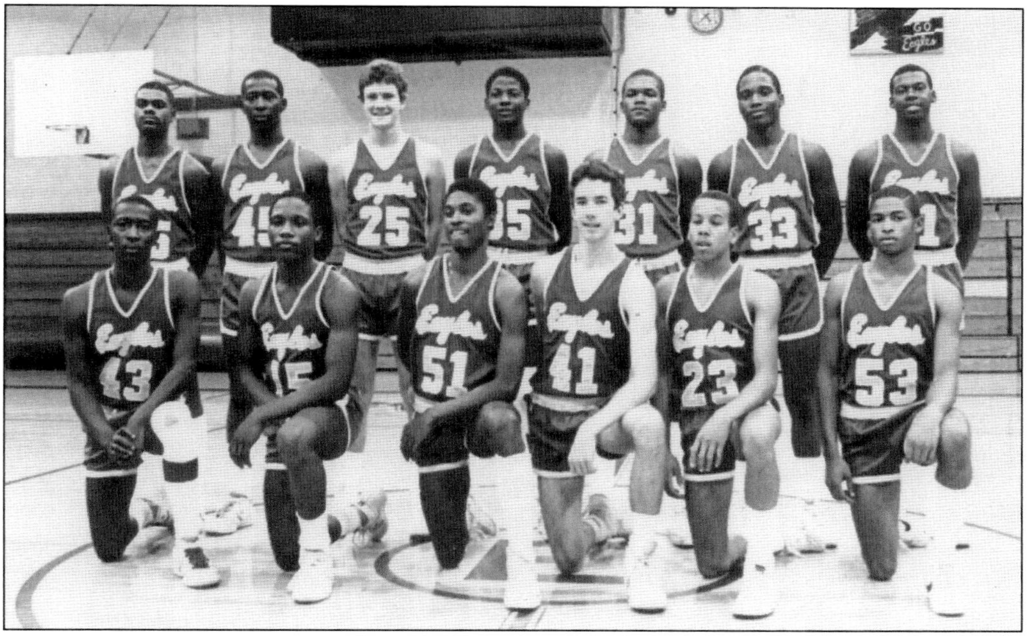

Eastern's basketball team is seen posed in the gymnasium in the early 1980s. (Courtesy of Tal Jobe.)

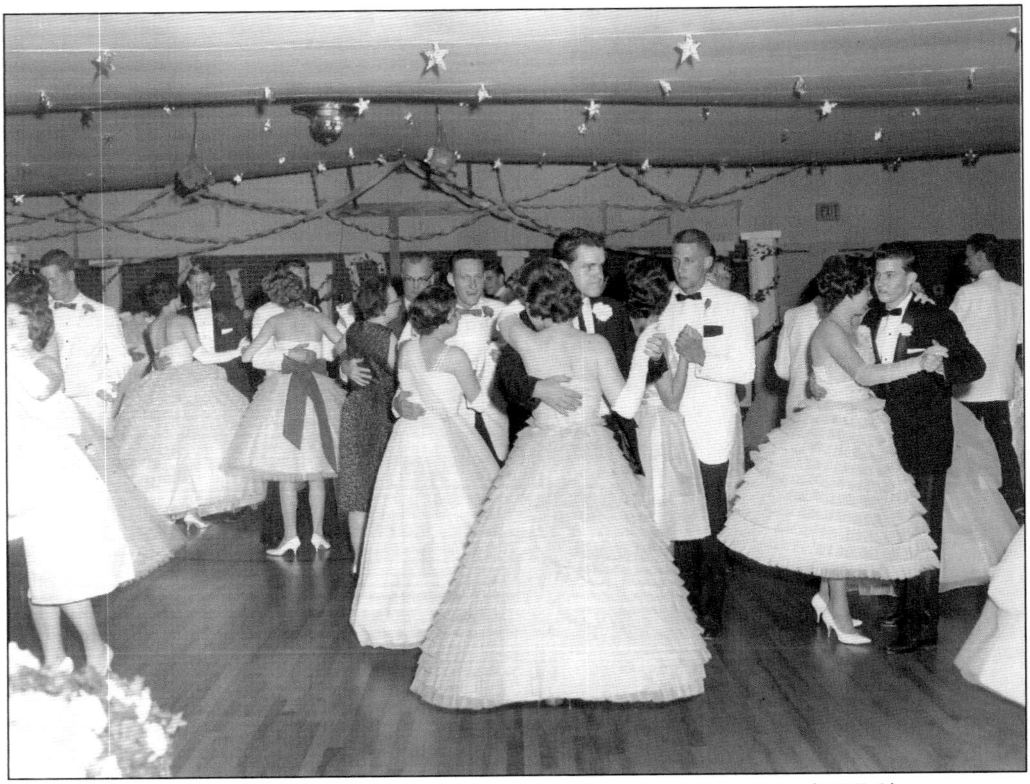

Eastern students enjoy the first junior-senior prom in the new gymnasium. (MHM.)

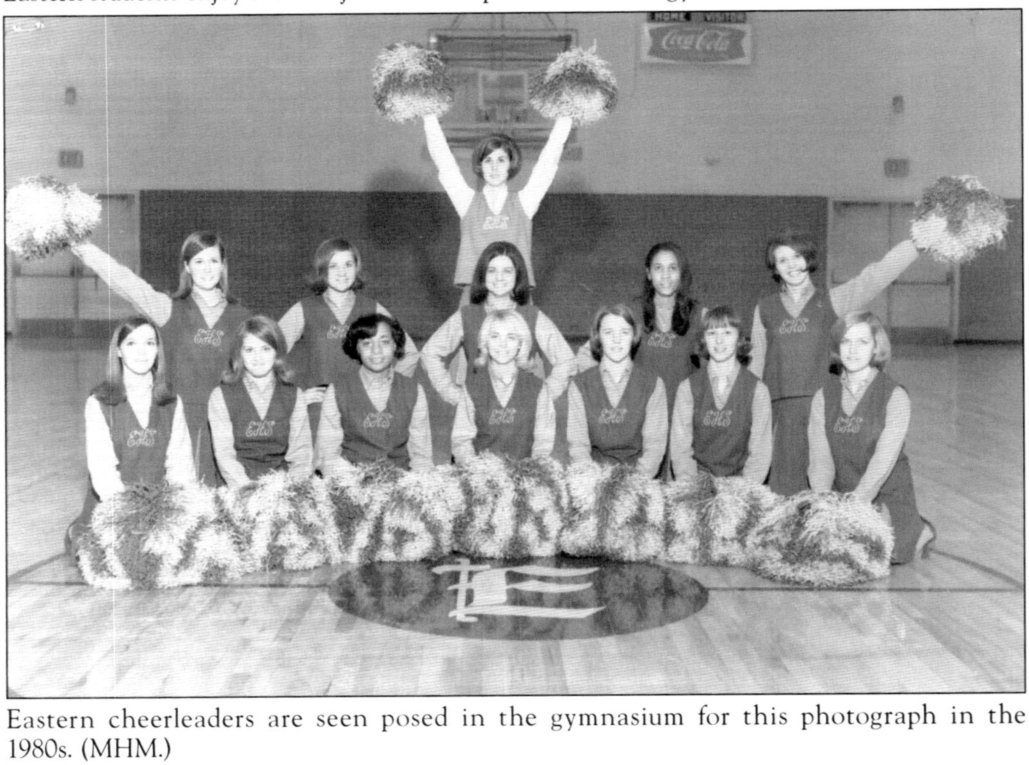

Eastern cheerleaders are seen posed in the gymnasium for this photograph in the 1980s. (MHM.)

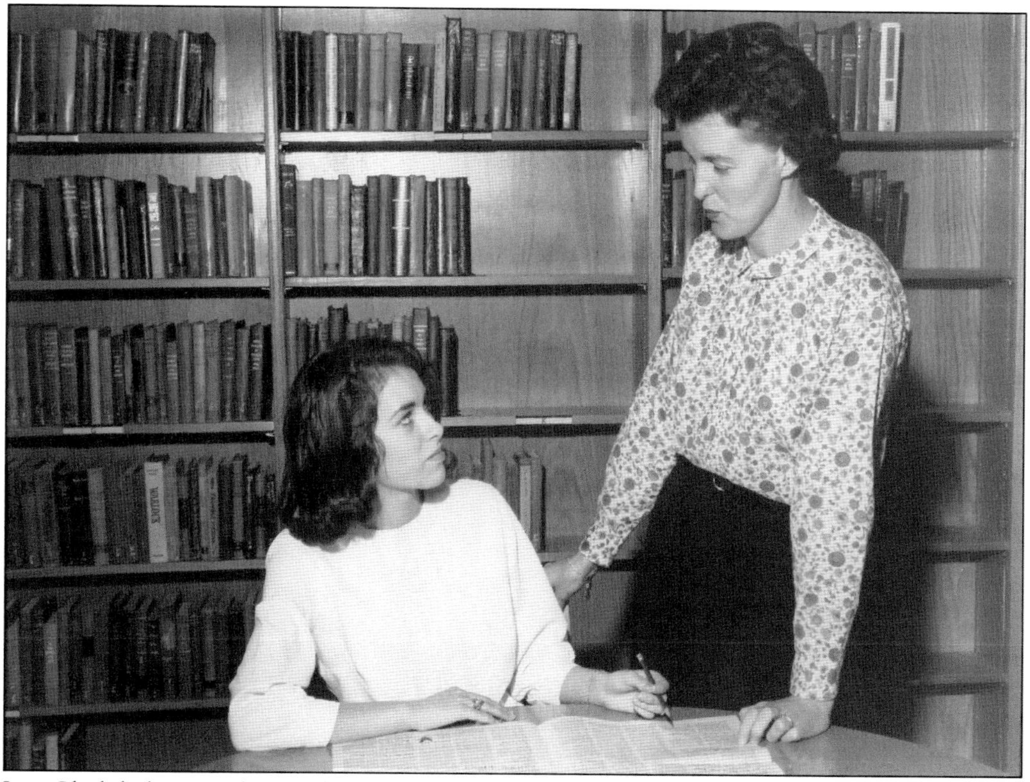

Lou Clark helps a student with the school newspaper. A business education teacher, Clark had a long career at Mebane and Eastern High Schools. (MHM.)

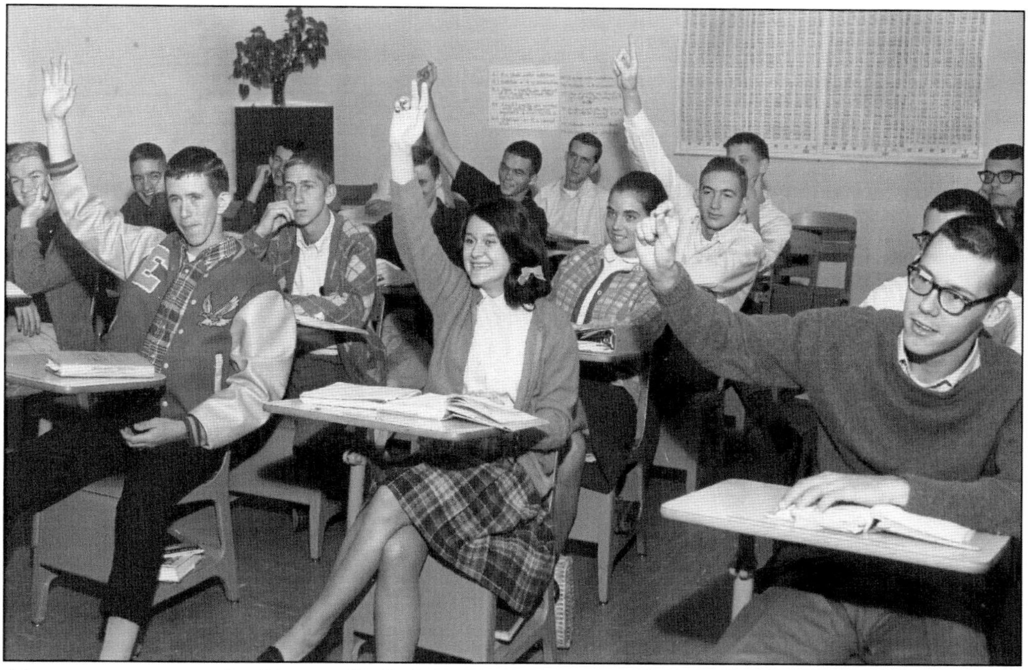

Almost everyone in this Eastern High School trigonometry class in the mid-1960s seems to know the answer. (Courtesy of Tal Jobe.)

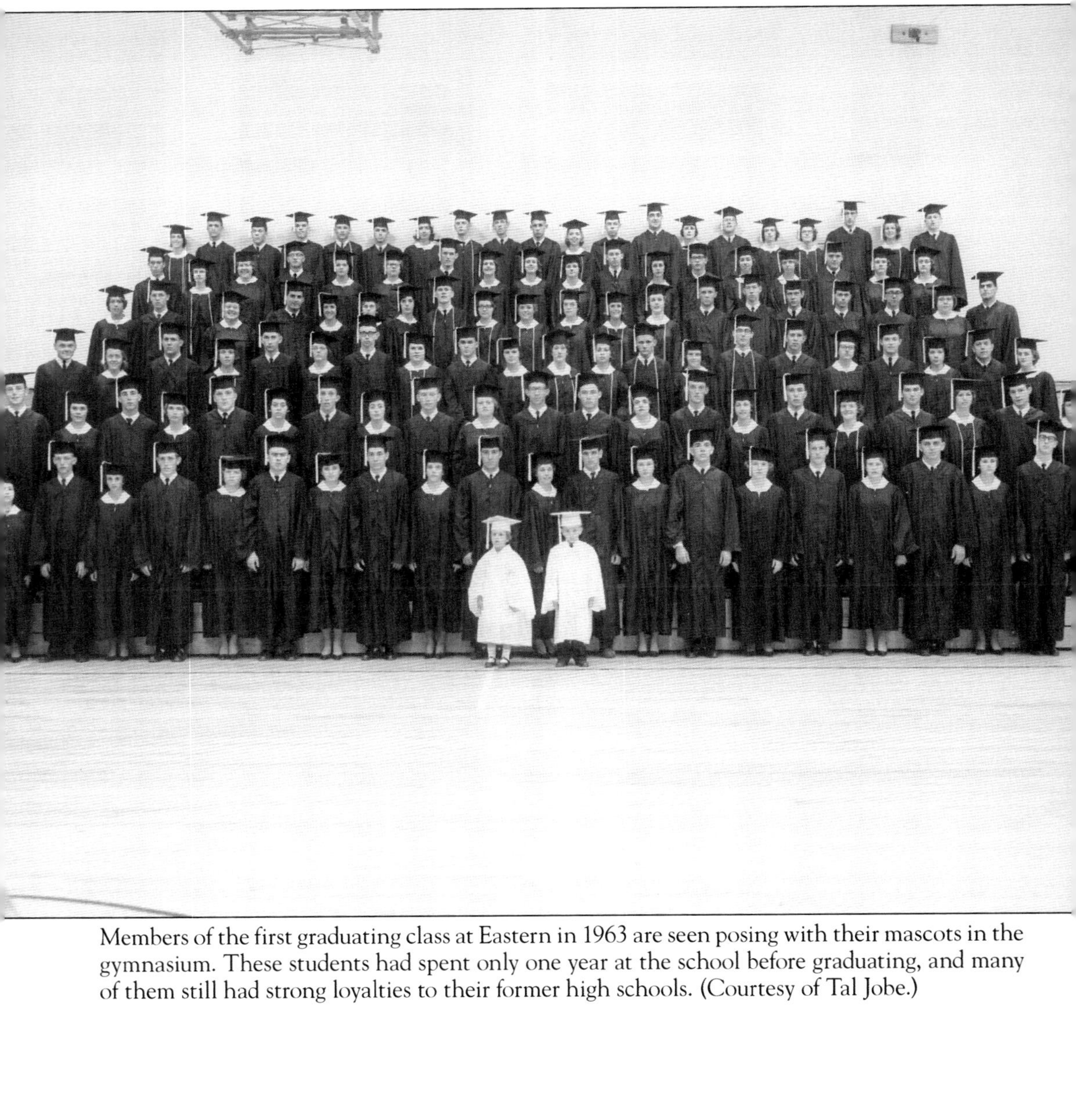

Members of the first graduating class at Eastern in 1963 are seen posing with their mascots in the gymnasium. These students had spent only one year at the school before graduating, and many of them still had strong loyalties to their former high schools. (Courtesy of Tal Jobe.)

Nine

Preserving and Celebrating the Past

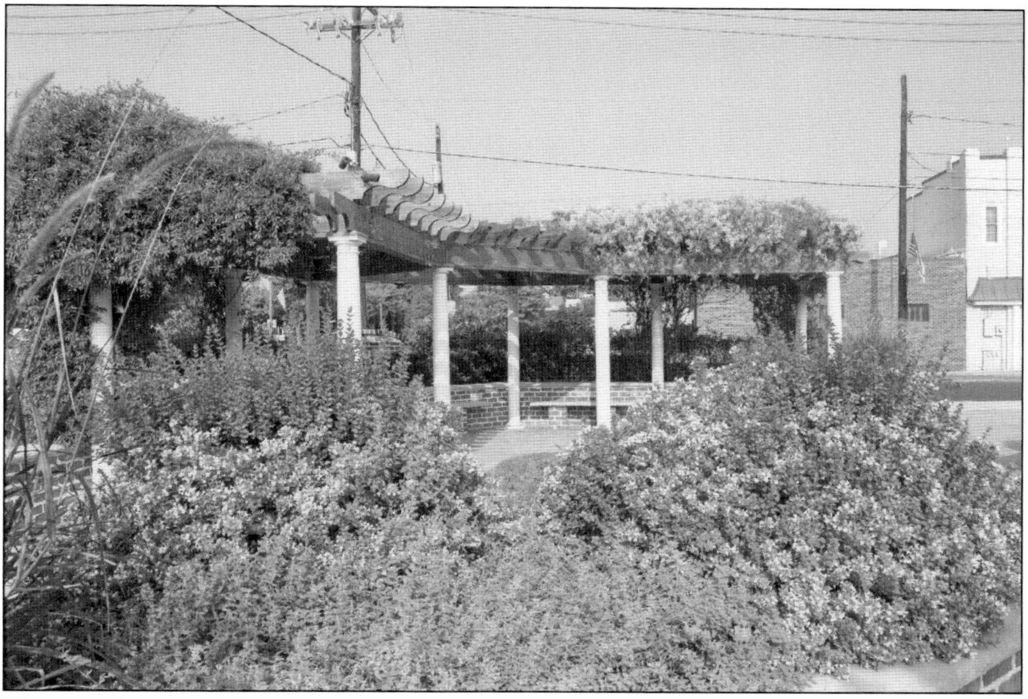

This is a side view of the Veterans Garden. The Veterans Garden is just one of many examples of how over the years the City of Mebane and its citizens have honored and celebrated the people and events in the little town's history. (Courtesy of Kelly Gauldin.)

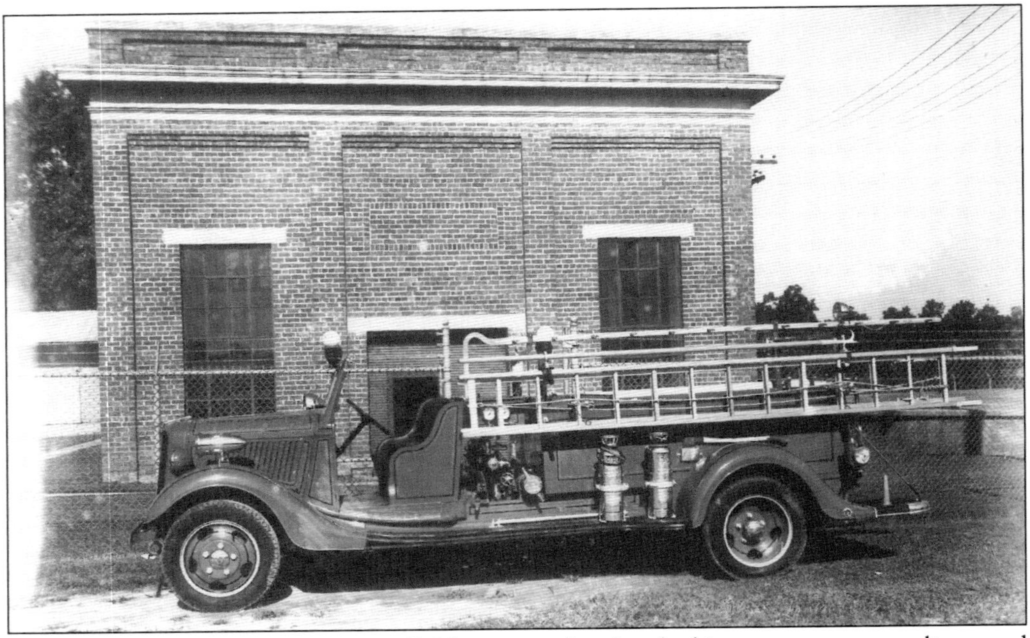

In the early 1920s, the growing city of Mebane paved and curbed its streets, ran water lines, and purchased its first fire truck, a 1923 LaFrance Brockway Torpedo, shown in this late-1920s or early-1930s photograph. Walter Dillard was the first fire chief. The first fire station was built in 1950 on Washington Street and is still in use today. (Courtesy of the *Mebane Enterprise*.)

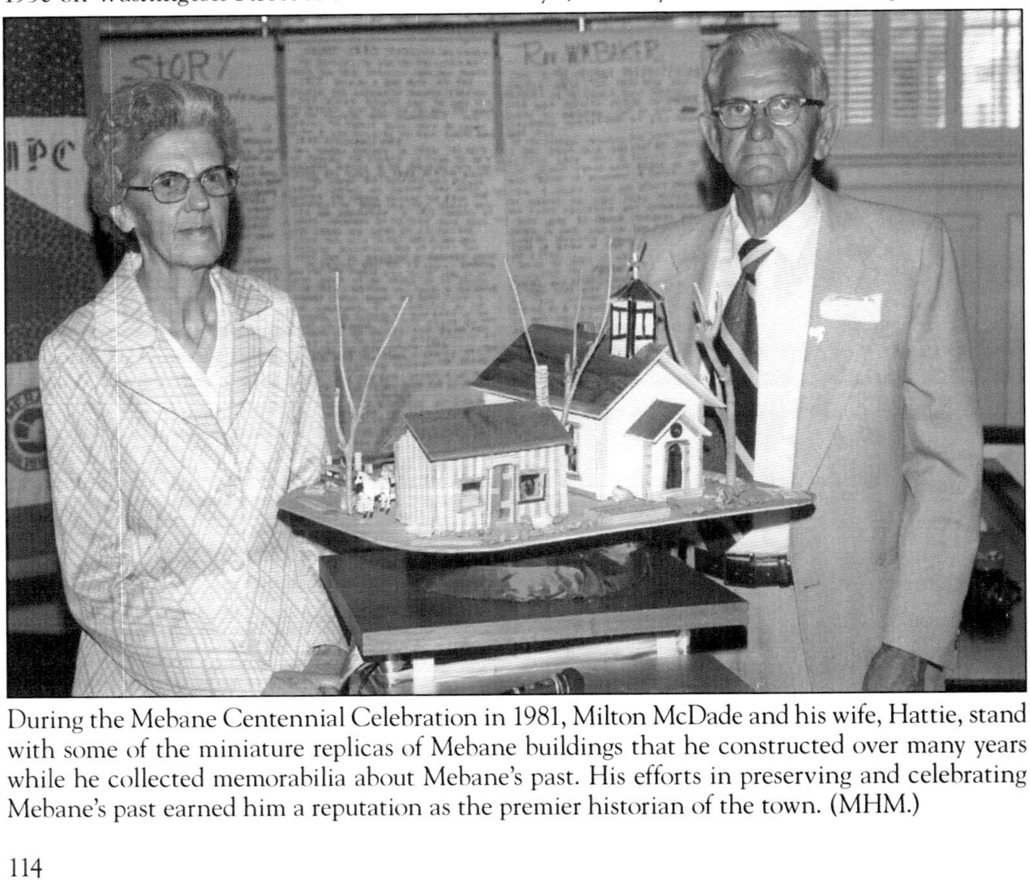

During the Mebane Centennial Celebration in 1981, Milton McDade and his wife, Hattie, stand with some of the miniature replicas of Mebane buildings that he constructed over many years while he collected memorabilia about Mebane's past. His efforts in preserving and celebrating Mebane's past earned him a reputation as the premier historian of the town. (MHM.)

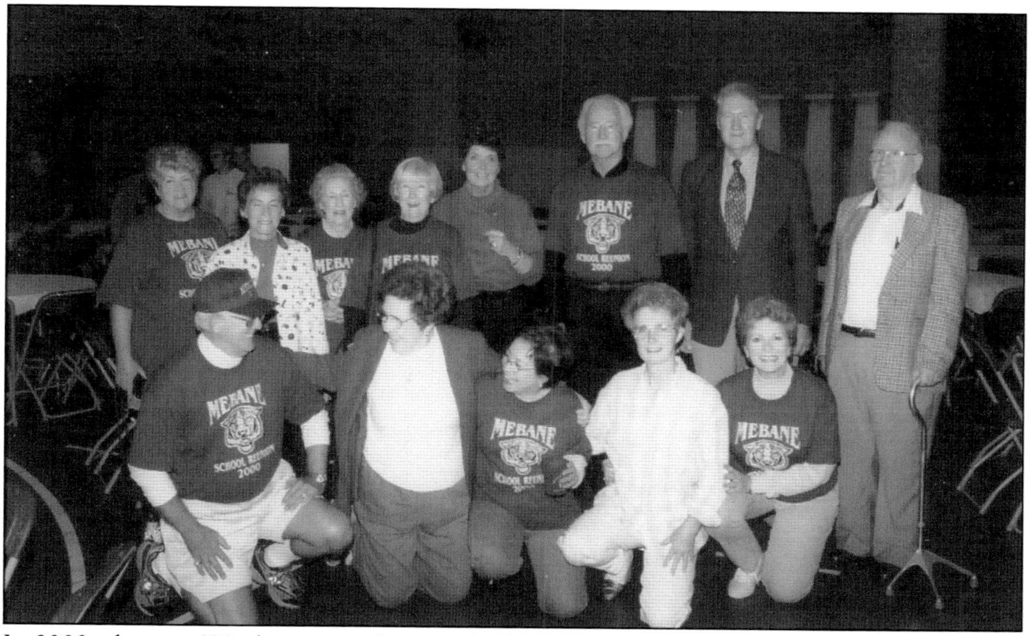

In 2000, close to 600 alumni, teachers, and other employees who had been at Mebane Public School between 1903 and 1970 gathered in the Mebane Arts and Community Center for a giant reunion appropriately called the "Blast from the Past." During the celebration, the planning committee posed for this photograph with Iris Abernathy (second from the left, first row) and Neal Smith (second from the right, second row). (MHM.)

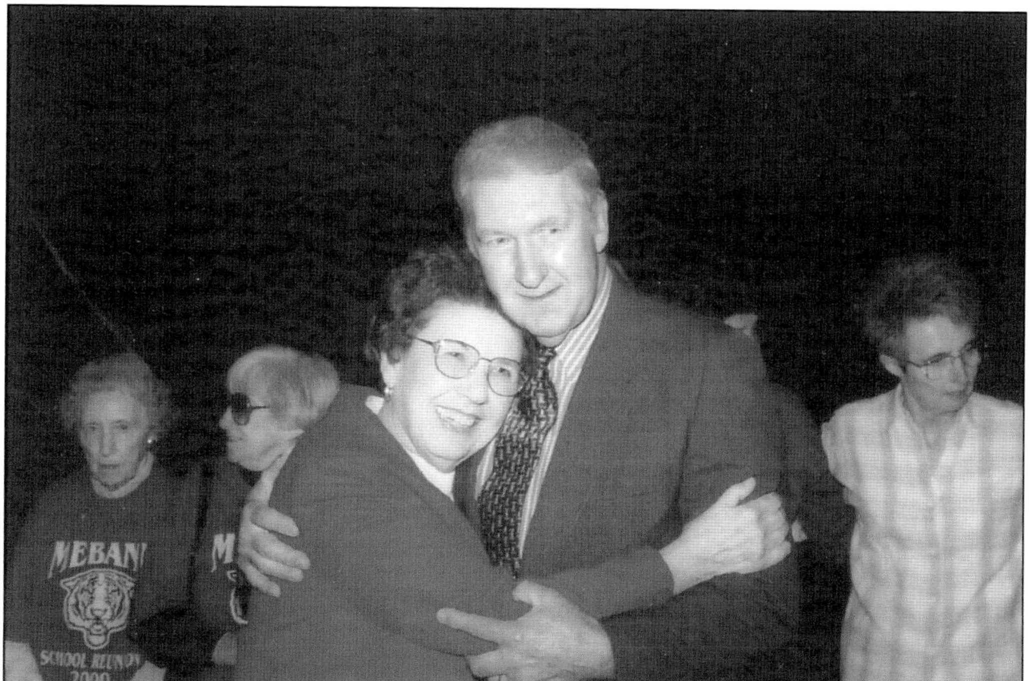

During the "Blast From the Past," teacher Iris Abernathy and former student Neal Smith embraced after meeting for the first time in many years. In the background are, from left to right, Velma Kelly, Colleen Payne, and Penny Butler. (MHM.)

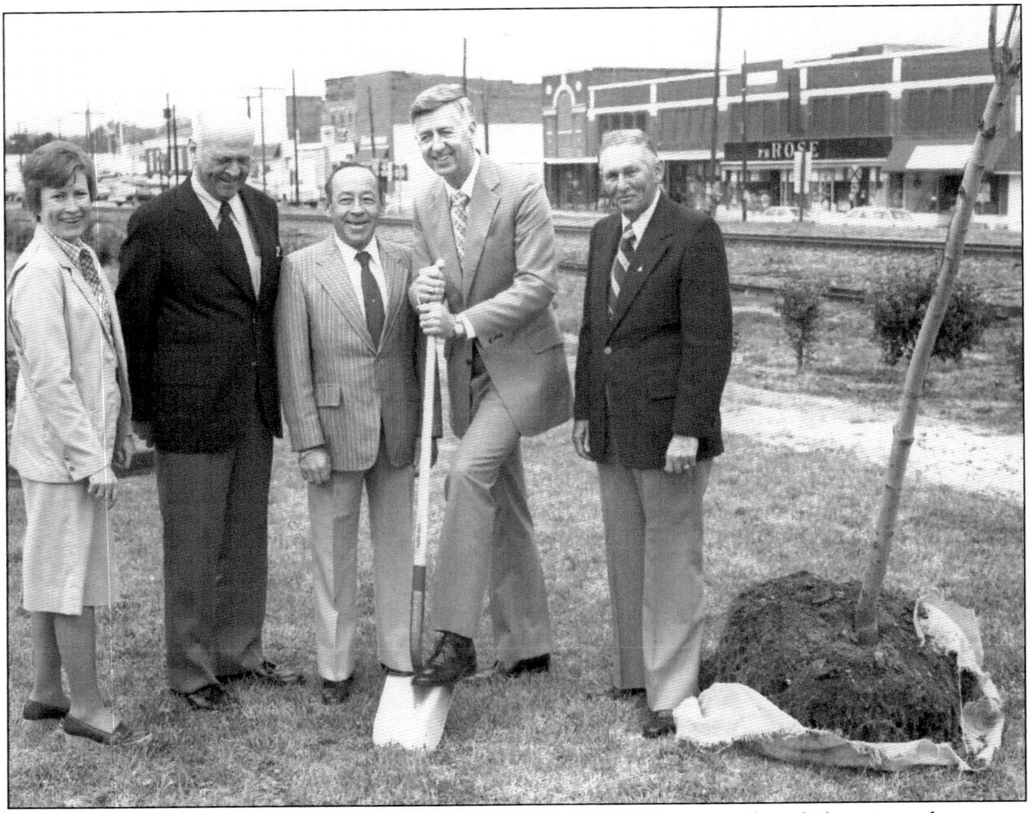

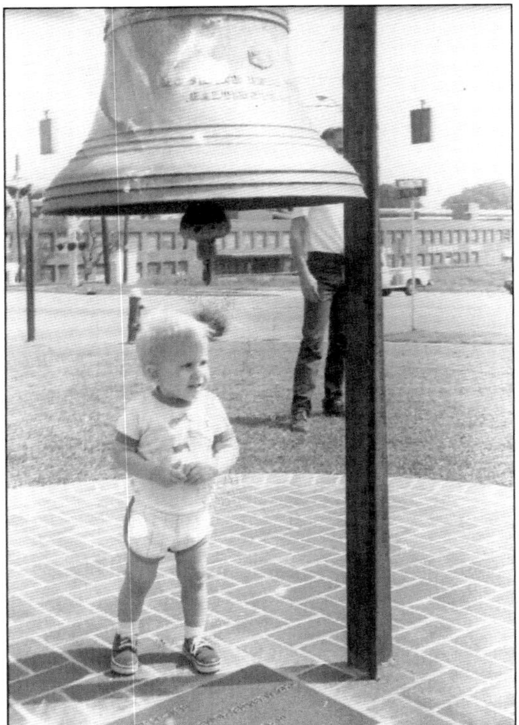

In 1981, after months of planning, the City of Mebane held a huge centennial celebration commemorating the signing of the charter that gave birth to the little town of Mebanesville, which was renamed Mebane two years later. Several major events were held over a period of several months. In this photograph, town officials inaugurate a tree-planting project along the railroad and Mebane's streets. From left to right are Joyce Dickey, George Ratterman, Bill Hupman, Mayor Glendel Stephenson, and Everette Pender. (MHM.)

Near the end of the centennial events, a child wanders under a replica of the Liberty Bell donated by Mebane Home Telephone Company. (MHM.)

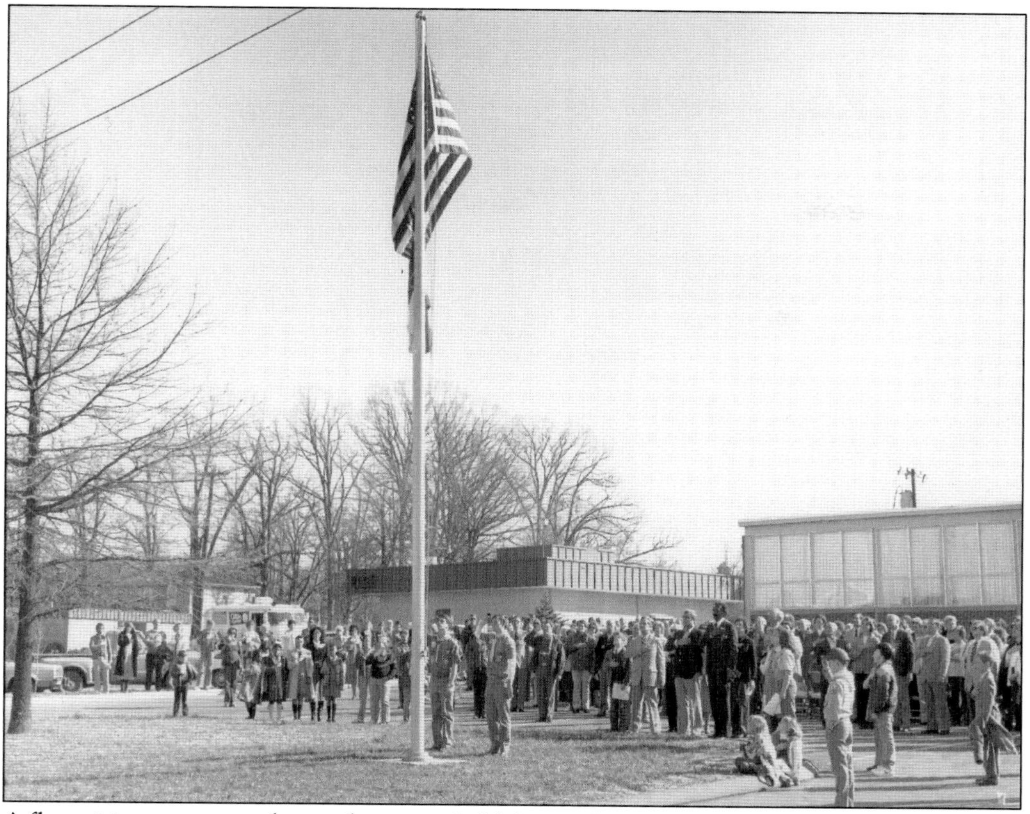

A flag raising ceremony, shown above, was held during the centennial celebration. Shown below, a time capsule, a gift from Walter Kidde Company, was buried near the flagpole to be opened on Thanksgiving Day in 2081. The marker was from the Siler City Monument Company. Among its contents are copies of local newspapers, minutes of the town board meetings, pictures of Mebane, a description of the centennial events, church bulletins, a telephone directory, state and town maps, and a list of town officials and employees. (Above, MHM; below Kelly Gauldin.)

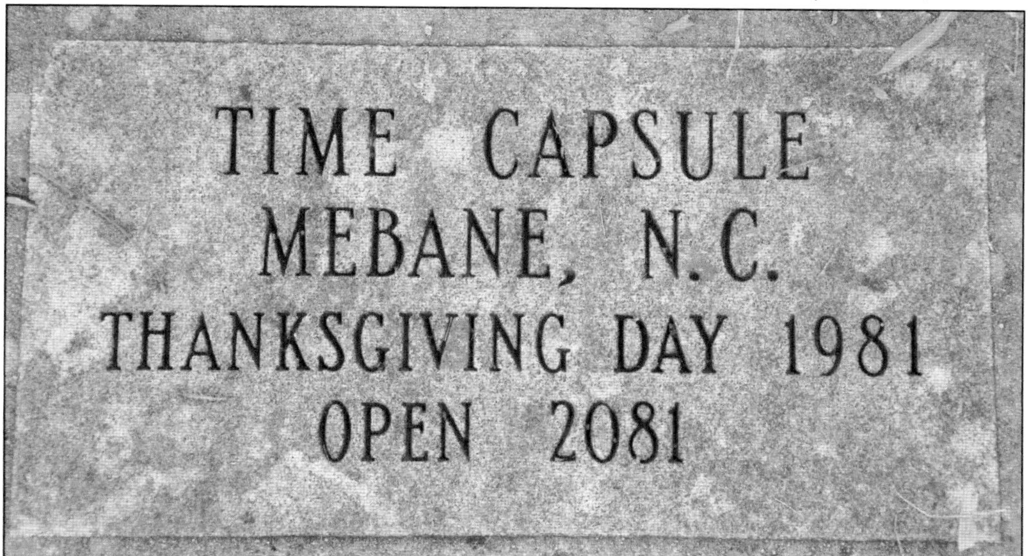

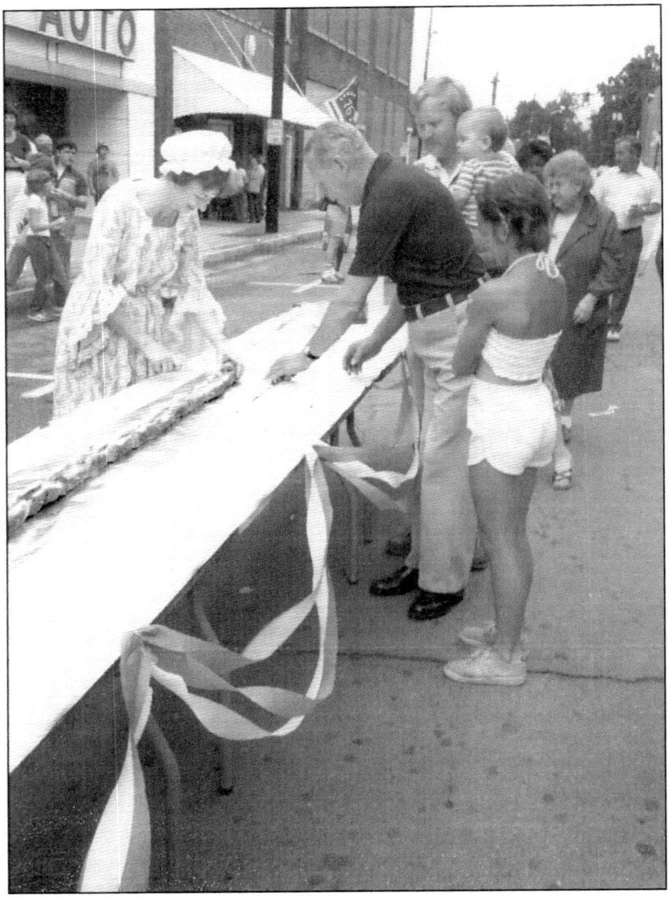

Several citizens enjoyed the 40-foot-long hot dog served on Fourth Street during the centennial on the Fourth of July. (MHM.)

The Mebane Dogwood Festival has been held every year in April for the past 23 years. The event attracts thousands of people to downtown Mebane for food, children's rides, arts and crafts, and several other forms of entertainment. (Courtesy of the *Mebane Enterprise*.)

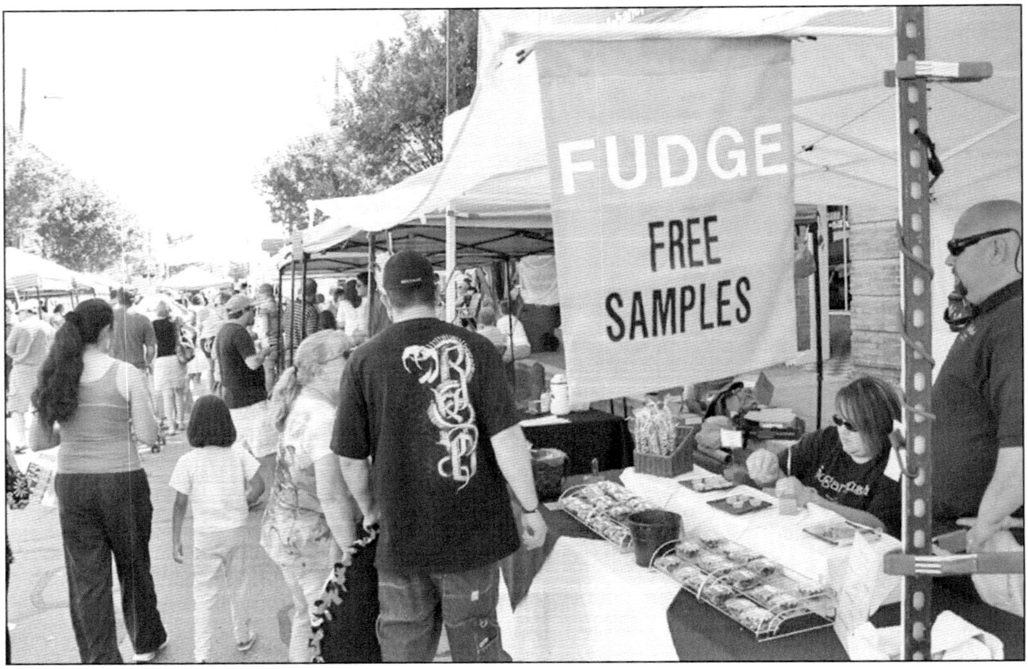

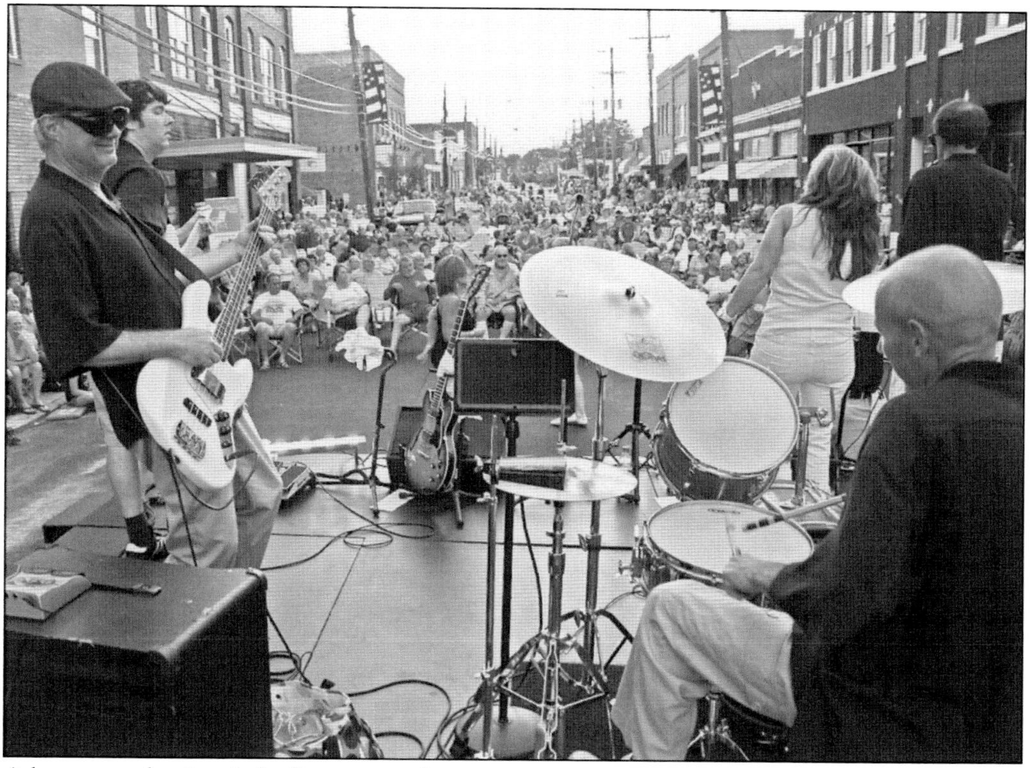

A large crowd enjoyed the live music of the Franklin Street Band in 2011 during a Clay Street After Work event sponsored by the City of Mebane, the Alamance County Arts Council, and local merchants. (Courtesy of the *Mebane Enterprise.*)

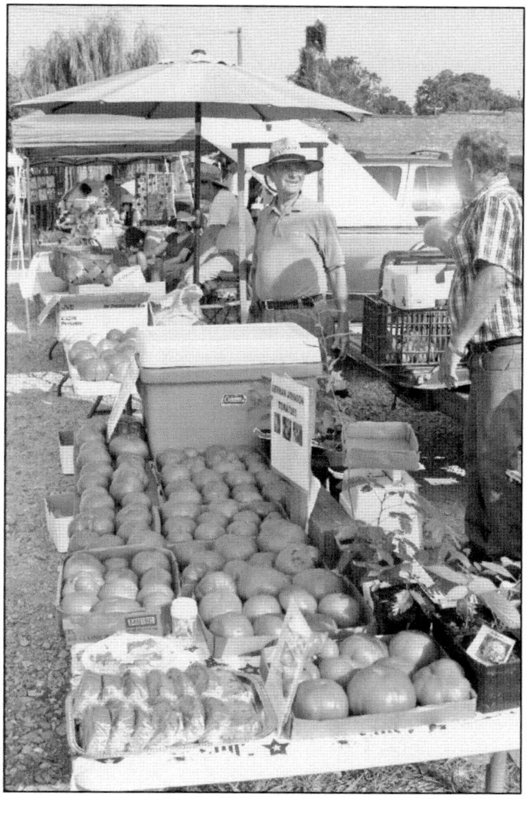

A reminder of days past, vendors at the Mebane Farmer's Market have sold fresh produce, jams, cakes, and other items during the summer months on the corner of Clay and Third Streets. (Courtesy of the *Mebane Enterprise.*)

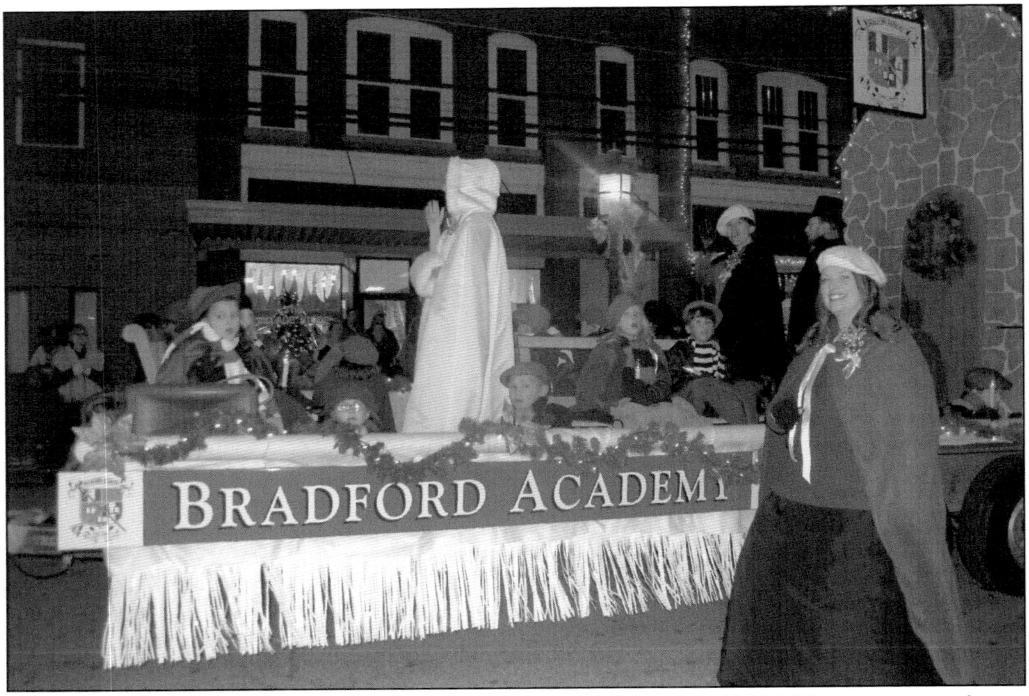

A Bradford Academy float passes down Center Street during the 2010 Christmas parade, an annual event for over 70 years. (Courtesy of the *Mebane Enterprise*.)

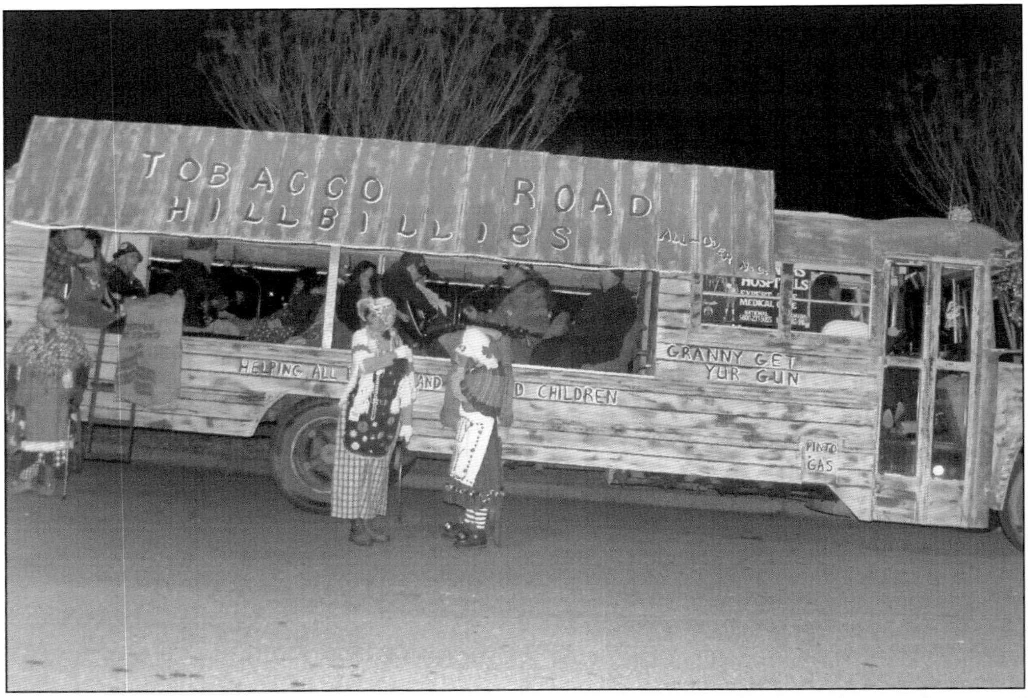

Members of a local Shriners Club perform as the Tobacco Road Hillbillies, always a big crowd pleaser, on a cold night during a recent Christmas parade. (Courtesy of the *Mebane Enterprise*.)

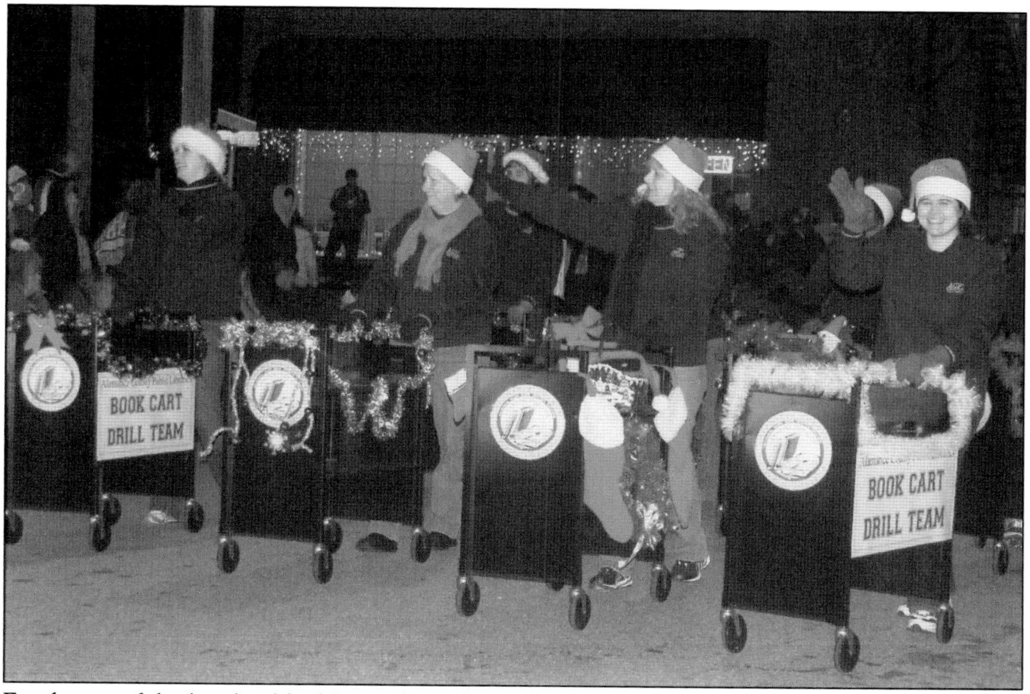

Employees of the local public library show their skills with a book cart drill team during a parade in 2010. (Courtesy of the *Mebane Enterprise*.)

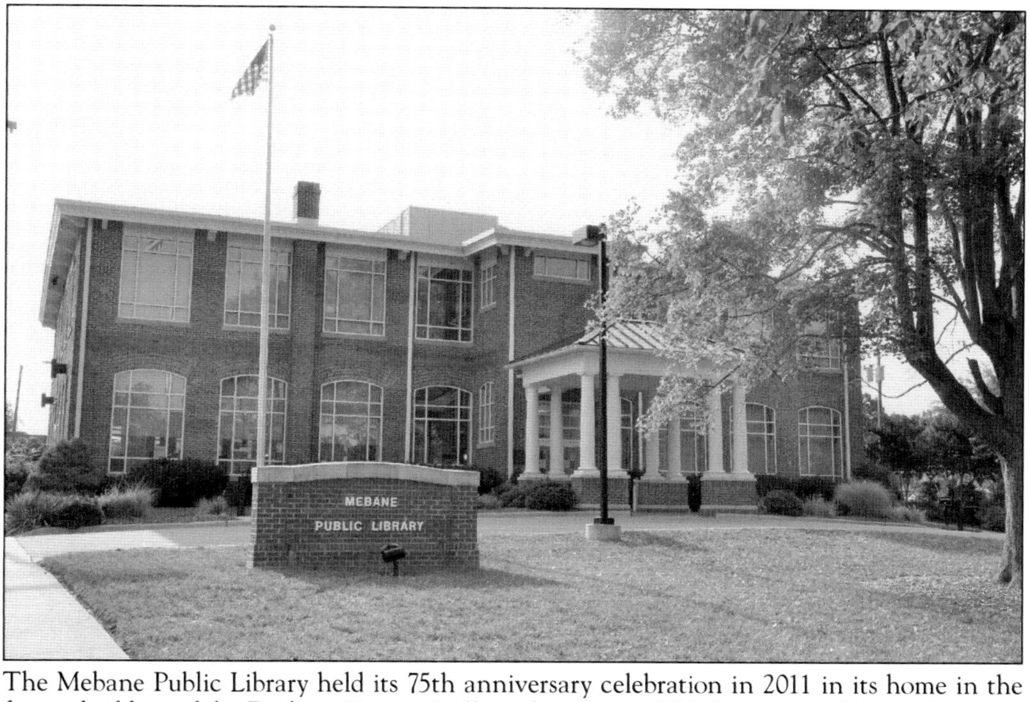

The Mebane Public Library held its 75th anniversary celebration in 2011 in its home in the former building of the Durham Hosiery Mill on the corner of Washington and Second Streets. The City of Mebane purchased and remodeled the building, and a local committee raised close to $100,000 from local businesses and citizens to pay for the furnishings. A grand opening was held in 2005. (Courtesy of Kelly Gauldin.)

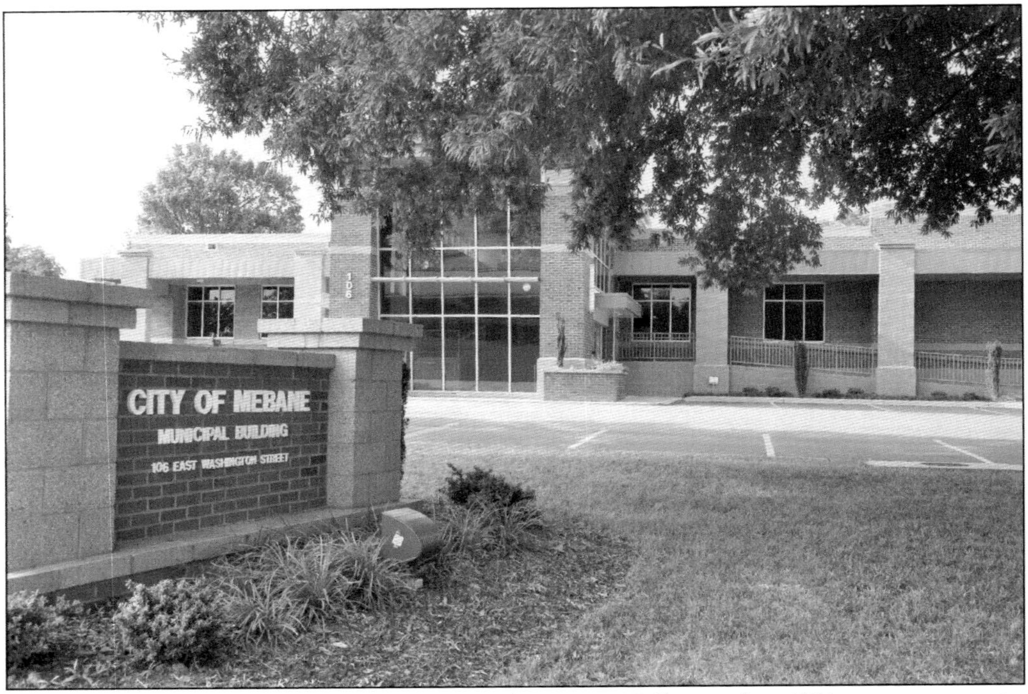

After years spent in crowded headquarters, Mebane City Hall moved in 1974 to its present site across from the railroad on Washington Street, the former home of May Apparel. The building was extensively renovated in 2009. (Courtesy of Kelly Gauldin.)

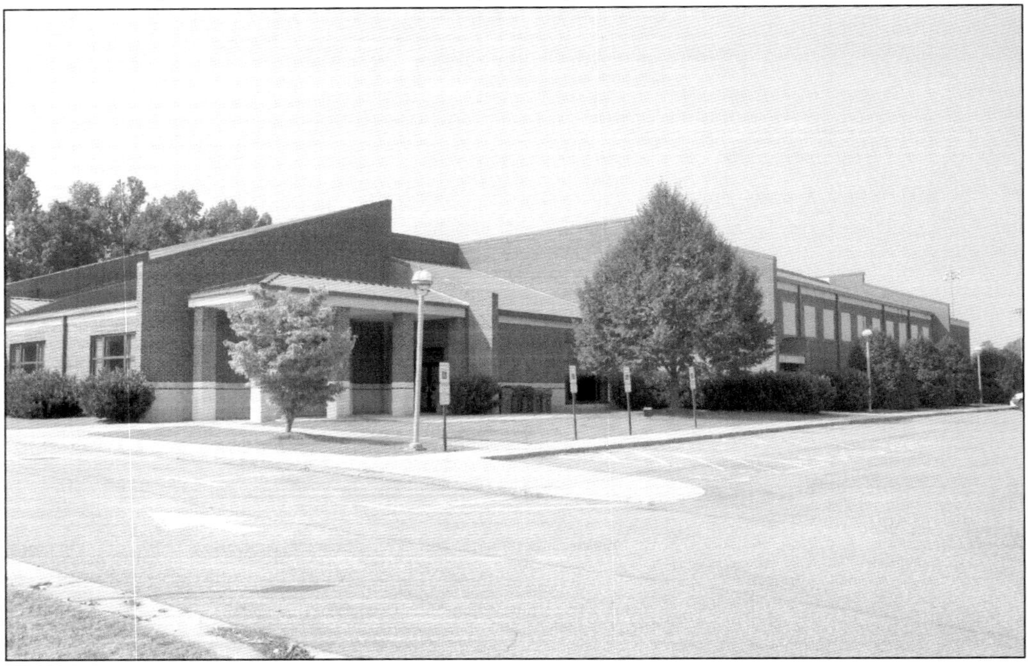

The City of Mebane completed construction of the Mebane Arts and Community Center in the mid-1990s. The large building provides a combination gymnasium/multipurpose room and several outdoor athletic fields and sponsors many inside and outdoors events every year. (Courtesy of Kelly Gauldin.)

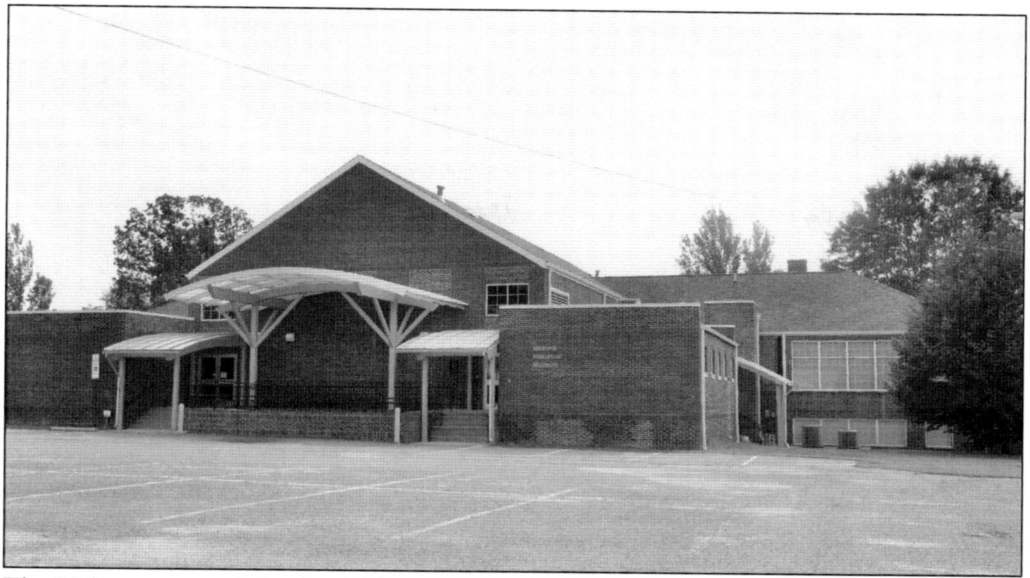

The Mebane memorabilia that Milton McDade collected over many decades was first housed in a small building in his backyard before being put in storage at the Mebane Public Library and then in the basement of the police station on Center Street. Thanks to the efforts of the Mebane Historical Society and the City of Mebane, these materials and others are stored and exhibited at the Mebane Historical Museum on Lee Street, which opened in 2009. (Courtesy of Kelly Gauldin.)

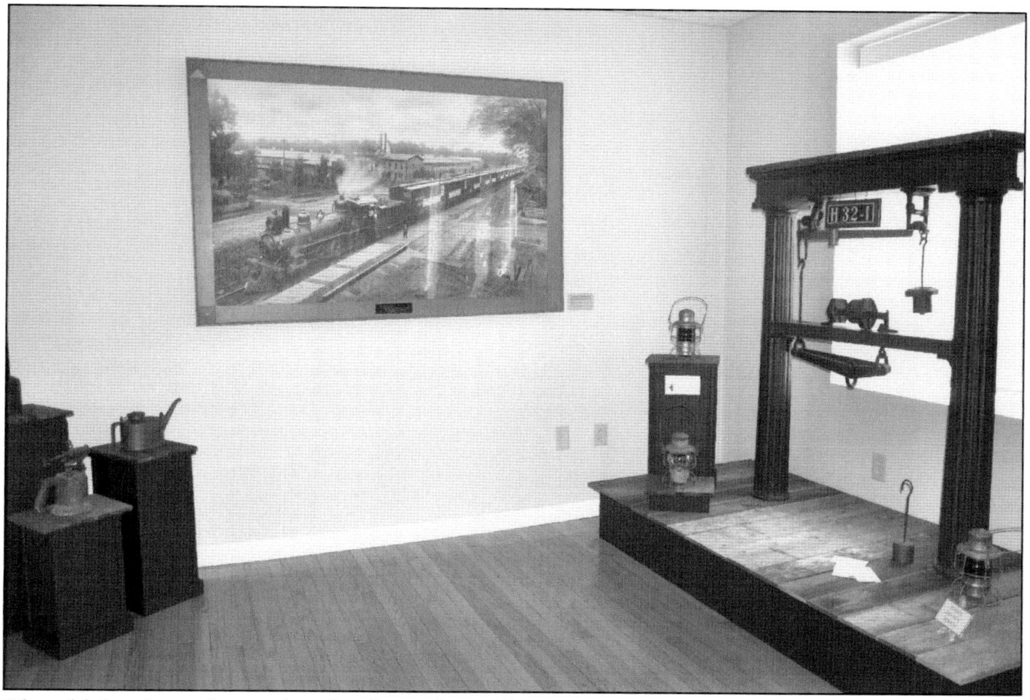

The old freight and postal scales from the Mebane Depot were put on display in the Mebane Historical Museum near the iconic 1906 Waller Holladay photograph of a train leaving White Furniture Company with a large load of furniture for the workers building the Panama Canal. The depot was closed and torn down in the 1970s. (Photograph by Kelly Gauldin.)

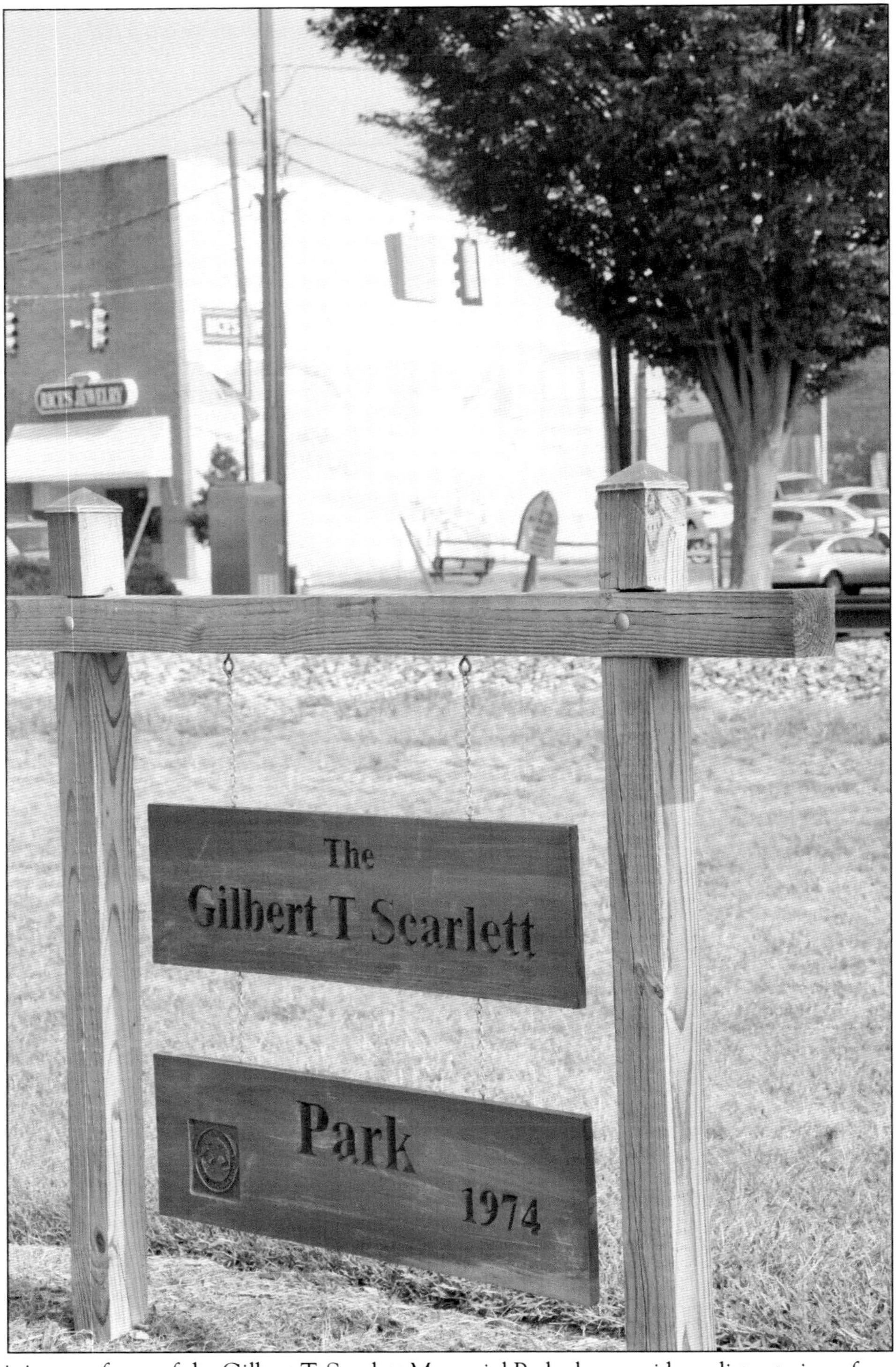

This image of part of the Gilbert T. Scarlett Memorial Park also provides a distant view of part of the train mural painted on the side of Rice's Jewelry in the 1980s. During the Christmas holidays, the park is the site of a beautiful light display of Santa and his sleigh and reindeer. (Courtesy of Kelly Gauldin.)

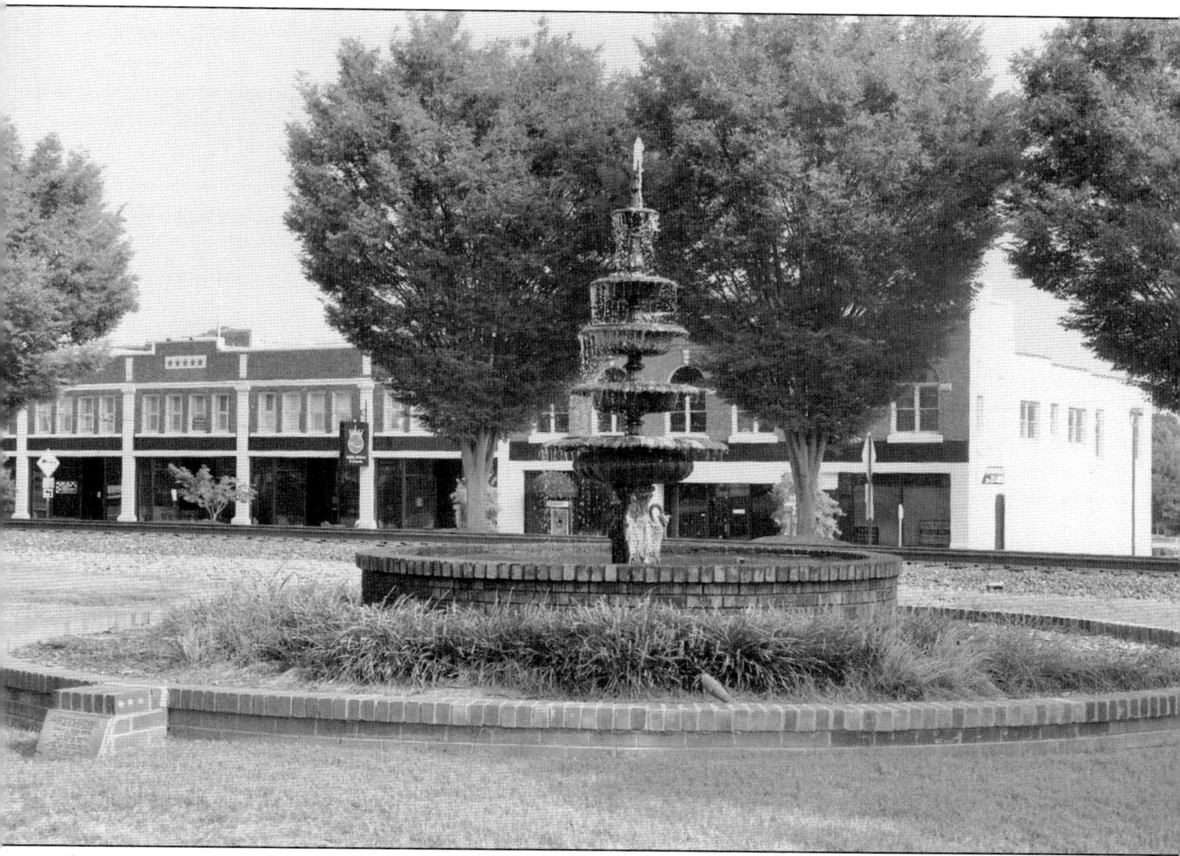

This picturesque fountain located in the Scarlett Memorial Park is one of the many areas around town included in the beautification projects provided by the City of Mebane and many local organizations. (Courtesy of Kelly Gauldin.)

BIBLIOGRAPHY

Bamberger, Bill and Cathy N. Davidson. *Closing: The Life and Death of an American Factory*. New York: W.W. Norton and Company, Inc., 1998.

Bolden, Don. *Alamance in the Past: A History in Photographs*. vol. I and II. Burlington, NC: P.N. Thompson Printing, 1979 and 1981.

Lasley, William Kerr Jr. *Alamance County*. Charleston, SC: Arcadia Publishing, 1999.

Mebane Enterprise. Various issues.

Smith, Ricky N. *Change for a Dollar: A History of First Savings and Loan*. Chapel Hill: Chapel Hill Press, Inc., 2011.

Trelease, Allen W. *The North Carolina Railroad, 1849–1971, and the Modernization of North Carolina*. Chapel Hill: The University of North Carolina Press, 1991.

Troxler, Carole and William Murray Vincent. *Shuttle and Plow: A History of Alamance County, North Carolina*. Graham, NC: Alamance County Historical Association, 1999.

Vincent, William Murray. *Historic Alamance County: A Biographical History*. San Antonio: Historical Publishing Network, 2009.

Whitaker, Walter E. *Centennial History of Alamance County: 1849–1949*. Burlington, NC: Burlington Chamber of Commerce, 1949.

THE MEBANE HISTORICAL SOCIETY

Local citizens established the Mebane Historical Society in 2001 to collect, preserve, and promote the history of Mebane. The society's headquarters were located in several temporary places for years until the City of Mebane carried out a major renovation of the Mebane Recreation Center and generously donated part of the space to the society and the Mebane Historical Museum. Close to a thousand people attended the grand opening of the museum on January 23, 2010.

The Mebane Historical Society operates the museum, which is located on the corner of Jackson and Second Streets near downtown Mebane. The museum features exhibits on two floors. The society presents a historical program for its members and visitors on the third Monday evening of each month, provides guided tours of Mebane, designs educational programs for local public schools, and assists the City of Mebane and other agencies in promoting Mebane.

The museum is currently open from 10:00 a.m. to 2:00 p.m. Wednesday through Friday and from 10:00 a.m. to 3:00 p.m. on Saturday.

The museum is funded by modest membership dues, grants, donations, fundraisers, and other sources. Membership forms are available at the museum and on its website, www.mebanehistoricalsociety.com.